THE VALLEY
ITS · PEOPLES

Puritans and Victorians both suffer from the misconception that certain generations were too "civilized" or restrained to enjoy themselves outdoors or to experience the glories of nature. Individually they walked, rode, swam, and disported themselves in the Valley. View Near The Laurels, *an 1847 lithograph, depicts The Laurels, West Newbury, which was a favorite picnic spot in the 19th century, and who knows how old the tradition was then? Courtesy, Historical Society of Old Newbury, Newburyport, Massachusetts.*

THE VALLEY

ITS · PEOPLES

AN

ILLUSTRATED HISTORY

of the

LOWER MERRIMACK

PAUL HUDON, 1939-

Illustrations edited by Helena Wright

"Partners in Progress"   by Thomas W. Leavitt

Sponsored by the Merrimack Valley Textile Museum

Windsor Publications, Inc.
Woodland Hills, California

Portions reprinted by permission of the publisher, E.P. Dutton, Inc., from *November . . . December* by George Bower. Copyright ©1977 by George Bower.

Excerpt from "The Gift Outright" from *The Poetry of Robert Frost* edited by Edward Connery Latham. Copyright 1942 by Robert Frost. Copyright ©1969 by Holt, Rinehart and Winston. Copyright ©1970 by Lesley Frost Ballantine. Reprinted by permission of Holt, Rinehart and Winston, Publishers.

Windsor Publications, Inc.
History Books Division

Publisher: John M. Phillips
Editorial Director: Lissa Sanders
Administrative Coordinator: Katherine Cooper
Senior Picture Editor: Teri Davis Greenberg
Senior Corporate History Editor: Karen Story
National Sales Manager: William Belger
Marketing Director: Ellen Kettenbeil
Production Manager: James Burke
Design Director: Alexander D'Anca
Art Production Manager: Dee Cooper
Typesetting Manager: E. Beryl Myers

Staff for *The Valley and Its Peoples*
Editor: Annette Igra
Designer: John Fish
Text Editor: Rita Johnson
Sales Manager: John Dowiat
Sales Representative: Diane Murphy
Editorial Assistants: Clareen Arnold, Susan Block, Patricia Dailey, Phyllis Gray, Greg Harris, Karen Holroyd, Judy Hunter, Mary Mohr, Hedy Oliver, Phyllis Rifkin, Susan Wells
Typographers: Shannon Mellies, Barbara Neiman
Layout: Lisa Sherer, Shannon Strull, Melinda Wade
Production Artists: Janet Bailey, Beth Bowman, Ellen Hazeltine, Chris McKibben

Library of Congress Cataloging in Publication Data

Hudon, Paul, 1939-
   The valley and its peoples.

   "Sponsored by the Merrimack Valley Textile Museum."
   Bibliography: p. 184
   Includes index.
   1. Merrimack River Valley (N.H. and Mass.)—History,
Local. 2. Merrimack River Valley (N.H. and Mass.)—
Description and travel. 3. Merrimack River Valley (N.H.
and Mass.)—Industries. I. Leavitt, Thomas W.,
1935-   . Partners in progress. 1982. II. Merrimack
Valley Textile Museum. III. Title.
F72.M6H8   1982   974.2'72
82-50186
ISBN 0-89781-047-3

For my family,

four generations of workers in the Merrimack Valley

An important feature of the system of industrial capitalism introduced at Lowell was the corporation boardinghouse. In order to ensure a proper home environment for the thousands of single young women who came to work in the textile mills, boardinghouses supervised by matrons were built by the corporation. Merrimack Mills and Boarding-Houses, *an 1848 engraving, shows the brick blocks of the Merrimack Corporation along Dutton Street, with the mill in the background. (MVTM)*

Contents

By 1856 a wider panorama of Lawrence had unfolded. As seen from the Clover Hill residence of Pacific Mills agent William Chapin, this view documents the remarkable growth of the city during its first decade. The farmhouse of John Fallon, who succeeded Chapin in 1871, marks the comfortable retreat of mill management away from the noise and smoke of the factories along the river. This lithograph by John B. Bachelder is one of twenty in the artist's Album of New England Scenery. *(MVTM)*

Preface

There are at present one dozen towns on the lower Merrimack and they're located along the water with unexpected balance, six on either side. Tyngsborough, Dracut, Methuen, Merrimac, Amesbury, and Salisbury lie one next to the other on the northern side, in the direction of the current. In the reverse, upstream direction, West Newbury, Groveland, North Andover, Andover, Tewksbury, and Chelmsford take up the southern side. In addition, there are four cities: Lowell, Lawrence, Haverhill, Newburyport. The oldest of the lower Valley towns was Newbury (1635), and the most recent is Merrimac, which was separated from Amesbury in the year of the Unites States' centenary (1876). As a comparison of maps will show, however, the passing of time not only adds to the inherited stock of the past, it also subtracts. Rowley, Billerica, Dunstable, and Bradford began with frontage on the Merrimack, but each has since been trimmed and shaped to make room for other communities. Bradford, indeed, has disappeared altogether, though it was there on the river for more than two centuries, from the year it was separated from Rowley (1675) to the year it was absorbed into Haverhill (1897). And, if Newbury is still on the map, it no longer touches the water of the Merrimack since the separation of Newburyport (1764) and West Newbury (1819).

These 16 communities, however, do not compose the latest chapter of one, continuous story. Instead, there have been several stories: Pennacook and Puritan and Yankee, each in turn has held the stage and written the lines being told on the lower Merrimack. In more recent times, since the 1800s, the story of the region has unfolded out of the needs of the industrial corporation, whether the purpose was site development or product research or manufacturing. The rise of the corporation has ensured the domination of economics over all other plots and subplots of the last century and a half. So, the later peoples who came to the cities and towns of the lower Merrimack—from every corner of Europe and from the Middle East, or in more recent years from Hispanic America and from southeast Asia—were informed by the rules of economic survival before reaching the American political and social structures.

Beginning, again and again, may be *the* American Dream, and if that is the case the residents of this region have done their share toward keeping it moving. What follows, then, is not *the* story of the lower Merrimack, but a number of stories about displacements and departures. Some of these are local stories mainly (Chapters I, II, III), while some are of national significance, though centered in local events (Chapters IV, V, VI). But in all cases the story tells of change, and each change involved a people to make it happen. In that sense, at least, the current tale of the lower Merrimack, "Finding the Future," is like those that have come before.

The list of acknowledgments published elsewhere in this volume is a long one, but I would like in addition to recognize the special help of John Roberts for the topographical information in Chapter I, and the work of Thomas Dublin in the story of the Lowell mill girls related in Chapter VI. I am also indebted to Peter Molloy for his research, recently published, on the construction of the Great Stone Dam at Lawrence. Most especially, I thank Julian S. Miller of Haverhill for his two years of patient work at transforming the manuscript diary of Isaac Merrill into six volumes of typescript. For him, this was a labor of love, no doubt. For us, it retrieves the personality of Merrill and casts a light on this place as it will not be again.

It remains only to add that any errors, of fact or fancy, are my own.

— Paul Hudon

I

THE STRONG PLACE

Here were huckleberries still hanging upon the bushes,
where they seem to have slowly ripened for our especial use.
— Henry David Thoreau, *A Week on the Concord
and Merrimack Rivers*, 1849.

All of us now living in the Valley of the lower Merrimack have seen
the stone walls that mark the landscape of its towns. They are as familiar
as the river itself and seem to have grown directly from the soil, as indeed
they have. The walls were made by the hands of English settlers who
farmed the Valley's soil, but the stones lay for 10,000 years, disturbed by
nothing but the frost that heaved and pushed them out of the earth. It
needed the European view of things to arrange them into boundaries,
separating yours from mine. Robert Frost, a Valley poet, passed the word
to us: good fences make good neighbors. As we look at them, however,
some of these walls are in peculiar places; they enclose stands of trees,
separate forest from forest, so it is impossible to say what is being kept in
or why anyone should be kept out.

Henry David Thoreau was delighted by the sight. He was glad, he
said, to see nature reclaim the land from the grubby industry of the

*A Pennacook village on the bank of the Merrimack River in modern Andover, known
as the Shattuck farm site, is depicted in this diorama. Researched by Dr. Frederick
Johnson of the R.S. Peabody Foundation for Archaeology and constructed circa 1950,
it represents typical aboriginal village life of the Late Woodland Period, about AD
1400, just prior to European settlement. Activities shown include drying fish,
grinding corn, and building snowshoes and canoes. Courtesy, R.S. Peabody
Foundation for Archaeology, Andover, Massachusetts.*

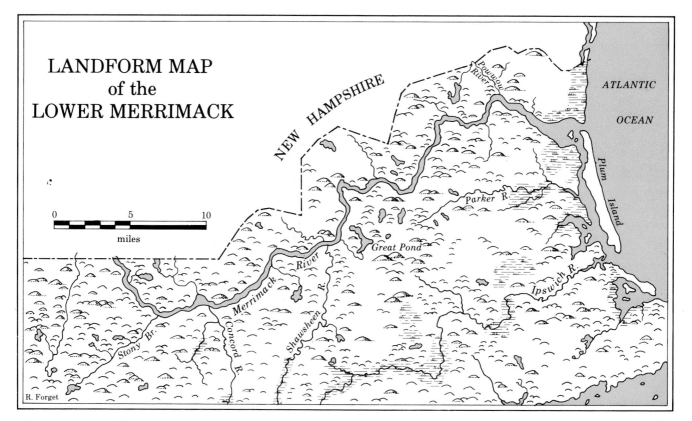

LANDFORM MAP of the LOWER MERRIMACK

NEW HAMPSHIRE

ATLANTIC OCEAN

Powwow River

Parker R.

Plum Island

Great Pond

Merrimack River

Ipswich R.

Shawsheen R.

Concord R.

Stony Br.

0   5   10
miles

R. Forget

The basic structure of the land underlying the Valley settlements is shown in this landform map of the lower Merrimack area. Its numerous hills and ponds are visible, along with the marsh areas around the rivers. Map made by Robert Forget for The Valley and Its People.

Yankee farmer. The spiritual Mr. Thoreau, also a poet of the Valley, found it hard to sympathize with his neighbors, and they returned the compliment. His observation nevertheless is accurate. The stone walls that no longer have a purpose present us with a double exposure of time: they show us where the land used to be farmed. Like the remnants of fruit orchards stranded on the median of our local interstates, or the lilacs we occasionally find in the wild, the stone walls remind us that the use we make of this place does not exhaust its possibilities.

The Valley is littered with the objects of its former tenants. It has been home not only to many people—individuals in the hundreds of thousands. It has been the home also of several peoples—groups large or small, surviving for centuries or merely decades. So what is left now is a multiple exposure rather than a double one, as though four or five family portraits were projected at the same time onto a single screen. Some of these people would be familiar to us; some would look like intruders. And it would be impossible not to have favorites. But all of them belong here. They might not all be in the same focus, some after all being projected over a long distance from the past. Each is a face that at one time was the witness to the river and its Valley. The business of filtering out one image from

the others begins with objects, things having weight and color, things that resist human manipulation. Objects participate in the response to questions posed to the past, and none will make a grander response than the place itself.

For most of its length, the Merrimack runs directly south toward Massachusetts Bay. In fact, there is geological evidence that the river did at one time empty into the Atlantic in the vicinity of Boston Harbor. That, however, was many thousands of years ago, before Pleistocene glaciation covered the entire northeastern United States with ice and altered the surface of the Valley. Glaciation occurred in this area as long as half a million years ago, but the last glacier began its descent from the north only 70,000 years Before Present. This ice sheet is known as the Wisconsin Glacier and lay over the Valley one mile thick, gray-brown in color, holding a great scattered mass of debris in a frozen clutch. It reached to Cape Cod, then extended east-southeast along the continental shelf across Long Island, New York, New Jersey, and Pennsylvania. About 18,000 years ago, the flow of ice stopped and some 3,000 years after that the glacier began its slow retreat. Ten thousand years ago the Merrimack was finally uncovered, free of ice.

The topography of the Valley was created in the recession of the Wisconsin Glacier. The most prominent result of this process is what geologists call drumlins but the rest of us call hills. We have Powow Hill in Amesbury and Ames Hill in Tewksbury. Ayer in Haverhill, Whortleberry on the line between Tyngsborough and Dracut, Holt in Andover and Robbins in Chelmsford are only a handful among so

Located in the Byfield section of Newbury, the "Haystack" boulder was named in obvious reference to its shape. Deposited by the glacier, this outcropping of quartz hornblende diorite represents an erratic formation in the otherwise gentle, rolling coastal plain of the Merrimack Valley. From John Henry Sears, Geology of Essex County Massachusetts, *1905. Courtesy, Peabody Museum of Salem.*

many others. None of them is very impressive, perhaps, few of them rising much more than 400 feet above sea level. Yet all of them together give the lower Merrimack its characteristic rolling landscape. In any season, there is something in them of color or shape or light that leads one to think that beauty can be explained after all. Moreover, these hills and the lakes and ponds between them create those sudden cascades of water, abundant falls that have been so important to the region's economic history. The drumlins or hills are shaped in an oval, with a blunt end where the debris from the glacier was collected in front of some larger obstruction, most likely an outcropping from the solid bedrock. The other end is streamlined, showing that the glacier smoothed the clay as it receded. Because they are oval and not round, the hills have a long and a short axis. The direction of the long axis is the clue that tells the direction in which the ice moved away from the Valley. The combined angles of the glacier and the river amounted at several points to about 90 degrees; their relative movement was at right angles.

The drumlins are made of a material called till, which is a mixture of sand, clay, and boulders. This sediment was deposited directly by the glacier, but in differing configurations. Where there was no obstruction to gather it up into a hill, it spread rather evenly; and because the till contains so much clay it prevents sufficient drainage. These areas are called moraines and today have a wet soil in spring. In other places, the sand and smaller rock debris within the glacier flowed along its fissures, those cracks that develop in any mass of that size. When deposited on the surface of the earth, these materials formed eskers—long, winding hills seeming to cover the remains of prehistoric serpents. Today they are likely subjects of commercial mining for gravel. There are several such systems in the region of the lower Merrimack, and one of them begins near Nickle Mine Hill on the Dracut/Methuen town line.

Some fissures in the glacier must have opened entirely, and this caused large blocks of ice, called dead-ice, to be cut off and left behind as the ice flow retreated north-northwest. These chunks of dead-ice melted in isolation. When this happened in a slight depression of till, a bog or swamp resulted. Great Swamp in Tewksbury and Spruce Swamp in Dracut are examples of this, as is Tadmuck in Westford. Where the depression was deeper and there was a proper bedrock foundation, the same process formed lakes and ponds. Lake Cochichewick in North Andover, the largest body of water in the region, as well as Chadwick in Haverhill and Johnson's Pond in Groveland, may have formed in this way.

Even today, the land of the Valley is reacting to the glacier, or to the absence of it. Freed thousands of years ago from the immense weight of ice 5,000 feet thick, the land is rebounding still. The adjustment this causes in the earth's crust may explain the earthquakes that have been recorded here since the 17th century, and that the Native Americans reported had been part of their relationship with the god of the place.

It is uncertain when exactly the first human inhabitants entered the Valley of the lower Merrimack. We can be sure, however, that the people of the first settlement lived in the Valley for long centuries—for millenia, really—during which time the Valley underwent slow and profound transformations. Spruce forests replaced tundra, and pine subsequently replaced spruce. Temperature was the regulating factor in this process and, in the warming temperatures that began 8,000 years ago, the forest changed again to a variety of hardwoods: oak, hickory, and maple. As one vegetation cover displaced its predecessor, new species of animals came to exploit the new habitat. The change was far from dramatic: the transformation from tundra with its mosses and lichen to hardwood forest took more than 4,000 years. The place changed, and the only constant was the need for humans to change with it. To put it simply, when there were elk and caribou, the aboriginal settlers were hunters of elk and caribou; when the cultivation of beans and corn became possible, they were part-time farmers.

The story of these vast stretches of life in the Valley relies on records that offer little hope of achieving an exact picture of its communities. The edges are blurred where, indeed, edges can be found at all. Fossils and pollen borings tell what the flora and fauna of the Valley were through many thousands of years, while artifacts of stone or bone display human skill both in the making of them and in their use.

The people of the first settlement lived in the Valley for 9,000 years, developing more than one culture during that time. It seems clear that settlements were present in the period archeologists call the Middle Archaic Period (8,000-5,000 BP) and probably some occurred before that, in the Early Archaic Period. Through those millenia, and into the three phases of the Woodland Period (2,000-300 BP), the Valley natives underwent the change from an exclusively hunting economy to a partially agricultural one. That change was never totally articulated. The gathering of berries was done in the years before settled fields were planted and harvested, while hunting and fishing remained crucial to the subsistence of the tribes down to the time when the written record begins. The women of these tribes farmed, it seems, and hunting remained a male occupation. The crops consisted of a variety of squashes, beans, and corn. Modern studies have confirmed the legends telling that the cultivation of corn was introduced into this region from the southwest. That direction of the compass was always associated with good things in the minds of the Native Americans. It was the direction, for instance, in which worthy souls of the dead would go to enjoy endless days of delight.

The last Native American people to occupy the lower Merrimack called themselves the Pennacook, but that is somewhat misleading because it applies not only to one particular tribe of that name, but also to a loosely knit confederation of tribes associated by common allegiance to the sachem of the Pennacook. The Pawtuckets (or Wamesits), the Pentuckets, and the Agawams were the principal tribes of this so-called confederation living on the lower river, and they recognized their commonality with the tribes of the upper Valley. The sachem regularly divided his time between a winter residence at Pennacook (now Concord, New Hampshire) and a summer stay at Wickasauke (now Tyng's Island) some few miles upstream from Pawtucket Falls. The Pennacook had no written language and relied solely on oral traditions, on stories told from generation to generation to preserve what they prized of their history. Also, they relied on place for instruction, which demonstrated the continuous cycle of a human history, turning and returning in season with the freeze and the thaw of land and river.

The economy of the Pennacooks, though partially nomadic, had its center in the river they called *Merroh Awke*, meaning Strong Place. (The Massachusets tribe, living to the south of the Pennacooks, called it River of the Sturgeon.) It is difficult to say how far the Pennacooks' treks after game took them, but the broad river with a swift current was always home. True, they did not favor settlement directly on its shores. They preferred rather to locate on or near the smaller streams and creeks, which are tributary to the Merrimack. They especially sought ecotonal zones, areas where two systems of fauna meet and overlap. There was a larger number of species in the ecotones of the Valley, so food might be available on the same site for more than one season. The choice of location, the decision to move or not to move was made for the reason of food. Knowledge of where food was abundant, and when, was the central concern of the Pennacook community. It was the stock of accumulated skill. The primary lesson was to eat when possible. One witness to their habits was amazed to see them able to go for days with little food and some days with none at all. But at other times they would eat "not ceasing till their full bellies leave nothing but empty plates." They lolled at their meals in "the Turkish fashion," he said.

The Pennacooks were powerless to ignore the demands of survival in the Valley, so they naturally saw in *Merroh Awke* the face of strength. They respected power and always were impressed by its display. Some of their leaders were reputed powwows, persons who could make things happen rather than simply suffer them. Part of the authority of their leader Passaconaway was based on the powers they said he had to make water burn, rocks move, or trees dance. They believed he could transform himself into a flame, survive, and return as himself, the Child of the Bear. This attitude toward displays of power may explain why Passaconaway decided not to offer resistance to the English settlers. Their superiority was obvious and to counter their will was as futile as resisting the sleet of winter or the summer drought.

They saw, however, that power was good as well as evil. Evidence of this attitude can be found in the names they used to describe the places around them: The Smile of the Great Spirit, The Beautiful Waters of the High Place, The Beautiful River with the Bright Strong Current and Pebbly Bottom. They seemed to reason that if everything might be withheld, then anything was a gift. The greatest gift, however, was the yearly run of fish that came up the Merrimack: shad, alewives, salmon that came late in winter with the waking of the earth. The tribes of the lower Valley gathered at the Pawtucket Falls to gather the harvest. It was a time of reunion and thanksgiving. Each year the river was at the center of their renewal; each year the river gave proof of concern and paid the tribute that secured the contract between people and place. Now, however, came alien settlers, for whom the river was not the center of life, but its frontier.

Left: *Chief of the Pennacooks Papisseconewa, better known as Passaconaway, was always friendly to European settlers. This mid-19th century lithograph portrays him wearing a conical cap and bear's head, the symbol of Passaconaway and his tribe. Courtesy, Merrimack Valley Textile Museum (MVTM).*

Below: *Sponsored by the Andover Historical Society, a team composed of Massachusetts Historical Commission staff and field school students worked for two summers excavating the site of a Pennacook village. Field school team members expose a hearth during their 1981 excavation. Courtesy, Massachusetts Historical Commission.*

Below: *Long important to the Valley's economy, the Merrimack River salmon,* salmo salar, *provided food for Native Americans and immigrants until the 19th century. Progressive improvements are expected to insure the salmon's return to the river during the 1980s. Courtesy, Peabody Museum of Salem.*

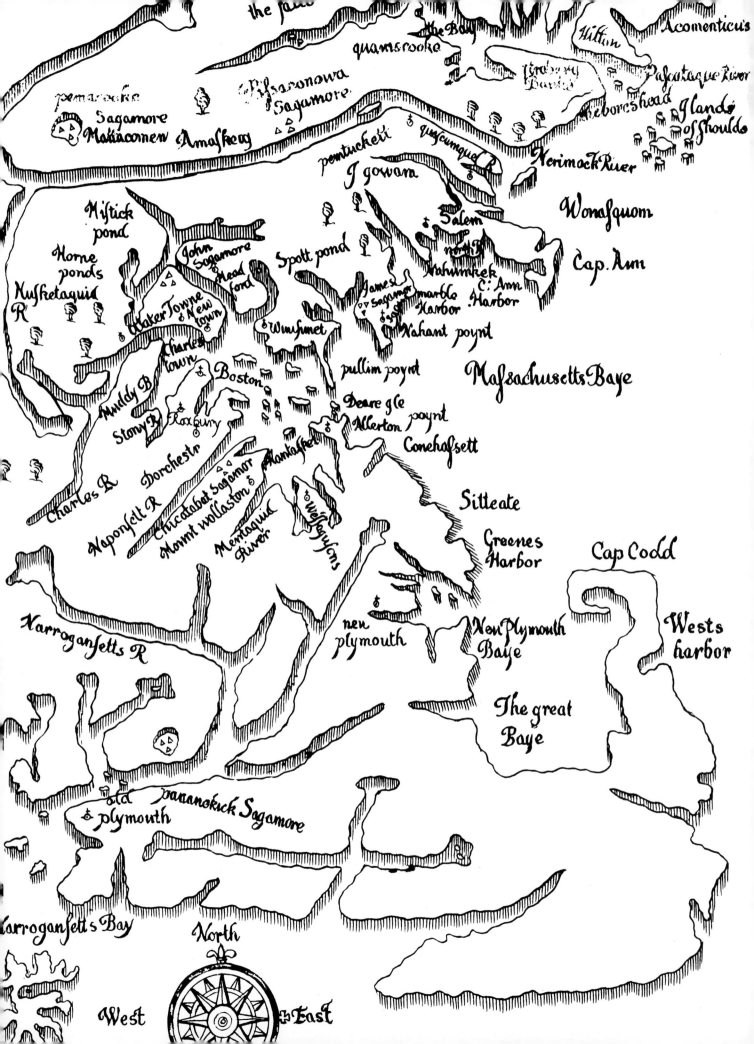

II

"UNDER THE VISOR OF RELIGION"

[Chelmsford] . . . WHICH BORDERETH UPON
MERRIMACK RIVER NEAR TO PAATUCKET, which we do
find a very comfortable place to accommodate a company of
God's people upon; that may with God's blessing and
assistance live comfortably upon and do good in that place for
church and commonwealth.
— Petition of the towns of Woburn and Concord
"for the erecting of a new Plantacon on
Merremacke River," 1653.

The people of the second settlement came over the ocean, from the
East, and at that time the mouth of the river was obscured by the sand
dunes of an island that lay across it. Voyagers sailing south from the Gulf
of Maine or north from Massachusetts Bay could not easily sight the
river, particularly as they preferred to sail the safe waters to the east of
Cape Ann and the Isles of Shoals. These natural outworks kept strangers
at a distance. From the St. Lawrence to the Plata, rivers were a special
objective during the 100 years and more when Europe's explorers
charted the waters of the New World. The sailors who came, and the

Engraved for William Wood's New England's Prospect, *published in London in
1634, this map was intended to show Europeans what is now eastern Massachusetts
and southern New Hampshire. The Merrimack River is identified and runs from left
to right across the top portion of the map. Wood's account of the New World is that
of a scientific observer, as indicated by this detailed map with its numerous place
names. (MVTM)*

princes or merchants who sent them, dreamed of finding a water passage to the Orient. The Orient held treasures of silk and spices, wealth in trade. It was a dream that died hard, but when Europeans awakened to reality they saw that the Merrimack was not a passage but a frontier.

The name and origin of the first European to see and hear the waters of the Merrimack remain unknown. It may be that the river and its valley were visited by travelers from Europe centuries before Columbus made his voyage in 1492. The facts of that tale, however, are thin and uncertain, so we are left with controversy until the opening of the 17th century, when the written record of this story begins.

Even that presents us with debate. In 1613 the French explorer Samuel de Champlain published a map to accompany his account of the voyages he had made to North America. The map clearly shows a large river on what is now the coast of Massachusetts, somewhat north of a place he called Beauport (present-day Gloucester). The river can only be the Merrimack, though the map bears no legend. What is not at all certain is when, and to what extent, Champlain investigated the site. Apparently he was not impressed; he did not return nor did he send others to settle the place. In 1608 he founded the city of Quebec far to the north, and so began the events by which France came to occupy the valleys of North America's great waterways—the St. Lawrence, the Mississippi, and the Ohio. These giants seemed to promise control of the continent, and compared to them the Merrimack was a minor stream indeed. However, it suited the purpose of English Puritans well enough. When Champlain died in 1635, he was the governor of New France. In that same year the English planted their first settlement on the Merrimack.

It was the celebrated John Smith who, in 1614, discovered the Merrimack for the English crown. Smith was a hero in his own day, and he is known for his adventures in Virginia and his storybook rescue by the Indian princess Pocahontas. But Smith traveled elsewhere, and he was a practical man of business as well as a figure of romance. In particular he had a talent for selling an idea. He not only found the river; he also suggested the name "New England" and helped organize the settlement of the region. By 1620 he had marshaled enough support to persuade Parliament to establish a council for that purpose. This body was to act as an agent, a sort of development company, allotting rights and territories in the king's new lands across the sea. Officially it was called the "Council established at Plymouth in the County of Devon for the Planting, Ruling, Ordering, and Governing of New England." However, the key to its enterprise was not in the character of the English who remained by the estuary of the Plym, ordering and ruling. The key to success was in the character of the English who emigrated to New England, to plant. In the later 1620s there were groups in several parts of England, in the south, in the east, and in London, who began to coordinate a response to the opportunity advertised by the Council. They were not all alike, but they were all charmed by the prospect of New England. Also they were Puritan, though not yet ready to accept that nickname foisted on them by their enemies.

In March 1627 the Council of New England granted the right of colonization to a group of Puritans calling themselves the Dorchester Company. The grant was bounded by the oceans on the east and west, by the Charles River on the south, and by the Merrimack on the north. This made for a rather narrow tract with its western end trailing off into mystery. Nevertheless, only two years later, in March 1629, the same tract was granted a second time, again to a Puritan group—now described as "the governor and company of Massachusetts Bay in New England." It was a trading and colonizing company like the first, but with this difference: the governor and company of Massachusetts were allowed the right to leave England; they were allowed to establish a legal government across the sea. This is a unique exception in the history of English colonies, and it speaks volumes about the amount of influence—and bribes—that Puritans were able to concentrate on the Council and on the king.

Obviously, they had great expectations. Massachusetts Bay was a special place to these Puritans only as they could be, there, what they had it in their souls to be. Today's view of them is obscured by three centuries of commentary, but these English men and women saw themselves in the clear light of their own conviction. They thought and spoke of themselves as the Remnant, the remains of Israel, the Lord God's one chosen beloved. Despite every prejudice of our century we can invoke to deny it, all the evidence forces the conclusion that the Puritans lived in sacred time. Just as we hope to continue the Republic of Jefferson and Madison, they thought to continue the epic of the Old Testament; when they talked of Massachusetts Bay as Zion in the wilderness, it was no metaphor. And, like the ancient Jews, they waited on God's direction. Words and events were messages and signs; the most remote circumstance was a coded transmission of God's intent that only needed deciphering. The discovery of New England, then, the mere fact of its existence, was proof to them that God had reserved it for Puritan rule.

However, God is no democrat, and if he sent the Puritans to settle the Merrimack Valley he was not sending them to rule themselves. There is nothing Puritans spoke so harshly against as democracy. In their opinion, asking for leadership from the people was asking the crew, ignorant of all mathematics, to navigate the ship. Instead, the right to leadership belonged only to those they called the saints, those God had elected to share his vision. Intended for solitary bliss in the next world, the saints were obliged, while still in this one, to contract with one another, and this covenanted society or congregation is what they called the church. The Puritans were at pains always to mark a clear difference between the community of saints, which was the church, and the place of its worship, which was the meetinghouse. The church was a living community of men and women endowed with God's power to teach and rule. Not everyone was delighted with the rule of these saints, so matters of discipline would soon enough disturb the peace of the Valley towns. Lydia Perkins Wardwell of Newbury, for example, was publicly flogged for appearing naked before her judges in protest against their misuse of authority. One author reacted with indignation to the severity of the judgement:

And this is the discipline of the church of Newbury in New England, and this is their religion, and their usage of the handmaid of the Lord, who in a great cross to her natural temper, came thus among them, a sign indeed, significatory enough to them, and suitable to their state, who under the visor of religion, were thus blinded into cruel persecution.

If instruction and punishment were often confused in the minds of the Puritans, it was because both were taken as legitimate means to rescue mankind from its willful destruction. The word of God would be translated directly into law, to ensure that society would become a great schoolhouse where even the greatest dolt of Christendom might do right provided only that he obey civil law. This way, the state would also guarantee the delivery of truth to future generations, so that the children of Adam and Eve would not live like beasts of the field.

In March 1630 John Winthrop and Thomas Dudley, governor and deputy governor of Massachusetts, gathered with several hundred other Puritans to hear a parting instruction from John Cotton, master of the church at Boston in Lincolnshire, England. Master Cotton went to II Samuel for his text:

Moreover, I will appoint a place for my people Israel, and will plant them that they may dwell in a place of their own and move no more.

The entire government of the Massachusetts Company then boarded ship and sailed off to build the New Jerusalem, a city upon a hill as a beacon of direction to mankind, forever.

Such was the vision of the English Puritan. However, he was more certain of the destiny that brought him than of his capacity to live it. For the irony is that the saint was never certain of his sainthood. God gave signs of favor, and wealth was one of them, but no man or woman could ever

be sure of being God's chosen. Constantly under the obligation to survey their lives for signs of election or destruction, the Puritans lived at the edge of doubt. Who can wonder that they feared savages lurking in the wilderness?

The General Court of Massachusetts, sitting at Boston, was anxious to occupy the tract granted by the Council of New England, but it took half a century of persistent effort to secure the frontier of the Merrimack for the Puritan cause. The process began in 1635 with the planting of Newbury at the mouth of the river. Four years later the General Court authorized the settling of Rowley, an unusually large parcel that later was divided to make up the towns of Bradford, Groveland, Georgetown, and Boxford. Also, Rowley was oddly shaped, squeezed between Newbury and Ipswich on the coastal end of town and fanning out to some 18 miles where it fronted on the Merrimack. In 1640 Salisbury and Haverhill were established and six years later, Andover. Chelmsford and Billerica were both settled in 1655, plotted side by side with their northern limit on the river. Billerica at the time included all of contemporary Tewksbury and parts of Lowell and Wilmington; Chelmsford also comprised parts of Lowell and what is now Westford. In 1668 Amesbury became autonomous after 20 years as Salisbury-new-town. Puritan occupation of the lower Merrimack Valley was completed in 1672 with the establishment of Dunstable, an enormous

Grief and mourning were expressed in elaborately carved gravestones, such as this example with its cursive death's head at the top. The Reverend Thomas Barnard was the third minister at Andover, and during his term the North Parish and South Parish divided. These later became the towns of North Andover and Andover. Photo by Gayton Osgood.

area of 200 square miles, equal to an English dukedom, according to one proud local historian. Most of that tract presently lies in the state of New Hampshire, but it also included Tyngsborough, which is now the first town touched by the Merrimack as it flows into Massachusetts. (On May 10, 1643, the General Court organized Middlesex and Essex counties.)

The procedure followed in making these towns was always the same, and it required the approval of the General Court. Whoever occupied the Merrimack Valley would owe political allegiance to the Puritan theocrats; they would have no squatters. A group of families in a town already incorporated—at Charlestown or Ipswich or Woburn—would petition the General Court and argue that crowded conditions required that they move on; their economic survival demanded more land. They then had to show that a qualified minister would go with them to undertake the covenanting of the saints, and to assure that right teaching would guide the new community. Also, there were economic considerations. The free male heads of households, those who signed the petition, were expected to provide the capital to begin the new town. These were constituted the proprietors and shared in the division of common lands in proportion to their contribution. Typically, the larger landowners were also members of the church, so that economic and spiritual power resided in the same individuals. The proprietors might benefit from two and three divisions of land until the entire grant had been put to private use, though that might take more than one generation.

Population was low. Billerica was established by 25 families, and the great expanse of Dunstable was at one time occupied by half a dozen families. Numbers grew moderately through the whole colonial period. At the time of the War of Independence, in 1775, Haverhill had fewer than 2,000 inhabitants, while Newburyport, with over twice that number, was the metropolis of the Valley.

The process of occupying the Valley was not so neat as the recitation of town names and their birthdates seems to indicate. Expansion often brought conflict within the towns and this sometimes led to separation, as in the case of Amesbury. Distance and the difficulty of travel also encouraged subdivision. Thus the northern end of Rowley, fronting on the Merrimack, was chartered as the town of Bradford in 1675. Or, again, in 1709 the farmers in the south end of Andover were allowed their own meetinghouse because the original North Parish (1646) was too distant for their convenience. Squabbles over the location of the meetinghouse led to the same solution in Newbury (1725), in Haverhill (1726), and in Chelmsford (1729).

This wholesale parceling of the Valley's real estate did not go unchallenged by the people who called themselves the proprietors of New Hampshire. The charter of 1629 bounded the authority of the governor and company of Massachusetts Bay at three miles north of the Merrimack, but in 1629 everyone assumed that the Merrimack ran out of the west. It was soon found that the river ran from the north and not out of the west. Did the charter still apply? Was the Merrimack still a political frontier? Yes, legally it was, according to the Puritans at Boston, and they insisted that the charter be followed to the last letter of the title. In 1658 Governor John Endicott ordered a survey of the river's course. The surveying party determined that the Merrimack began at the mouth of the Winnepesaukee River, so the official claim of the government at Boston extended to three miles north of that line. In fact, the Bay government ruled the towns of New Hampshire for nearly 40 years, from 1641 to 1679, and in that period planted the town of Dunstable. However, the claims of rival proprietors were revived after 1680, and the political face of the Valley became obscure again for another half century.

Besides marking the political frontier with New Hampshire, the Valley was a physical frontier, separating wilderness from civilization, heathen from Puritan. If the Puritan condemned the wearing of long hair, after the manner of "barbarous Indians," the Pennacook replied in kind against the "bastard Englishman" for his filthy habit of growing hair of his face. Nevertheless, the Pennacook tribes were remarkably unwarlike. The great chief Passaconaway always counseled against resistance to the English, and he repeated this advice in his last meeting with the tribes at Pawtucket Falls in 1660. His son Wannalancet followed the same policy of deference. If the policy was intended to save the Pennacooks from destruction, it failed totally. The Pennacooks disappeared, pressed by the land hunger of the Puritans and ground between the wheel of English ambition and the stone of French rivalry.

Still, while they survived, the Pennacooks were a puzzle to the English newcomer, challenging his need to find a role for them in God's plan. According to one Puritan invention, these savages were the lost tribe of Israel, those cut off from the life of God. Cotton Mather called them "the veriest ruins of mankind," so degenerate that they were barely distinguishable from the forests they inhabited. Obviously decoyed by God for the instruction of his darlings, the Pennacooks were taken as the living example of the Puritans' future should the Remnant ever separate from the saints.

What the Puritans saw as the laziness of the Indians was glaringly offensive. According to the Puritan ethic, labor and toil was a way of social education, the gentlest means to virtue for the majority of mankind (that is, those who are not saints). "Wee heartily pray you," Governor Endicott was advised by the authorities in London, "that all bee kept to labor as the only means to reduce to civil, yea to Godly life; and to keep yough from falling into many enormities, which by nature wee are all too much enclyned into." Besides this moral benefit, labor brought economic dividends. Labor begat property. John Cotton wrote "that in a vacant soyle, hee that taketh possession of it, and bestoweth culture and husbandry upon it, his Right it is." True enough, the "soyle" of the Merrimack Valley was vacant after a fashion because the Pennacook population had been much reduced by a plague several years before the English came to settle. This plague, too, was sign to the Puritans that God intended the Valley for their cause.

Many saw the sin of the naked heathen but few attempted his salvation. One who did was John Eliot. For 60 years this extraordinary man labored to bring the hope of Christianity to the Bay Indians. From the Charles to the Merrimack, the entire breadth of the Puritan grant, Eliot established so-called praying villages where Christianized Indians were gathered on lands reserved for them by the General Court. In 1653, two years before the court sanctioned the bounds of Chelmsford and Billerica, it provided for the establishment of Wamesit, a praying village for Pennacook converts at the junction of the Concord and the Merrimack. There, and at the falls nearby, Eliot preached the good news of the Gospel to the Pennacooks in their own language. He told them of their sin in Adam and of their relation to its redemption by the Christ. He gave what he had, freedom as he found it. Eliot, however, did not expect the Pennacooks to forsake the Valley to live in the sacred time of the Puritan, and his genius was to separate culture from theology. Wamesit was a semiautonomous village ruled in part by the local chief, Numphow, and according to tribal law, in part by General Daniel Gookin, who had been commissioned by the Court to deal with Indian affairs. In the end, isolation from the rising sea of English values was impossible. There is now a church opposite the falls at Lowell named to honor Eliot, but the Christian community at Wamesit had already vanished before he died in 1690.

The tribal life of the Pennacooks, Christian or not, never recovered from the shocks suffered during King Philip's War. King Philip was a Wampanoag chief—his true name was Pometacom—who led an alliance of tribes in war against the English from July 1675 to August 1676. Most of the conflict was fought on the southern and western ends of Massachusetts and in the towns of Rhode Island, but in March 1676 danger was present and real on the Merrimack. General Daniel Denison makes this clear in a letter to the Secretary of the Commonwealth:

> I received your intelligence the Substance whereof
> I had 2 houers before by ye way of Billerica and
> Andouer, together with certaine intelligence that the
> enemy is passed merrimack their trecks seene

yesterday at wamesit and 2 of their Scouts this
morning at Andouer who by 2 posts one in the night
& againe this Day about 2 of the clocke importunes
for helpe as doth Haueril . . .

None of the river towns was seriously molested, though nearby Groton was reduced to its last outpost. Few of the Pennacook tribes joined Philip, choosing instead to follow Wannalancet and remain friendly to the English. This attempt at neutrality only generated suspicion on both sides, and the Indians at Wamesit, being cultural half-breeds, were the object of particularly strong feelings. In November 1675 a party of Philip's men burned a barn in Chelmsford. The culprits got away, so the inhabitants of the town punished the Indians nearest at hand. That these Indians were neutral did not matter, nor that they were Christian; it did not matter even that most of them were women and children and all were unarmed. Despite the protest of Lieutenant James Richardson, who owned the barn, 14 men of Chelmsford took up their guns and trooped to the wigwams at Wamesit in a cloud of indignation and fear. In the confrontation that followed, two rounds of buckshot wounded five women and children, killing one boy. A murder trial followed the incident, but the two men accused were acquitted.

One incident among so many cannot tell the story of the dissolution of the Pennacook people. Once the English had arrived in the Valley, the native population had no recourse but flight. They had no defense but to put distance between themselves and these intense strangers who were bent on eradicating any deviation from one, absolute ideal.

Wannalancet twice withdrew from contact with the English and both times he returned. Each of these treks left him with less land and fewer followers, so that before his end he had become a relic surrounded by a residue. Some of his tribes deserted him to take up with his nephew Kancamagus in war against the English. The last known about Wannalancet is that in 1696 he was made a ward of Colonel Jonathan Tyng, the redoubtable Indian fighter of Dunstable. Tyng, along with Major Thomas Henchman of Chelmsford, received the lands of the praying Indians at Wamesit from the General Court as payment for military service in maintaining the Merrimack frontier. These two sold shares to 44 others and together they pastured their sheep at the place, behind a proper English stone wall.

A threat like King Philip's depended on the combined efforts of many tribes and on the unlikely chance that any Indian leader could unite them long enough to achieve the destruction of the Puritan towns. By contrast, later military action at the Merrimack frontier relied on the political presence and sustained will of the French in Canada. For decades the French and their Indian allies, operating out of fortified settlements in the district of Maine and elsewhere, did what they could to dislodge the English. The effort was not continual, but when the kings of France and England were at war in Europe, they were at war everywhere. On this continent the contest ended in 1759 when the English took Quebec City, but in the Valley the struggle was most intense in the last decade of the 17th century. Amesbury, Haverhill, Andover, Billerica, Chelmsford, Dunstable: all had crops and barns burned, inhabitants killed or taken prisoner. Each town has its tale of terror and daring, but none more popular than the story of Hannah Duston.

Hannah was taken by Indians during a raid at Haverhill in mid-March 1697, then dragged off into the isolation of their settlements deep within the upper Valley. This was little more than a week after Hannah had given birth to a son—one of 13 children. She was carrying the infant in her arms and was accompanied by Mary Neff, a widowed townswoman who had been acting as her nurse, when both

During the centuries following Hannah Duston's exploit, her legend grew. Artifacts accumulated and, like pieces of the True Cross, were displayed for the public. Here a 19th-century descendant displays the cloth in which the scalps were purportedly wrapped. Courtesy, Trustees of the Haverhill Public Library.

Hannah Duston's exploits are well remembered in the Merrimack Valley. The monument to her erected on June 1, 1861, in Haverhill was the first monument erected to a woman in the United States. That one was replaced in 1879 by this bronze statue designed by Calvin Weeks of Haverhill. Courtesy, Trustees of the Haverhill Public Library.

were captured at Hannah's house. En route, the Indians killed the child and several adult prisoners also from Haverhill. Hannah and Mary were not alone with the Indians, however. An English boy who had been captured at Worcester a year and a half before was also a member of the party. There is no doubt that Hannah was telling the truth when she later claimed to have prayed to her God, but after six weeks of captivity she signed for herself the warrant of her fate. One night near the end of March, she and Mary and the boy, Samuel, killed 10 Indians and removed their scalps. Hannah and her companions took the scalps as proof and returned to Haverhill by canoe, on the current of the Merrimack. Mrs. Duston became the heroine of the Valley. As Robert Caverly wrote in *The Merrimac and Its Incidents* (1866):

Her noble deeds are held in high renown,
Sacred like *heirloom* in that ancient town;
And long as Merrimac's bright waters glide
Shall stand that mother's *fame*, still by its side.

Her action improved morale, no doubt, and the General

Court was happy to give her and her accomplices a bounty of 50 pounds. However, the security of the Valley depended less on the occasional heroic deed and more on the daily tending to business. The primary concern was to keep the towns alive, economically. One town order at Newbury, dated August 7, 1690, proclaimed, "in his majesty's name," that all the "soldiers" of the town "are required to carry their arms and ammunition with them into meadows and places, where they worke, and if any man doe refuse or neglect his dewty as above expressed he shal pay five shillings for every such neglect." In July of the previous year, the "select Men" of Dunstable twice petitioned the General Court, for a supply of meat and for the defense of their gristmill, saying that without its help they "must be forced to draw off and leave the towne." The danger of desertion so alarmed the Bay government at Boston that it warned the inhabitants of Dunstable and Chelmsford in 1694 that they would forfeit the property they left undefended. The court also imposed a heavy fine for evasion of military service. Still, only two years later, two-thirds of the citizens of Dunstable had left the place, and the court itself provided 30 pounds for the minister's salary.

Despite fire, despite death and abduction, the Puritans were still on the Merrimack when the new century began in 1701. Nevertheless, the decade of the 1690s was a watershed in the history of the Valley, separating the story of the Puritan experiment from all the other stories that have been told of this place. The violence of warfare on the frontier was only part of it. The smallpox epidemic of 1691 and 1692 added to the insecurities of daily life. Longer-lasting tensions were generated by the political legacies of the 1680s. The charter of 1629, so prized by the Puritan fathers for the independence it gave them, was revoked in 1684. Worse still, in 1686 the royal government at London made Massachusetts a part of the larger unit, the Dominion of New England, governed by the king's appointed servant, Sir Edmund Andros. The project collapsed in 1689 when James II was replaced by William III in what the English call their Glorious Revolution. It did not escape the notice of the Bay leaders that their deliverance from the tyranny of Andros had relied on the incompetence of James and on the abilities of his son-in-law. God might be made responsible for both, the Puritans reasoned, but how would this help the anxieties that came with the realization that the political future of Massachusetts depended not on law, but on personality and circumstance?

One consequence of the Andros episode was to depress the maritime sector of the Bay economy, and another was to call into question most titles to the land in the agricultural sector. And for the residents of the lower Merrimack, there was worse news still. Robert Mason, who had reactivated his family's claims in New Hampshire, was a political ally of Andros and a member of his Council. Mason had pressed his family's claim to New Hampshire with enough success to whet his appetite for more, and before his death in 1688 he had read his grant to run south beyond the Merrimack. In fact he claimed all the land of Essex County, down to Salemtown, the first jewel in the Puritan Crown of Glory. Mason's claim might have had no legal base, but what of that? Who would have thought that the charter would be taken? And without that charter the Puritans had no more right to the Valley than Mason had; moreover, Mason also had the friendship of King James. Mason died in 1688 and James was harried out of England in the following year, so the Merrimack towns were not cut off from Massachusetts. Still, the 1690s began in confusion and uncertainty.

Enemies were everywhere. The soldier in his red coat, the judge at the land court in his robes, Mason at Portsmouth dispatching his requests to Andros and the king. Why not, then, spectral enemies? God or the Devil, any man might know himself well enough to believe in either, or in both if he accepted the final grace. So when some citizens at Andover in 1692 gave evidence of dealings with the Devil, of witchcraft, that is, some of the town's citizens believed them, while others could not.

The real consequence of the witch hysteria at Andover, as in the other Puritan towns, was to divide the community. "We were all exceedingly astonished, amazed and consternated and affrighted even out of reason," one witness later testified. There were public trials where the gentlefolk of Andover tore at each other with accusations and evidence, and no one was safe. The town's leading citizens, Osgood, Johnson, Faulkner, two of them daughters of the minister, were accused. Goodwife Foster, aged widow of one of the town's original incorporators, died in prison after 21 weeks of ill-treatment. After nearly a year of such conflict the magistrates and the ministers burst the bubble and imposed silence. If enemies were everywhere, they would choose which to confront, and for their purpose the French and the Indians, even the political maneuvers of English royalists, were a better choice of enemy to keep God's Remnant undivided on the frontier.

From the perspective of our century, trained as it is in the vocabulary of psychology, the Puritans might be described as anxiety neurotics. And well they might have been, living as they were in a valley where the wilderness was a constant lesson in the difficulty of subjugating nature, including their own. Also in the language of psychology one can say that they confronted time with the vigor and desperation of a narcissist. However, ultimately as little profit derives from a 20th-century definition as from a 17th-century one. Only one thing can be said of the Puritans with certainty: they knew a prophecy. The entire world might be made fit by nature for the habitation of men, but the Puritans would make the Merrimack Valley a place fit for the habitation of saints.

III

LAND AND RIVER AND SEA

The land was ours before we were the land's.
She was our land more than a hundred years
Before we were her people.
— Robert Frost, "The Gift Outright," 1942.

In *Magnalia Christi Americana*, written in 1702, Cotton Mather tells the story of a Puritan divine who ventured north of the Merrimack during that first decade of settlement. He had gone beyond the bounds of Massachusetts to preach to those other Englishmen, "the inhabitants upon the River Pascataquack," to instruct them in God's holy purpose. They were not having any. When the preacher got to the part about the "main end of Planting this Wilderness," one member of the involuntary congregation objected. "Sir," he cried out, "you are mistaken, you think you are preaching to the People at the Bay; our main end was to catch fish." Not fishers of men, alas, but trawlers after an income. The story became popular, repeated as late as 1825 by Nathaniel Adams in his *Annals of Portsmouth*. Its endurance shows that the Merrimack was a real boundary, fixed in the thinking of the settlers on either side. Those in Massachusetts had a religious purpose and those in New Hampshire an

Governor William Dummer (1677-1761) left land in Byfield to support the academy that bears his name. The son of a silversmith, he served the Commonwealth in several terms as lieutenant governor and governor. Courtesy, Essex Institute, Salem, Massachusetts.

economic one. It would be difficult to decide who was more pleased with the difference, and the convenience of the line between them.

In fact, the religious and economic motives cannot be separated so surely. The Puritans were never angels for want of being saints, never willing to live on air. The leaders at Massachusetts Bay in particular were clear-sighted in calculating what the New World might contribute to their incomes. John Winthrop in his native Suffolk was both lord of Groton Manor and a lawyer who competed successfully for preferments. In 1628 he was admitted to the Inner Temple, a closely kept sanctum at the very top of the legal profession. Still, he was hard pressed financially, squeezed between rising demands on his income and the inflation that destroyed his real earnings. When he wrote down the pros and cons of resettlement, before leaving England, he spoke of himself in the third person:

> His meanes heer are so shortened (now 3 of his sonnes being com to age have drawen awaie the one half of his estate) as he shall not be able to continue in that place and imployment where he now iss, his ordinary charg being still as great almost as when his meanes was double.

Winthrop decided on Massachusetts because he could not maintain his scale of living, and his station in society, if he stayed in England. He moved geographically in order to stay in place, economically and socially. Both economics and religion are powerful motives for action. Both, after all, offer rewards. Keeping them distinct and in balance is an equation difficult to maintain, and the resolution is not hereditary. From generation to generation, the need to earn a living pressed hard on the Puritan resolve to establish Zion in the wilderness. That commitment disappeared with the wilderness, and the tamed Valley revealed a new ideal of economic independence and political equality.

Land and its tillage was the chief livelihood of the great majority of the English; it naturally became the chief attraction for those with a thought of removing to Massachusetts Bay. John Smith—a first-rate promoter—knew his audience when he described the advantage of New England to the husbandmen in Old England:

> Here should be no hard landlords to rack us with high rents, or extorted fines to consume us; here every man may be master and owner of his own labor and land in a short time.

Smith wrote this in 1614, the year he explored the coast in both directions from the Merrimack. In 30 years, settlers began arriving in the Valley to test Smith's promise that in this place industry and time would make a man free of all masters.

Like the settlers in other parts of Massachusetts Bay, the settlers of the Valley were attracted first to those areas already cleared by the Indians. They also chose the areas nearest the coast, because these offered rock-weed, kelp, and eel grass in fall and winter as stable bedding and in spring as fertilizer for corn, potatoes, and roots. And like migrants everywhere, the settlers of the Valley at first tried to duplicate as nearly as possible the life-style they had left behind. They sought the security of the familiar.

However, some crops would not adapt well to the conditions of the Merrimack Valley. English wheat in particular was a disappointment, though the other English cereals—oats, barley, and rye—did well. The settlers readily adopted Indian corn as well as the Indian practice of using fish as fertilizer. Fish were plentiful and free to those in the Valley; and, one writer maintained, even the lightest soil would produce 40 bushels of rye to the acre when manured liberally with fish. If any Puritans noticed that they were taking lessons in agriculture from the heathen savages, they were quiet about it.

Not so with fruit trees and orchards. The English needed no instruction on this topic. An apple orchard is mentioned at Salisbury-new-town (Amesbury) as early as 1649, though its stage of maturity is not known. The cultivation of apples was extensive, pursued as much for the cider as for the fruit. By 1764 Middlesex County alone produced 33,436 barrels of cider, or enough to give each family seven barrels. Productivity seems to have been a source of local boasting—and some humor. One historian of Bradford claimed that some apple trees of that town were large enough to yield 8 or 10 barrels of cider. The trees of one citizen reportedly produced a superior cider "which for many years bore the highest price in market of any made in the state." Pears were also prized, though grown in smaller quantities, and Governor William Dummer produced a distinctive variety on his land in Byfield (Newbury). A hardy winter pear was developed at Bradford, which also produced outstanding quantities of peaches and plums throughout the 18th century.

The care and breeding of livestock was a second area in which the English farmer distinguished himself from the native worker of the land. Oxen and horses, cows and sheep each had a particular role in the Valley's economy, and all eventually provided edible flesh to supplement native game and fowl. Oxen were of special value. They extracted boulders and stumps while clearing the fields; they pulled the plow at planting and hauled the grain to the mill after harvest. They drew in hay, apples, and firewood. At Newbury-port, at the mouth of the Merrimack, they were used to move heavily loaded drays from wharf to warehouse and back again. Horses seldom were used for

John Winthrop (1587-1649) typifies the Puritan elite of the first period of settlement. A lawyer and landowner in old England, he practiced both professions in New England and also served as the first governor of Massachusetts. (MVTM)

sheep, because they require a smooth grass pasture rather than the roughage goats can consume. "Until the land be often fed with Cattell, Sheepe cannot live." Goats, cows, and oxen had to prepare the way. Still, the sheep population increased rapidly in the last quarter of the 17th century. In 1660 John Cutting at Newbury had a total of 47 sheep, an enormous number compared to the usual three to twelve in a flock. Near the end of the century the town counted 5,635 sheep. Most of these were gathered into four flocks, and though they belonged to individual farmers in town, they were cared for by municipal shepherds on common land.

Finally, trees growing on the land produced abundant harvests from a variety of species suitable for a number of uses. In *New England's Prospect*, written in 1633, William Wood speaks of the red oak, the white, and the black. "As these are different in kind, so are they chosen for such uses as they are most fit for. One kind being more fit for clapboard, others for sawn board, some fitter for shipping, others for houses." He also described the New England walnut, cedar, fir, and pine, the ash and elms. Pine was doubly valuable, for the rosin, turpentine, and pitch it provided were essential for building and maintaining ships. The pines themselves, of course, were used for masts. Some of these magnificent pines were more than 200 feet tall and 40 inches in diameter.

After 1685 these larger trees were reserved for the use of the Royal Navy, and tree wardens roamed the forests of the Valley marking what pines they chose. The bulk of the lumber business was centered in the upper Valley of the

anything but human transport, so oxen remained crucial to the economy of the Valley, as to the rest of Massachusetts Bay, well into the 19th century.

Cows were few at first; for the first 50 years a herd of 12 was considered large. The ratio of cows to oxen may be used as a measure of the maturity of a settlement. In 1766 Haverhill, already in the second quarter of its second century, counted 716 cows and 252 oxen, while Ashfield, in the Berkshires, settled only 20 years before, counted 35 oxen and 31 milkers. In addition to milk, the cows yielded butter and cheeses. Goats were kept for the same purpose and were valued because they required so little care.

Sheep, on the other hand, demanded a great deal of care. By 1600 the English husbandman had already had more than four centuries of caring for sheep, but conditions in the Valley presented new problems. For one thing, there were the wolves. Unlike pigs and goats, sheep are not fighters and so were helpless against these predators. Even with the bounties offered for wolves—their heads were often nailed to the meetinghouse door—it was not much before 1700 that they were eliminated from the Merrimack towns. Pasturage presented another difficulty in raising

Livestock had an important role in the domestic economy of the Merrimack Valley. Sheep provided wool, a renewable resource, for clothing and blankets, and edible flesh. They required smooth pastureland and protection from predators. (MVTM)

Lumber was an important economic asset in the Merrimack Valley. Numerous local sawmills developed from the 17th century on to mill the wood necessary for buildings and tools. A riverside sawmill of the 18th century is depicted here, with its shipyard at right. Lumber could be floated down the Merrimack to the coastal shipyards. (MVTM)

Merrimack, where scores of sawmills, built on the tributaries of the river, prepared timber products for export. Most of this trade was moved overland toward the coast by teams of oxen, because the Pawtucket Falls at Chelmsford prevented using the river as a means of transportation. The lumber operations below the falls, in the lower Valley, were generally more for home markets than for export, though exports were made as long as a surplus was at hand.

The English fished the Merrimack even before they settled the Valley. Sturgeon were a prized catch, growing, it was claimed by some, to 12 or 14 feet. These great fish were pickled and sent to markets in Europe. Of course, the English were attracted also by the same teeming runs of anadromous fish that had been so vital in the yearly cycles of the Pennacooks' economy. Shad and alewives, salmon and eels were staple fare. Unlike the Pennacooks, however, the Europeans converted fish into cash, feeding a market far beyond the population of the Valley. The quantities taken from the river by Europeans were consequently much larger, and within 50 years of settlement the fish population began its decline. The original stock was so large, however, that even after years of decline the quantity taken was still considerable. As late as 1790, 60 to 100 fish were caught daily at Amesbury during the summer run of the salmon.

Henry David Thoreau, who spent his earliest years at Chelmsford, could still remember in the mid-1840s "the tales of our seniors" who had been "sent on horseback in *their* childhood from the neighboring towns, perched on saddle bags, with instructions to get the one filled with shad, the other with alewives." Finally, a historian of Chelmsford, writing in 1820, tells that the annual catch of salmon, shad, and alewives in that town was 2,500 barrels, and that this was far less than in former times, "so that they are rather desirable as a luxury, than as an article of cheap living."

Trade provided a further source of income for the first generation of Europeans in the Merrimack Valley. The trade for furs with the Pennacooks and other natives was highly lucrative, but it could not survive the destruction of hunting grounds by the advance of European agriculture. Trade on the sea was another matter. Considerable sea fishing was done from the port on the Merrimack side at Newbury, though in absolute numbers the size of this operation never matched the men and ships operating out of the southern ports of Essex County. On the other hand, the Newbury river front was a thriving center of coastal trade with the other British colonies as they developed.

A kind of internal commerce existed for the first decade of Massachusetts Bay, the earlier arrivals providing the necessities of life to those who followed. This market of immigrants was significant, considering that more than 12,000 Puritans arrived during the 1630s.

But the beginning of the English civil wars in 1640 put an abrupt end to this flow of settlers, and a boom economy went bust. The economic necessity this presented was accepted as an opportunity, seen as heaven-sent, of course. "It pleased the Lord to open to us a trade with Barbados and other islands," John Winthrop wrote. Fish, clapboard, planks, and other lumber products became immediately available for ready markets. In 1641 Sam Winslow at Salisbury-new-town contracted to supply 30,000 pipe staves yearly, presumably to make casks used in shipping. The cultivation of hemp and flax was begun and, according to Winthrop, these enterprises prospered. What had seemed at first to be the end of the economy became instead the stimulus for growth and diversification. Pork, beef, and oxen, either salted or on the hoof, were taken from the meadows of Valley towns and transported to the West Indies or to tobacco and sugar plantations in Virginia and the Carolinas. On the return voyage the ships might bring cotton for making yarn and cloth, or sugar and molasses for distilling into rum. There were distilleries at Haverhill and Newbury well before the mid-18th century, and they were quite important to the commerce of the region, since rum was both a commodity and a medium of exchange. The General Court did not fail to control and support this trade by establishing corn, at a fixed price, as the standard of exchange. In 1652 Massachusetts Bay set up its own mint, and transactions could be made in coin rather than in products.

Several Merrimack towns became commercial towns. The river was, and is, navigable by coastal shipping for some 11 miles, to Bradford and Haverhill. Haverhill, on the northern side, was ideally located for trade with upcountry towns; goods were carted by ox team overland to the riverside at Haverhill, avoiding the falls at Amoskeag and Pawtucket that made the Merrimack unsuitable for rafting. In the third quarter of the 18th century, James Duncan, a successful Haverhill merchant, built facilities at Lebanon, New Hampshire, to grind flaxseed and to make linseed oil, and kilns to produce potash used in making glass, soap, and fertilizers. The oil and potash were carted from Lebanon to Haverhill, where they were put on board ship and sent downriver for export. The empty carts were then filled with imported goods that had come upriver to his warehouses. In just over two years the gross value of shipments sent by Duncan into the northern town amounted to $96,000, a considerable amount in the Valley's pre-Revolutionary economy. And he was only one merchant among others with this sort of operation at Haverhill. By this time—about 1750—the economies of British colonies had found specialized products and crops, and these were the source of cash income for whole communities. The towns of Essex County cultivated onions that were exported in large quantities. The towns of northern Middlesex County were noted for the growing of hops; Tewksbury was a particularly large producer. The hops were used at local breweries or sent to other cities, such as the 3,000 pounds shipped to New York on the schooner *Bernard* in February 1763. The towns of the lower Merrimack Valley were rooted, deeply and surely, in the broad estates of the British Empire, from

Barbados and the West Indies to the Carolinas and New York, and of course to the home islands that met their need for manufactured goods—porcelains, cutlery, textiles.

Rather than separating the three sectors of the Valley economy from 1635 to 1763, land and river and sea were combined to support individuals, families, and communities. Once the settlers had survived beyond the first generation of scarcity, even a small farm could turn an extra cow or pig into imported clothing or a teapot or steel cutlery.

The towns of the Valley never were exclusively agricultural. Even pioneers will not live by bread alone, if they are given a choice. The communities required artisans and professionals to duplicate as completely as possible, and as soon as possible, the style of life they had known in Old England. Not having the cash to attract them, the towns offered land and privileges. In 1638, only three years after incorporation, the selectmen at Newbury granted Richard Dummer the right to erect a corn mill, and they agreed to allow no other provided that Dummer could meet the town's need. John Hoitt, brickmaker, was enticed from Ipswich by the townsmen at Haverhill in 1650, seduced by the offer of free land and clay pits, provided he furnish the

The Merrimack River's juncture with the Atlantic was an important connection for trade and commerce. Lumber and agricultural products sent downstream were processed or wholesaled through Newburyport, where incoming foreign goods were marketed and distributed. Imports from faraway lands reached the Valley's hinterland through traffic on the river. (MVTM)

townspeople with bricks. In 1656 the town of Chelmsford gave Samuel Adams 450 acres and the right to build a sawmill, on the condition that he supply the town with boards at three shillings per hundred. In the same year, Chelmsford gave William How 12 acres of meadow and 18 of upland, "provided he set up his trade of weaving and perform the town's work."

The differences in the amount of land granted are evidence that the freemen of Chelmsford valued some services more than others. The bestowing of land and privilege was made to fit the service to the community. Edward Whittington and Walter Wright, weavers at Andover, were granted land in 1673, "for encouragement of erecting a fulling mill, which they promise to set about in the spring." Shipbuilding and commerce were similarly encouraged from Newbury (in 1650) to Haverhill (in 1681). Such arrangements were made for blacksmiths, tanners, carpenters, and other artisans, and of course for ministers, teachers, and physicians. This method of dealing with the shortage of skilled labor resulted in a network of social relations in which individual rights were balanced according to the values of communal obligations.

Puritans had a strong sense of community. This was shown, for instance, in their notion that truth was held by the congregation of saints, and no individual, however august his station, was allowed to claim dispensation to teach or impose discipline unchecked by others. Even Governor Winthrop was reprimanded on this point. Likewise, property was not allowed to be unrelated to communal need and control. In part this came from the practice of centuries that put property at the service of families rather than individuals, and the practice continued in early New England. So in 1640, the General Court of Massachusetts awarded Winthrop's wife, Margaret, 3,000 acres in order to enlarge the Winthrop estate for the benefit of the governor's children.

Some of the economic development in the Valley

Following the capture of Louisburg by the British, the Acadian population was resettled in New England and other British colonies. Some were quartered in Andover with Jonathan Abbot, with whom they developed a friendship. When the Frenchman Jacques Hébert departed for Allenstown, New Hampshire, in 1770, he sent Abbot this elaborately decorated powder horn as a token of esteem and thanks. Courtesy, North Andover Historical Society.

required more than could be given or managed by one individual. In March 1717 Ephraim Foster and six other freemen at Andover addressed a petition to "his Majesties Justices of the Generall sesions of the peace now wholden att Ipswich for the county of Easex." They required "for our selves and in Behalf of our partners,"

> ...that we may have Libberty to erect a wire [sic] in Marrimick River against henery [Henry] Boddals which we say is much in the Senter of our upper Towns.

The weir was intended, of course, to draw fish from the river. The catch would be sold at profit to the partners, a profit equal to, consistent with, and contained by the service done to the community in growing food at fixed prices. Some undertakings needed the support of whole towns, such as the Great Bridge over the Concord at Billerica, which was built and maintained by Dunstable, Chelmsford, Billerica, and Groton, all the settlements that used it.

The principle of economic cooperation had its political consequences for the towns of the Valley, however, as for all the towns of Massachusetts Bay. Despite strong attachment to a tradition of command, the Puritan fathers found that the participation of all freemen—church members or not—in political decisions was the only way to ensure peace and tranquillity and to prevent dissension from easily destroying the community. Despite themselves, the Puritans became democrats. It was consensus democracy that allowed only one set of values and left no room for minorities, but it was democracy nonetheless. Town meetings became the form of participation and they made it clear that property, not sainthood, should admit individuals to the process of control.

At Rowley in 1674 and 1675, after death had removed the strong hand of the Reverend Ezechial Rogers, the rule of the saints was challenged by a handful of citizens, with Abraham Jewett in the lead. They said it was the town (the freemen), and not the church (the saints), that paid for the minister's salary. It was the town, then, that had "Libberty" to choose the minister. This was contrary to the idea of church rule, at the center of Puritan life during the first generation. The controversy at Rowley was soon lost in the demands of Philip's War, but the trend away from church rule continued until equality and participation, the ideals of secular authority, prevailed against the Puritan virtues of subordination and command. In 1701 Boston celebrated the accession of Queen Anne, as was done throughout the British Empire. The Reverend Samuel Willard was shocked that in these festivities government officials were given a place of honor before the clergy. But it was done, and Boston must have been the last English-speaking city to

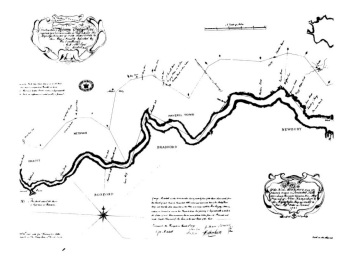

The boundary line between Massachusetts and New Hampshire was disputed until the settlement of 1739. This map, made in 1741, traces the Merrimack River from Pawtucket Falls (now Lowell) to the Atlantic and denotes the New Hampshire boundary following the river's course some three and a half miles to the north. Note that Boxford, rather than Andover, is incorrectly given river frontage. Courtesy, Trustees of the Haverhill Public Library.

think of it as news. The citizens of Massachusetts Bay were beginning to share a common inheritance with the other English colonies, and the inheritance was secular.

Yet one value of the Puritan past survived. The conviction remained that thrift, industry, and perseverance would be rewarded. This notion, often called the Puritan work ethic, was defended even when no longer nurtured by the Puritan theology that had been its matrix. The point is made by the career of the Reverend William Symmes at North Parish in Andover. The good pastor assumed his duties in November 1758 and stayed a rather long time, until 1788. Through those three decades, heavy with change, Symmes preached a liberal version of Puritan doctrine. That is what his congregation expected of him, and why they had "called" him rather than another to be their minister. However liberal his teaching on grace and predestination, he still defended the work ethic. "Beware sloth. Till the land," he said in 1785. "It is not God's ordinary method to rain down bread for the food of man." That wealth indicated God's favor had always been doubtful. On the other hand, it became increasingly certain that wealth won the respect and even the deference of other citizens, and it gave access to political power.

The face of the Merrimack as a frontier aged beyond recognition until even the memory of it was dissolved by time. The frontier against the wilderness and the military frontier against the French—even the political frontier with

New Hampshire—all were gone before the War of Independence in 1775.

The Indians and their French advisors made one final, devastating raid on Haverhill in 1708, killing 16 people, abducting 31. After this, the military operations were carried to the towns of the Valley, and they contributed their share of men and materiel to bring the war to the French in Canada. In 1763 the treaty was signed by which the French king relinquished all his territories and rights on this continent. The lands of the west suddenly became safe—safe from French military attack and safe from the sudden loss of legal title to the land. There was a surge of population, and the frontier began its relentless move westward.

On August 10, 1737, the members of the General Court of Massachusetts gathered at Salisbury, on the Merrimack, while the members of the General Court of New Hampshire met at nearby Hampton. This put both representative assemblies within negotiating distance of the Commission, which was then making another attempt to settle the disputed boundary between them. It was a major effort but, like one made six years before at Newbury, it failed. In desperation, the Commission appealed the question to the highest authority, the king.

Both Massachusetts and New Hampshire hired agents to argue their case before the king's Privy Council, where the decision would be made. It may be that the lords of the Council were predisposed against Massachusetts, which had the reputation among officials at London of being too independent. It may be that New Hampshire's agent, John Thomlinson, was genuinely superior to his rival from Massachusetts in presenting his case. Or it may be that Thomlinson played with the inspiration of a gambler, because he had bought the claims of the Mason family to New Hampshire in 1738.

For whatever reason, when King George made his decision on March 5, 1739, the case went for New Hampshire. The Privy Council decreed a line three miles north of the northern side of the Merrimack, from its mouth to three miles north of Pawtucket Falls, and from there due west until it met with His Majesty's other dominions. At one stroke, Massachusetts lost 28 towns it previously had claimed, some of them in the Merrimack Valley. The men of Massachusetts protested mightily against the decision, but there was no appeal. At this time, in this place, neither the will of God nor the will of the people was substantial enough to challenge the will of the king that fell between them.

The lower Merrimack Valley had acquired its permanent dimensions. The irony is that in 1739 New Hampshire and Massachusetts were more alike than ever before and the difference between them was fading with each passing year, until the populations on both sides saw the need for united action.

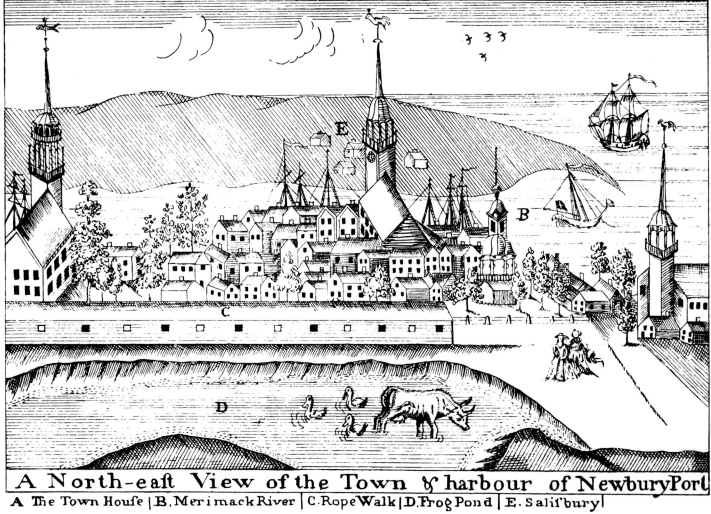

A North-east View of the Town & harbour of NewburyPort

A The Town House | **B.** Merimack River | **C.** RopeWalk | **D.** Frog Pond | **E.** Salisbury

IV

THE VALLEY IN A CHANGING AMERICA

Every order of things which has a tendency to remove oppression and meliorate the condition of man, directing his ambition to useful industry, is, in effect, republican.
— Robert Fulton, *Address to Congress*, 1807.

For a work of this kind will never be perfected by the abilities and labours of one man.
— Oliver Evans, *The Young Mill-Wright*, 1795.

The spring of 1775 called the men and women of the Valley towns to another year of labor: preparing of land, the planting of seed, the long months of care and risk to be outlived. They waited for signs from the place itself, as the generations had come to know the signs in the nearly 150 springs since the first European tilled the soil of the Valley. The great flocks of migrating geese had already passed, late in the winter; beavers left their lodges and returned to the work they had deserted since before the first snows of the previous year. The river ran with fish. And, more to the point for the thousands of farmers on the lower Merrimack, the bud of leaves on the elm was as big as the ear of a mouse, indicating it was

Newburyport, the smallest city in Massachusetts, was created out of Newbury land beginning in 1722, when the Third Parish was set off from the First. The enterprise of the "waterside" people (those living adjacent to the Merrimack) resulted in Newburyport's successful petition to become a separate, incorporated town in 1764, and a city in 1851. This engraving shows the importance of maritime economy along the river—there are more masts than church spires! (MTVM)

safe to plant the corn.

However, the spring of 1775 was unlike any other, before or since. The farmers at Chelmsford and Amesbury, at Bradford, and Dunstable, scanned the horizons beyond the Valley. They looked to Boston and Philadelphia and London for political signs, and most of them seem to have understood that soon they would reap a harvest of dragon's teeth. For one year now, since March 1774, relations with the king and Parliament had been in their final stage of collapse; a decade of strain was about to break into open conflict. In that month Parliament had ordered the port of Boston closed and in three separate acts had reorganized the government of Massachusetts, investing more power in a governor appointed by the crown. To emphasize the point of these changes, the London government named Major General Thomas Gage, a military man with 20 years of loyal service in America, as its first governor of Massachusetts under the new rules. At issue were commerce and politics, money and authority.

The towns of the Merrimack Valley answered Parliament, measure for measure. To the closing of Boston's port, they responded each in turn with a resolution, voted at meetings and binding on all citizens, not to buy British goods and not to consume them. Closing the ports on the Merrimack was a vital step in making that boycott effective in Massachusetts. To the subversion of the state's royal charter of 1692, the towns responded with defiance: they ignored the legislature convened by Gage at Boston, and instead sent delegates to the assembly of "patriots" that met at Concord and later moved on to Cambridge.

The center and the means of resistance among the people of the Merrimack Valley were the town and town meeting. Town meeting was an institution developed by the townsmen themselves, in the Valley as in other regions of New England. It was not imposed and it was not imported, except that some basis for it came with the English immigrants in the habits of their daily dealing with one another and the needs of agricultural village life in medieval England. In New England the habits of centuries were transformed by the demands of frontier living. Town meeting was used to mediate internal conflict, a way of preventing disagreement among individuals from exploding the community. In short, it set boundaries on aggression, and it made clear to individuals how much aggression the communities could tolerate. Also, since 1632 the towns had elected delegates to the lower chamber of the General Court, and this gave them some measure of control over their own economic and political well-being.

But the events of 1774 transformed the town meeting. In fact, they tempt the use of that ancient phrase *annus mirabilis,* Year of Marvels. For townsmen at Dracut, Tewksbury, and Andover debated not only this incident or that act of Parliament; they debated also the very basis of society, its nature and capacities. In other words, what a man owed to the public and what he reserved for himself and his own.

The towns of the Valley were not alone in challenging the authority of Parliament. Beyond them, the other towns of Massachusetts and the 12 other British colonies had their backs up. Not that the townsmen of the Merrimack Valley felt they had much in common with the people of the other regions where the drama of political revolt was being played: the coastal plains of the Carolinas, the area of Chesapeake Bay, the Hudson Valley. There were economic ties among the regions, certainly, but they did not hide from these men and women the great variations in social organization, political structure, and religious beliefs that made British colonies so different from any nation on earth.

Why the men of Georgia and Virginia, Pennsylvania and New York, should have overlooked their differences to concentrate attention on one point of community is a question that may have no satisfactory answer. Their one common link was their relationship with England. It was as siblings that they had a bond, and it was as siblings that they united in rebellion against the Mother of Parliaments. Their concentration of purpose achieved its focus at Philadelphia in September 1774 with the meeting of the First Continental Congress. The townspeople of the Merrimack Valley agreed, formally at town meeting, to ally themselves with the decisions of this Congress and to follow a unified direction in their economic and political resistance to Great Britain. The language of the resolution of the Andover townsmen is typical:

> Dec. 26, 1774: The town accepts every article & clause of Continental Congress requesting non-importation, non-exportation and non-consumption of British goods. Anyone over 21 who neglects to sign, shall have his name published in "Essex Gazette" as an enemy to the country.

The language of the resolution incidentally also reveals the underside of the town's freedom. Once a legal vote was taken in due process, there was no room for minority opinion. And God help the individual who, for whatever reason of courage or folly, stood against the town. Though he might not be banished he would be made to feel the crushing weight of exile among his own, a sinner among saints.

Eventually the 13 colonies formed a united political structure, and because they could not rely on a common tradition of place—which, after all, was England—they looked to antiquity for their model. They founded a republic. But the thoughtful men were worried because their trusted authorities said that such a republic was not possible. James Harrington and John Locke, who had defended England's "Glorious Revolution," the venerated French

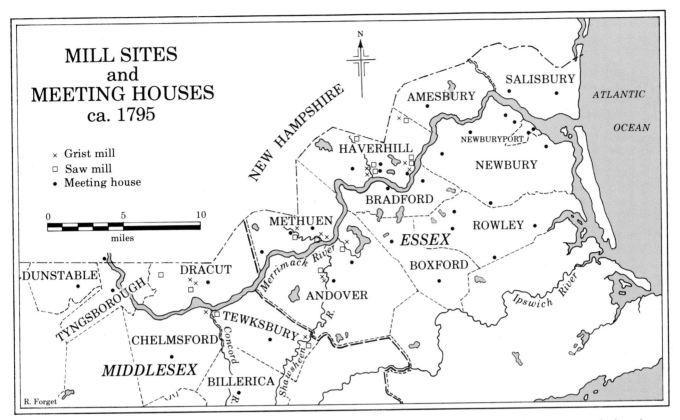

MILL SITES
and
MEETING HOUSES
ca. 1795

× Grist mill
□ Saw mill
• Meeting house

0   5   10
miles

NEW HAMPSHIRE

SALISBURY

AMESBURY

ATLANTIC

OCEAN

HAVERHILL

NEWBURYPORT

NEWBURY

BRADFORD

METHUEN

ESSEX

ROWLEY

Merrimack River

DUNSTABLE

DRACUT

BOXFORD

Ipswich River

ANDOVER

TYNGSBOROUGH

Concord R.

TEWKSBURY

Shawsheen R.

CHELMSFORD

MIDDLESEX

BILLERICA

R. Forget

Osgood Carleton's 1798 Map of the Commonwealth of Massachusetts, *based on individual town surveys of 1794-1795, provided the basis for this map of the Merrimack Valley. Carleton's key, which included numerous symbols, has been reduced here to show gristmills, sawmills, and meetinghouses as primary indicators of settlement patterns within the towns. Map made by Robert Forget for* The Valley and Its People.

philosophe Montesquieu, even that strange "young" man from Geneva, Jean Jacques Rousseau, all agreed that republics composed of so various a society as the British colonies, spread as they were over so large an area, could not survive.

On the level of theory, republics were small, composed of persons who enjoyed a near equality of income so that no one might master another. Women and servents, the propertyless in general, were excluded from the *res publica,* the public thing, precisely because in private things they were dependent on those with property. They might be bought. In many cases, they *had* been bought. The freeman was male, over 21, and in charge of his own economic life. Inevitably, this made him a taxpayer. Finally, the theory went, the republic's freemen shared a common reservoir of interests and values: they knew what needed protecting and which means of protection were honorable.

This theory of a republic spelled out what the allied towns of the Merrimack Valley had become in practice. But even here, on a local scale, there were difficulties in making the structure work. For instance, in January 1764, two miles of the waterfront of the Merrimack at Newbury were set off as the town of Newburyport, and the charter of incorporation left no doubt why this was necessary:

... the town of Newbury is very large, and the inhabitants of that part of it, who dwell by the water side there, as it is commonly called, are mostly merchants, traders and artificers, and the inhabitants of the other part of the town are chiefly husbandmen, by means whereof many difficulties and disputes have arisen in managing their public affairs.

Those whose livelihood comes from the sea have economic needs different from those who live by the land, so that, at Newbury, it was easier to divorce the two than to live in rancor and misery. How, then, would it be possible to unite more than two million persons living along so many hundreds of miles of the Eastern Seaboard? At least the townsmen of Newbury had a century and a half of experience at the business. What did the inhabitants of the 13 colonies have except their own government and suspicions of all the others? Furthermore, the republic model was drawn from antiquity and there was the example of antiquity itself; all the educated men at the time knew the story of Rome, how power had corrupted the Republic of Rome into the Empire of Rome. So, it was against all reason that participants in the events of 1774 disregarded the voices of the past. They made a republic, and for two centuries Americans have been working at keeping faith with that great gamble.

Those who lived from March 1774 to March 1775, found it difficult to judge when the point of breach was passed, the point at which all the parties, or most of them, agreed that no return was possible—or at least that none was desirable. The thick of battle narrows all points of view and in the end offers only one route of escape. For the king and his minister the breach was discovered in November 1774, when they decided that what the colonials had been naming defense of liberty they would name rebellion. Despite impassioned pleas for conciliation from Edmund Burke and others in the House of Commons, the king's government sent 12,000 troops to Boston. They arrived in March 1775. Eight hundred of these troops were sent by Gage on the historic march into Middlesex County on April 19, 1775, to search out and destroy hidden arms. Neither of the military engagements that resulted, on the green at Lexington and across North Bridge at Concord, had the scale of modern war. But these "embattled farmers," as Longfellow later described them, surely "fired the shot heard round the world." The national leaders, Franklin and Jefferson, later

A rare survival, this Revolutionary War helmet was worn by Michael Titcomb of Newburyport, who served in the Washington Life Guard from 1776 to 1779. Titcomb, trained as a cabinetmaker, also had a mast yard in Newburyport and was appointed first lieutenant of the Merrimack *in 1798. Courtesy, Essex Institute, Salem, Massachusetts.*

claimed that no one had talked of independence before hearing the news of the events at Lexington and Concord. Those events revealed the breach. These British subjects were certainly at the end of one road, so whichever road they now chose would have to be a beginning. The slow waters of the Concord River left the scene of battle at North Bridge, joined the swifter current of the Merrimack at Chelmsford, and rushed, free, toward a destiny in the Atlantic. In April 1775, after a year of continual correspondence, Americans suddenly realized that they had been calling to each other from a common future.

The year of rapid movement was over. Now began the years of tedious work, the slow drudging toward the vision seen in the clear light of spring. Endurance was needed rather than speed, stamina more than outrage. Perhaps, after all, the long generations of contention with the unyielding soil of the Valley were not lost on these farmers become soldiers.

Only the minutemen of Chelmsford, of those from the Valley towns, reached Concord before the battle ended. Others joined in the bloody pursuit of the British as they retreated back to Charlestown. That retreat was the beginning of a siege, for Gage soon found himself surrounded by the people he had come to rule. The first major engagement in the War of Independence, at Breed's Hill and Bunker Hill, was in fact his attempt to loosen that circle. He succeeded, but at a fearful cost. "We have lost some extremely good officers," he reported to London. "The trials we have had show the rebels are not the despicable rabble too many have supposed them to be." He ended with an assessment that became a prediction. "The conquest of this country is not easy; you have to cope with vast numbers. In all their wars against the French, they never showed so much conduct, attention, and perseverance as they do now." But the king and his government could not hear what they chose to ignore. It took six years of war and two of negotiation to bend their willful ignorance into something like accommodation.

Gage was correct nevertheless. There were many in Massachusetts with combat experience, and some had gained the confidence of command in the French wars. One of these was Colonel James Frye of Andover, who rode to Breed's Hill with cheering news for friend and stranger alike. "This day 30 years ago," he told them, "I was at the taking of Louisbourg [Nova Scotia]. This is a fortunate day for Americans. We shall certainly beat the enemy!" There were hundreds from the Valley at Charlestown on this day of battle, June 17, 1775. Nearly 75 came from Haverhill alone, and more than 50 from Amesbury. There were the men of Tewksbury led by John Trull and those of Methuen under John Davis. One company came from Newbury with Captain Jacob Gerrish, and two from Newburyport, led by Captains Erza Lunt and Benjamin Perkins. They did not

Families in the Merrimack Valley were under the constant shadow of death, from infancy through adulthood. In an epidemic of cholera or typhoid in the fall of 1778, multiple deaths occurred among the Fletcher, Swallow, and Woodward families of Dunstable in the space of a week. These stones record the ominous toll to those families. Courtesy, Richard Graber, Andover, Massachusetts.

beat the enemy that day, but they responded with valor to the reminder that they were Americans.

The victory that escaped the men of the Valley so close to home was pursued into the middle and southern states of the Union. For six years the townspeople of the Valley made their contribution to the common effort at independence. This meant not only the soldiers who were sent every year at town charge to serve in the Continental Army. It meant also the supplies of food and clothing Massachusetts required of the towns. Toward the end, for instance, in 1780, Amesbury sent 33 oxen, weighing 900 pounds each, to help feed the army, while in the following year Haverhill contributed more than 16 tons of beef for the same purpose. The women of the Valley were at their spinning wheels and looms, making blankets and clothing for the soldiers of the republic.

The sea also was an arena of battle, one in which the ports on the Merrimack played a significant role. In June 1775, with hostilities just beginning, Bradford, Haverhill, Amesbury, and Newburyport cooperated to block the entrance of the river to British ships. These towns, however, were not satisfied with merely a defensive policy. Following the practice of the 18th century, Congress commissioned private vessels to harass enemy shipping. Thus Congress was able to disrupt enemy commerce at little or

no cost to the public, while the privateers, as they were called, stood to make a handsome income from "prizes" taken on the seas. It is difficult to say how many privateers were commissioned from Newburyport, but it was probably more than 100, for there were 61 in the years from 1780 to the signing of a treaty three years later. These 61 vessels carried 518 guns and just over 2,000 men. Privateers were also commissioned out of Salisbury.

Some of the experienced sailors of the Valley did serve on the vessels of the republic's young and small navy, and they challenged the great warships of His Britannic Majesty on the high seas. Two Newburyporters, cousins of the prominent Lunt family, were aboard the *Bonhomme Richard* as second and third lieutenants at the time of her encounter with HMS Serapis in September of 1779.

For two years the course of the war was inconclusive. However, the tide was turned in a series of sharp encounters in and about Saratoga, New York, during the summer and fall of 1777. This clear defeat of the British ruined their hope of dividing the 13 confederated states and, more important still, convinced the French that the Americans could win. In February 1778 the government of Louis XVI gave recognition to the United States of America and signed a military alliance, pledging loans, arms, and men. The French no doubt were motivated by revenge, hoping to return the injury they had received from Britain in 1763. But, whatever their purpose, it served America's well enough. The French alliance proved to be the decisive trick that turned the game in America's favor.

The war ended in October 1781 at Yorktown, Virginia, on a slip of land between the James and York rivers. Maneuvered into a dead end, British general Cornwallis found himself outnumbered by a combined American and

French force on land, and cut off by a French fleet from help by sea. He surrendered without a fight. Britain might have pursued the war, of course. She had by no means exhausted her economic and military resources. But the disaster at Yorktown produced political convulsions at London, which forced Geroge III to deal with the "rebels" he so heartily despised. The result, in 1783, was the Treaty of Paris, and his grudging acceptance of American independence. The republic was sovereign at last.

Winning the War of Independence was not the end of the revolution made by Americans. Looking at what was happening around him, John Adams concluded that people will make revolution only after it has been accomplished in the mind; in other words, there is no completing the design until the design is recognized. For the English king and his government, the design was completed when they conceded to relinquishing sovereignty over the 13 colonies now calling themselves the United States of America. But, for the 13 governments of the United States and for the peoples they represented, the story was only half told, the design only half recognized. With military decisions behind them, Americans now faced the political decisions they had neglected or shunted or escaped during the years of the war. The republic was sovereign but in what way should it rule? What structures would best translate the idea of the republic into reality? And there were conceptual problems as well. How can 13 governments make up one republic? How can sovereignty be shared when sovereignty is indivisible?

Finding solutions to these political riddles was complicated by the economics of the decade. It's not surprising, then, that political debates in the Valley were strongly marked by the commercial character of the region's economy, and particularly by the hard times of the postwar decade. After March 1781 the new republic was ruled by the Articles of Confederation, and the inability of the federal establishment to promote trade under this constitution fueled the demand by merchants that the constitution be changed. In the end they accepted an entirely new one, written at Philadelphia in 1787; they declared themselves satisfied that its provisions would promote commerce and so recognized, in that document, the end of the American Revolution.

Newburyport was the undoubted queen of the Merrimack at this time, but Salisbury, Amesbury, Bradford, and Haverhill were also merchant towns. Together they anchored the northern end of the wide circumference of Essex ports, billowing out into the Atlantic: Gloucester, Ipswich, Marblehead, Manchester, Beverly, and, to anchor the southern end, Salem, the second-largest town in New England. These ports of Essex County constituted commercial interests second only to Philadelphia. The men who controlled this formidable nexus of power were clear about their objectives and confident of achieving them. The political notions of the Essex men of commerce had a significant impact on the new federal constitution, and two men who were part of the establishment at Newburyport were well placed to make individual contributions.

One of these was Theophilus Parsons. In 1778 he was 28 years old, a young lawyer in practice at Newburyport. In that year Parsons was among the politically minded men from various towns of Essex County who gathered at Treadwell's Tavern in Ipswich to debate a proposed state constitution for Massachusetts. Parsons also wrote the *Essex Result*, a pamphlet that made public the opinions and findings of the meeting. They objected, the *Result* said, to the lack of a bill of rights in the proposed constitution, and they thought that the power of the state—executive, legislative, judicial—ought to be carefully divided and balanced. These changes were needed to safeguard the rights of the individual. Among the many readers of the pamphlet who found the changes sensible and just was John Adams, a friend of Parsons who helped put the views of the *Result* into the Massachusetts constitution of 1780. The structure of the federal establishment, debated and resolved at Philadelphia in 1787, also bears the obvious marks of the *Essex Result.*

The structure of government, however, was only one of the problems addressed by Parsons and his colleagues. The gathering of 1778 also talked about the structure of society because, for the men of Essex, the republic was a form of government in the middle, facing dangers from above—when power was concentrated in one individual—and dangers from below—when power was taken by people "of the lower sort." The men of Essex saw no better remedy against the tendency to drift to either extreme than to put the throttle of power in the hands of the men of wealth. This is done, according to the *Result*, by dividing the legislature into two houses, the one representing the "people," and the other representing property. In this view of things, wealth always indicated wisdom, goodness, education; it demonstrated high moral purpose and rigorous intelligence together with the ability and prudence to handle money.

In 1778 Theophilus Parsons was at the beginning of a long and distinguished career at law, nearly all of it at Newburyport. In 1806, however, he was appointed Chief Justice of the Supreme Judicial Court of Massachusetts in Boston. When he died seven years later, he left behind a number of important precedents, particularly in the field of shipping and insurance. For the men of Essex, 1778 was the beginning of an association, loosely organized but powerful enough over the next generation to affect national politics from time to time. In 1780 Governor John Hancock called them the Essex Junto, not meaning to be friendly. Thirty-two years later, Henry Clay dismissed them as the

*One of the great eccentrics of his day, Newburyport's Timothy
Dexter gained a fortune through commerce and shipping, although he began his career as a leather dresser. Lord Timothy,
as he styled himself, wrote an account of his life entitled A
Pickle for the Knowing Ones and kept a lion in his yard for
two weeks in 1795, among other oddities. Newburyport engrav-
er James Akin engraved this likeness in 1805, the year before
Dexter died. Courtesy, Essex Institute, Salem, Massachusetts.*

"Jackals of the Essex Kennel." The Essex Junto has had
fewer defenders than did their Puritan ancestors, whose
temper of mind they inherited. And like their sainted
forebears, the Junto became another perfect example of
how a point of view held too long becomes a blind spot.

A second Newburyporter played an individual role in
this political story of a changing America. Rufus King was
born at Scarborough in the District of Maine, but in 1787 he
represented Massachusetts at the Constitutional Convention at Philadelphia, and by that time he had been a resident on the lower Merrimack for 20 years. When he was 12

years old, his merchant father sent Rufus to the Dummer
School at Byfield in Newbury where he was instructed by
master Samuel Moody, as Parsons had been before him.
Later, after four obligatory years at the "colleges at
Cambridge," he returned to the Valley, settling at
Newburyport and reading law with Parsons. For three
years, during the 1780s, King was elected to represent the
town in the Massachusetts delegation at the Continental Congress. The Essex Junto could hardly have found
anyone more qualified to present and defend its views at
Philadelphia.

The next 20 years rewarded those who had wanted to
increase the authority of the federal government. With a
national trade policy, with public and private credit secure,
with the establishment of the Bank of the United States,
commerce and business in the young republic flourished.
The merchant towns of the lower Merrimack enjoyed a
long summer of prosperity.

The shipyards on the Merrimack—at Salisbury and
Amesbury, at Bradford and Haverhill, and of course at
Newburyport—recovered and surpassed their prewar productivity. In 1772 one witness reported 90 ships launched
at Newburyport alone. In the boom years that covered a
decade on either side of 1800, the Merrimack yards saw the
construction of over 1,000 vessels of all sizes and descrip-
tions. Twelve thousand tons were launched in 1810 alone.
And also in 1810, a year of relative decline, Newburyport
had 160 vessels in the European and West Indies trade, and
54 more in the Banks fisheries. Fortunes were made, great
and small. This prosperity was reflected in Newburyport's
appearance. Timothy Dwight, former president of Yale College, traveled widely throughout New England and New
York during these years, and he found the town one of the
finest on his itinerary. Its High Street became the site of
grand mansions in the newest Federal style. The town had
a new meetinghouse, and a new courthouse built in 1805
inspired by the famous Charles Bulfinch.

The capital accumulated in this commercial prosperity
was put to work, invested in "internal improvement,"
which was the rage of the era throughout the new republic.
Improvement in transportation was a particular favorite,
perhaps because results were so immediate and dramatic.
No fewer than four bridges were built across the Merrimack, all of them after a design by Timothy Palmer of
Newburyport, and some of them built with the help of
Palmer's mentor, the engineer Moody Spofford of Georgetown. The first bridge, the Essex-Merrimack, was finished
in 1792 at Deer Island, about three miles upstream from the
center of Newburyport. In rapid succession there came the
great bridge at Haverhill, 650 feet long, 34 feet wide; the
third connected Andover and Methuen; and the fourth, at
Pawtucket Falls, was built between Chelmsford and
Dracut.

The Middlesex Canal

Moving goods on the waters of the Merrimack no doubt began even before Paul White, merchant at Newbury, obtained the town's permission to build a wharf on the river. That was in April 1655, and it was the first grant for such an enterprise on record. The river was used in this commercial way well into the present century when coal, for example, was barged up to Merrimacport, to Haverhill, and to other locations. But it was natural that the heyday of commerce on the Merrimack should coincide with the golden years of prosperity that followed the ratification of the Federal Constitution of 1789. The proof and the symbol of the river's place in this flourishing trade was the Middlesex Canal.

Constructed between 1797 and 1803, the canal left the river at Chelmsford and ran for a distance of 27 miles before reaching Charlestown, its southern terminal. And it was no simple ditch: the course of the canal required building 20 locks, 8 aqueducts, and 48 bridges. The most impressive structure in the canal may have been the aqueduct that carried the canal 30 feet above the Shawsheen River at Billerica. By 1814 the Middlesex was one of a network of canals that connected the capitals of Massachusetts and New Hampshire.

However much a triumph of American finance and engineering, the Middlesex was costly for the region of the lower Merrimack, particularly for the merchants of Newburyport. In 1805 almost 10,000 tons of freight moved south through the canal to the port of Charlestown; nearly 90 percent of that was New Hampshire lumber, and all of it was diverted from the wharves at the mouth of the river. The lower Merrimack was pushed aside by the success of the Boston merchants competing with those of Newburyport, but what the canal took from commerce, it returned as industrial enterprise. Its proximity to the power of Pawtucket Falls made the canal another reason to choose Chelmsford as a site for the industrial production of cotton goods. The development of Lowell after 1821 brought over a decade of prosperous activity on the Middlesex. That ended with the construction of the Lowell-Boston Railroad in 1835; the railroad could move freight faster, and, unlike the canal, it was not stopped by the freeze of winter. The canal corporation struggled through the 1840s, but it did not survive the next decade. It was officially pronounced dead, its charter annulled, by the General Court in 1860.

Painted about 1825, this view shows the Middlesex Canal from the house of William Rogers in Billerica. At left, a man on horseback pulls a canalboat, while another man rides for pleasure at center. Jabez Warren Barton painted this watercolor as a companion piece to his view of Rogers' house. Courtesy, Billerica Historical Society.

Also at Pawtucket Falls, on the Chelmsford side, Newburyport capital created the Proprietors of Locks and Canals on Merrimack River in 1792, still in operation and one of the oldest corporations in the United States. The locks and canals were to provide a way around the falls for the timber that the merchants of Newburyport wanted to divert to their wharves at the mouth of the river. A decade later (1803) Newburyporters incorporated a company to construct the Newburyport-Boston Turnpike. Finished in 1806, the road was 34 miles long and as straight as engineers were able to make it. It cost $500,000 to build, an enormous sum, and included two hotels that the investors added to the original design. The investors obviously expected the route would be heavily traveled, but in this they were disappointed.

Manufacturing attracted less capital investment than transportation, but the need and benefit were widely acknowledged, as is shown in the following resolution passed at town meeting of Newburyport in 1786.

> We exceedingly lament, that in a country abounding with every material, the ingenuity and dexterity of whose people are exceeded by none, the practice of exporting unwrought materials, and importing manufactures, should be general, for we esteem it impolitic and uncommerical to export the former, till wrought to perfection or to import the latter, especially when wrought from materials of our own produce . . .

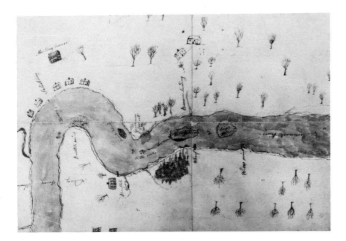

This manuscript map of the Merrimack River shows the bend at Salisbury Point, just below the ferry between Newbury and Amesbury, and continues to the edge of Newburyport. We can date this map at about 1790, since the Rocky Hill Meeting House, built in 1785, is shown at the top left, but Timothy Palmer's bridge, built in 1792 across Deer Island, does not appear. Courtesy, Historical Society of Old Newbury.

The residents of the towns of the lower Merrimack were anxious, as were all Americans, to establish economic independence, especially from the need to import the manufactured goods of England. The Newburyport Woolen Manufactory, the first incorporated textile company in Massachusetts, began operation in 1794. Across the Merrimack in Amesbury, Ezra Worthen also ran a textile operation using the waters of the Powow to turn the wheels of his mill. The ablest local machinist of the period was Jacob Perkins. A native of Newburyport, Perkins invented machines for making nails, milling coin, and making banknotes that could not be counterfeited. His success, however, was never equal to his ambition and the irony is that he eventually moved to London thinking to improve both his reputation and his income. In the meantime, the notes of the Massachusetts banks were for the most part engraved and printed at Newburyport.

Less glamorous, perhaps, but surely another bellwether of prosperity were the investments made by the citizens of the lower Merrimack in the banking and insurance industries so vital to commerce.

Finally, the culture of the town reflected growth. A wide variety of activities made their appearance, from singing schools and dramatic readings to traveling circuses with their wild assortment of educated pigs, acrobats, and ventriloquists. Newspapers began making weekly appearances. There were other publishers and printers at Newburyport. Edmund Blunt published Captain Lawrence Furlong's *American Coastal Pilot* and the *New Practical Navigator* by Nathaniel Bowditch, both signal contributions by native "Porters."

The agricultural sector of the Merrimack's economy shared in the prosperity of its commerce. Newbury, in particular, stimulated by the growing urban market at its back door, experienced a 25 percent increase in population between 1800 and 1810. Newbury farmers responded to the opportunity for a larger volume of sales by increasing the number of plantings, and by increasing the amount of fertilizers they used. The yield per acre of its farms was above average for the period: 40 bushels of corn, 200 of potatoes, 25 of barley, 20 of rye. Wheat as usual was more difficult to grow, yielding only about 10 bushels to the acre.

The towns of the lower Merrimack enjoyed a prosperous economy for 20 years after the Constitution of 1789. Many, perhaps most, of the townfolk enjoyed a happy prospect of plenty. Some leaders, however, reported having political premonitions—nightmares, in their definition of politics. They saw the face of opposition materialize before them, and the face belonged to Thomas Jefferson. By 1800, despite his thousands of acres and his slaves, Jefferson had somehow become accepted as a spokesman of the common man. Also, during the 1790s Jefferson was generally recognized as the most important of several leaders of an emerging po-

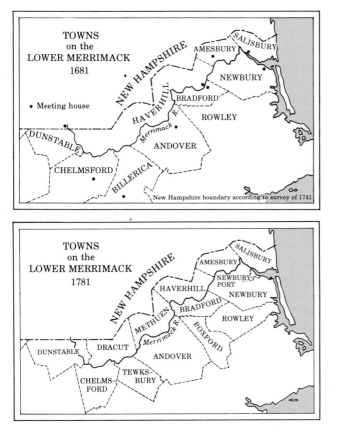

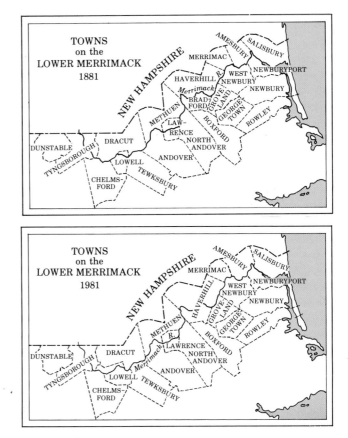

These township maps show the changing boundaries of Valley communities over time. Some towns that bordered on the Merrimack at one period no longer have direct access to the river. Maps made by Robert Forget for The Valley and Its People.

litical party who were called Republicans or Democratic-Republicans. The discovery of the common man was decisive as a prophecy of our political history. The discovery completed a train of thought begun by the previous generation, and it was the final evolution in political ideas of the new republic. It was inevitable as well that the thought produced a revolutionary device, politics by party. James Madison, also among the leaders of the new party, best justified the development of party politics. After all, he said, toleration was not new for Americans who had observed a wide variety of Christian forms without ever coming to open war. In the same way, he thought, political parties would make political toleration possible. Honest differences would lead to controlled opposition: parties were a mechanism to keep the Union together despite radical differences of opinion about how it should be run.

Today parties are accepted as a basic element of political life, but it was a difficult passage for that generation to negotiate. The Federalists, the party in power under Washington and Adams, clung desperately to the claim that the ability to lead was natural to some people only and that the ability could not be conferred by the votes of "people of the lower sort." The Puritans had thought that wealth might indicate the knowledge of God's plan and so confer the obligation to lead. These secular Yankee merchants of Essex were saying that wealth demonstrates superior ability to manage things and men and so bestows the right to govern. The mere fact that another party was emerging to challenge these natural leaders was a clear sign of perversion at the base of the republic. Nevertheless, Jefferson continued his "evil" ways, and the Democratic-Republicans pursued office and displaced Federalists in local and state elections. Finally, in the 1800 election, Jefferson was elected President of the United States.

The American system, the republic, was completed when John Adams, Federalist, peaceably relinquished the office of President of the United States to Thomas Jefferson, Democratic-Republican. Historians have often remarked that Jefferson, in March 1801, walked from his inauguration at the Capitol to a reception at the White House rather than ride in a carriage as Washington and Adams had done. This reportedly symbolized his coming from "the people." And, true enough, as a symbol it remains pleasing, but it ought not obscure the substance: that he was allowed office at all is astounding. There was no precedent, anywhere, for such an orderly transfer of power.

The Essex Junto remained in the forefont of opposition to

Jefferson after his election. Charges and stories were printed about Jefferson and his administration in the *Newburyport Herald and Country Gazette* that now would be considered ridiculous. Jefferson was an atheist, they said, and would bring the collapse of Christian morality; his prattling about the common man would bring the elimination of private property which was, after all, the foundation of the republic. The accusers pointed out that Jefferson was a friend of France and devoted to all the radical political ideas that the French Republic had been spreading to the rest of Europe since 1792. By contrast, feelings against the French ran so high at Newburyport that the town raised $30,000 to build a warship for use by the American navy. Launched on October 12, 1798, it was named the *Merrimack*, a 360-ton vessel carrying 28 guns. In mid-December it sailed to the West Indies to join a squadron under Commodore John Barry. With that, one historian of the town has said, "Newburyport had in effect issued its own declaration of war against France."

It may be that the Junto's diatribe against Jefferson was meant to immunize the voters of the Valley against the seduction of Jeffersonian rhetoric. But concerning trade and Jefferson's policies' detrimental effects on the commercial prosperity of the Valley, there were more than words at issue. The Essex men, and the Federalists in general, accepted the Constitution of 1789 because it gave the federal government the power to promote trade, and it didn't seem possible to them that the power might be used to damage commerce. After all, wasn't that why Americans had rejected the rule of Parliament? Yet, in 1807 Jefferson, with the support of his partisans in Congress, issued an Embargo Act that outlawed trade with both England and France. Jefferson's purpose was political: he wanted to maintain the neutrality of the United States during the intense and prolonged wars in Europe. However, the consequence of Jefferson's policy was economic: it put an immediate end to the years of prosperity that the port towns on the Merrimack had shared with the entire maritime sector of the American economy.

Jefferson's policies delayed American involvement in Europe's wars, but they also put new life in the waning political fortunes of the Essex Junto. When war against England finally came in 1812, under Jefferson's successor, they called it Mr. Madison's war. They thought it had nothing to do with them. How galling it must have been for the Valley Federalists in particular to see their old enemy, Joe Varnum of Dracut, sitting in 1813 as president *pro tem* of the Senate, acting Vice-President of the United States. Joe Varnum, proud of nothing so much as of his 500-acre farm with "more than 10 miles of good stone fence upon it."

The diehard New England Federalists favored secession over submission to this flagrant disregard of their interest. They convened at Hartford, Connecticut, in 1814, but in the end the Hartford Convention did not lead to a rupture in the Union. The majority understood that it was one thing, in 1764, to separate two square miles of river front on the Merrimack because merchants and farmers at Newbury couldn't manage to get along. It was quite another to cast away 40 years of monumental political invention by thousands of individuals and scores of towns.

Forty years lay between the Boston Port Bill (1774) and the Hartford Convention (1814). In that time the towns on the lower Merrimack had made their contributions to the military effort against England and had participated significantly in the political revolution as well. In that time the maritime economy of the region was well served by the power of the Federal establishment, particularly by the voice of the Essex Junto, strident and unreasoning as that voice often was. At the end of the republic's second war with England, in 1815, it seemed that the region had made its last contribution to the evolution of America and that the Valley of the lower Merrimack would become a political backwater.

Sloop-of-war Merrimack *was built at Newburyport in 1798 and was equipped with 28 guns. It typified American war vessels in the period when the Navy was being built. Courtesy, Peabody Museum of Salem.*

43

V

ENTERING THE INDUSTRIAL AGE

And now when upon the subject of the river, I think it proper to observe, that though in various ways this town in common with others upon its brink derive great advantages from this noble stream, it is obvious to any person who will take the trouble to reflect upon the subject that these advantages are much less than they might, indeed ought to be.

— Gardner Perry, *History of Bradford, Massachusetts*, 1820.

If you wish for increasing prosperity, you must move, like the planetary system, round a common centre, and that with increasing harmony. You must sacrifice at one altar and remember that you are members of one community, and interested in promoting the honor and prosperity of one town.

— Wilkes Allen, *History of Chelmsford*, 1820.

Nathan Appleton tells the story of how he and some others traveled to Chelmsford one day in November 1821, how they inspected the falls

A rare survivor, this throstle-type spinning frame was built by the Locks & Canals machine shop in Lowell during the 1830s. The frame consists of both wood and iron, a transitional feature typical of this period. It has 64 spindles, 32 on each side. Courtesy, Slater Mill Historic Site.

Represented here in its natural state, the river appears as it might have looked before the building of the dam, canals, and factories that would be called Lowell. Painted by Alvan Fisher in 1833, this landscape belies its time and place, as by this date the river was already lined with brick mills. Courtesy, Baker Library, Harvard University.

on the Merrimack at that site, and how in fact they had gone there only because the place offered waterpower. Patrick Tracy Jackson and Paul Moody were, like Appleton himself, natives of the Valley; the other three—John W. Boott, his brother Kirk Boott, and Warren Dutton—were Bostonians. Six men, prospectors as they've been called, in search of power to continue a business project already well under way at Waltham on the Charles. The two rivers, the ancient frontiers of Puritan Massachusetts, were again put to common effort, and like their "sainted" ancestors, these six new colonials came to the Merrimack Valley looking for place but found instead opportunity, an occasion in time.

The visit to Pawtucket Falls opened the industrial chapter in the Valley's story. Yet it was more than a local event, because the success of Appleton and his associates reached national proportions. The textile mills they built on the power of the Merrimack became an example to other Americans, and a proof to the rest of the world that the American republic was coming of age. Those mills were a demonstration that Americans had the technical and financial capacities to be a manufacturing nation. But it was not enough just to prove that Americans could do this; it was important, too, that the mills at Chelmsford prove Americans able to do it better than anyone had done it before, anywhere. Americans would learn from the past. The republic would avoid all the errors of tired old Europe.

England in particular was a model to avoid, and doing better than the English was still a need Americans had not outgrown. The record of British factories and factory cities

was like an omen to be dispelled, for there was no denying that British industry had brought many evils to the English. There were physical evils, such as unsafe workplaces and filthy living conditions, and moral evils such as greed and despair. There were social evils as well, all of them opening vast inequalities of wealth between those who owned the factories and those who labored in them. England might be a fit place for these inequalities, as England's political culture rested on centuries of class divisions. Americans, however, regarded social inequality as distinctly not American. Equality was the very soul of the republic and economic self-reliance was the base of all equality. Twenty years before an English settlement was made in the Valley, John Smith promised that "here every man may be master and owner of his own labor." More recently, Thomas Jefferson had constructed a political movement by glorifying farmers as the Lord's Chosen on earth. The self-sufficiency of farmers was not merely a virtue, it was *the* Virtue on which the republic was founded—its source of power. How, then, could this republic survive the inequalities that industrial production brought with it?

Concern with this question during the first generation after the ratification of the Constitution, for 30 years or so after 1789, is quite apparent. For instance, it was this concern that motivated Bailey Bartlett in 1801. A group of townsmen at Haverhill had petitioned the town "for leave to conduct the water by means of an acqueduct from Round Pond, so-called, into the settled part of town for private and public convenience." The request was referred to a committee with Bailey Bartlett as its chairman. He reported in favor of the petition, but attached conditions to the committee's approval. The first of these was that no one be allowed to buy more than one share of the stock until the subscription had been open for 90 days. At the end of this period, the remaining unsold shares might be taken by any of the shareholders. And, further, the company that built and operated the aqueduct was required to submit its regulations to the town for approval.

Bartlett, who was elected to Congress in his district, reflected the thinking of the citizens of Haverhill and the surrounding towns. The ideals of the common voter were a common inheritance, grown out of the Puritan notion of property and from the experience of two centuries in the Valley. The experience of the place taught that in some final sense all property was communal, and that private gain was not its only purpose. So, again, in 1803, the town of Haverhill granted a petition to erect a hay scales, certainly a useful enterprise in this farming community. But the town also exercised its right to control the price of service: one and a quarter cents per hundredweight for all hay loads over 600 pounds, and eight cents for each load under 600 pounds.

Like most Americans of the period, the citizens of

Haverhill were extremely wary of concentrations of wealth, because wealth generated social and political power, and like the framers of the Constitution, they wanted power distributed, not concentrated. These were the thoughts and fears that Appleton and his friends had to confront and overcome, when they came to build their mills at Chelmsford. They didn't ignore those fears, they didn't pretend to have a technical problem only or a financial problem only. They had a social problem as well, involving nothing less than the character of the American people and the definition of the republic. But they managed to solve it: for nearly 20 years they combined the ideals of republican equality and the needs of industrial production. Or so it seemed, for a time. American statesmen, such as President Andrew Jackson, and foreign celebrities, such as Charles Dickens, came to the Valley and marveled at the accomplishment. The radiance of American Virtue was a promise of hope that in the Merrimack Valley a better future had been found.

Until November 1821, the Valley of the lower Merrimack was like the valleys of scores of other rivers where water-power was providing a new sort of education. In England and in America, sites of falling water acted as a kind of lens, concentrating mechanical experience and mathematics and the hope of profit with a focus intense enough to put a brand on the future. The Puritan and Yankee residents of the Valley had used the waters of the Merrimack's tributaries, from the first decade of settlement, to power the mills—sawmills, gristmills, fulling mills—that the economies of their towns had demanded. But textile mills were different. They required many more workers and so presented managerial problems of organization and control. Also, textile mills were far more complex in their mechanics than even the most sophisticated grist- or fulling mill.

Beginning a textile enterprise meant designing and making an efficient wheel and wheel pit, it meant building an efficient transmission system of shafts, pulleys, and belts. Textile production also meant arranging the machines so the work could move easily from one to the next as each performed a step in a series that transformed fiber into yarn. Besides, each enterprise had to make its own machines. Since there were no machine manufacturers, each mill needed its own machine shop where the good ideas, those that worked, were arrived at collectively. The textile entrepreneur in 1800 or 1810 had to be part machinist, part millwright, part personnel manager, and he had to combine these various skills in himself or find others who would work with him or for him.

The technological demands of textile manufacturing were decidedly more complex than any known before, but there were sites on the tributaries of the Merrimack where the demands were well met. On the Powow at Amesbury

Ezra Worthen, with the help of Paul Moody and Jacob Perkins, began to operate a cotton-spinning mill in 1812. At Chelmsford, the following year, Phineas Whiting and Josiah Fletcher built a mill 60 feet long by 50 feet wide and 40 feet high "for a cotton manufactory" powered by the Concord River. Five years later, in 1818, Thomas Hurd bought their mill and fitted it with an impressive assortment of machines for making woolens. The choice of location was natural for Hurd, who came from Charlestown. Chelmsford and Charlestown lay at opposite ends of the Middlesex Canal, a waterway that Hurd no doubt hoped would link his mill with the Boston markets. Meanwhile, Moses Hale and Oliver Whipple were also developing the site on the Concord, complete with a power canal that they

Before Lowell and Lawrence were built, individual mills utilized the power of waterfalls. The Methuen Company's cotton mill, shown in this circa 1837 lithograph of the falls and mills on the Spigot River, represented the style of building typical in Lowell. Individual operations like this one persisted alongside the Lowell model until well into the 19th century. (MVTM)

began in September 1821.

None of this work was done in isolation; each site relied on news from other places where textile technology was being pursued aggressively, and no machinist scrupled at using the discoveries of others. Chance played a role in establishing these contacts. How quickly one could get news, how quickly it could be analyzed and adapted, whether, indeed, there was anyone able to decipher the news, all these factors depended as much on chance as on effort. But there were efforts made, and no contacts were sought out more eagerly than those with English mechanics, particularly those with managerial experience. Nearly all innovations in textile technology originated in England in the 25 or so years before 1800. Any Englishman who could dem-

Cochichewick Brook—became the renowned Davis and Furber Machine Company, maker of woolen machinery down to the present. But, in the early years, it was the technology of cotton manufacturing that was on the cutting edge of a revolution, and by far the greatest contribution made by an Englishman to the American textile industry was made by Samuel Slater.

Newbury native Paul Moody (1779-1831), an excellent machinist, trained first as a weaver with the Scholfields in the 1790s, and later as a machine maker with Jacob Perkins of Newburyport. After working as superintendent of the machine shop at Waltham, he transferred to Lowell along with his staff, tools, and patterns to make the necessary machinery for the new mills on the Merrimack. Moody's skill was an important component of the ultimate success of the Boston Associates. (MVTM)

Nathaniel Stevens (1786-1865) was born and raised in Andover's North Parish, where he established his woolen mill in a former gristmill on the Cochichewick Brook in 1813. The business he founded was carried on by his family at that site until 1972. The Stevens' company eventually acquired other mills in the Merrimack Valley, including two at Haverhill, one at Andover, and one at Dracut, in addition to those in other New England locations. The mills made woolen flannels and suitings, and during the Civil War they prospered with orders for blankets and uniforms. (MVTM)

onstrate firsthand knowledge of machines was respected for his high skills and sometimes as a business partner. In 1802 James Scholfield, a British immigrant, was first in the Merrimack Valley to card wool by machine. He used the waters of Cochichewick Brook in Andover's North Parish. Though a small stream, the brook offered a drop of more than 70 feet in little more than a mile; the Pennacooks were accurate in calling it "Place of Cascades." Scholfield stayed long enough to help Nathaniel Stevens, a native of the town, begin his enterprise of woolen manufacture in 1813. That operation was also located on Cochichewick Brook on a site formerly occupied by a gristmill. Stevens learned from Scholfield as well as from Moses Hale of Chelmsford, who became his father-in-law in 1815.

In Andover's South Parish, Abraham Marland, another English immigrant, began his cotton-spinning mill in 1804 at a site on the Shawsheen River. Only six years later he refitted for woolen manufacturing and so helped spawn a firm of machine builders who later—and again on

Slater was an early arrival from England, coming in the first year of the republic, 1789, and during his 22nd year. He carried only his indenture to document his seven years of experience at the cotton-spinning mill of Jedediah Strutt. Strutt himself was a former partner of Richard Arkwright, the inventor of the spinning frame, so while Slater was a first-generation American, he was a third-generation machinist of impressive pedigree. Within months of his arrival, Slater was in partnership with Moses Brown, merchant of Providence, Rhode Island, and in less than two years they organized the first successful cotton-spinning

Abraham Marland (1771-1849) was born in Lancashire, England, and immigrated to the United States in 1801. After an initial foray into cotton manufacture at Beverly and Lynnfield, Marland settled at Andover in the business of wool manufacture. The Marland Mills were known for their fine flannels and continued for 30 years after the death of the founder. In 1879 the mill was purchased by Stevens, who ran it until the early 1960s. Abraham Marland was instrumental in establishing the Episcopal Church in Andover. (MVTM)

mill in America. Located on the Blackstone River at Pawtucket, Rhode Island, the mill and others like it that Slater built in the Blackstone Valley were for two decades the most advanced model of cotton manufacturing in America.

While Slater led, others followed. In 1803 Charles Robbins, trained by Slater at Pawtucket, moved to New Ipswich, New Hampshire, and there, by the end of 1804, he operated a mill of 500 spindles, the first spinning mill of the Slater type outside the Blackstone Valley. Nathan Appleton was a native of New Ipswich, and though he had left the town when still a boy, he was well acquainted with Charles Barrett and the other locals involved in the project. He had this chance to take a close look at a cotton manufactory, especially after 1810 when his brother Samuel bought a quarter interest in the mill. Nathan was not impressed, not,

at least, with what he saw at New Ipswich. Slater's of course was not the only model, and though a potent one to its generation, it was not the model that came to dominate the Valley of the Merrimack. Rather, the mills at Chelmsford, established by Appleton and his friends after 1821, became the prototype, and those were organized on a model tested and proved at Waltham.

The mills at Waltham were organized by the Boston Manufacturing Company, and the story is reasonably familiar of how Francis Cabot Lowell, merchant of Boston, became, according to Appleton, the "animating spirit" of this most revolutionary enterprise. Indeed, his personal efforts were considerable, though none of them succeeded unaided. To reinvent the power loom he used what his memory was able to pirate from English designs. Lowell also used his very considerable ability at mathematics to synchronize four separate alternating motions of the power loom, while deriving all four from the simple rotary motion of a waterwheel. However, for mechanical experience and skill Lowell relied on Paul Moody, with the added consultation of Moody's own mentor, Jacob Perkins. Work on the loom was done in the back room at Lowell's store on Broad Street, Boston. This "machine shop" was the very frontier of American machine technology, and in the fall of 1813 it produced, in mahogany and metal, the first operating power loom in America. The cost of the model was $534.69. This loom was highly significant, because American experience with cotton technology had been confined to the preparation and spinning of the fiber into cotton yarn. Machine weaving, which transformed yarn into cloth, was still England's monopoly, and without power-loom weaving the American textile industry would remain incomplete and unable to compete with its English prototype.

The Waltham system of labor, a second innovation credited to Francis Cabot Lowell, was equally significant, and it seems to have been more nearly his solitary achievement. Before the Waltham mills, American textile entrepreneurs had copied the so-called Rhode Island system of labor, the labor system introduced by Samuel Slater in the last decade of the 18th century. Slater hired families, rather than individuals, so that men, women, and children worked in the spinning mills together. The families were generally sheltered in company housing and sometimes were a captive market for the company store. Like Slater's carding machines and spinning frames, this labor system was copied from an English model, so it roused all the nativist American fears about factory life. For the worst feature of the Rhode Island system was its natural tendency to generate a permanent class of factory workers, a class easy to collect but impossible to dissolve. This was the trap Francis Cabot Lowell set out to avoid. He proposed to hire single women primarily, young women between the ages of 15

As the prime mover behind the Boston Manufacturing Company at Waltham, Francis Cabot Lowell (1775-1817) deserves the credit for the system of industrialization in textiles that developed in the corporation towns of New England. His perseverance led to the introduction of the power loom, and his business acumen ensured its success. Although Lowell died an untimely death, his memory endures through the reputation of the city that bears his name. This silhouette, his only known likeness, descended through the family to Harriet Ropes Cabot. Courtesy, Harriet Ropes Cabot.

seduced from the land and self-reliance. To preserve the physical and moral well-being of these young women, Lowell proposed housing them in dormitory-like buildings, supervised by trustworthy matrons who would give them three wholesome meals a day and police their behavior. Whatever objections might be found against this Waltham system, it was distinctly American.

A third innovation by the Boston Manufacturing Company, one less often celebrated, was the size of its financial base. The BMC was chartered by the Massachusetts General Court with a capitalization of $400,000, far more than any previous textile manufactory. Lowell determined to raise only one quarter of that amount, divided into 100 equal shares, $1,000 at par. To help him in this was Patrick Tracy Jackson, a lifelong friend and former partner in the Indies trade. In fact, the Jackson-Lowell saga is a useful diversion in recollecting the ways of American power.

The tale begins by the Merrimack at Newburyport in the previous generation. Jonathan Jackson and John Lowell—fathers of the future textile magnates—were classmates together at Harvard College, and their chance meeting created a friendship that altered John Lowell's future and the lives of his considerable clan. Jackson was the scion of a prominent merchant family at Newburyport, and Lowell the son of the first minister of the town's first church. When both had returned to their native town, and John Lowell had begun his law practice, it was Jonathan Jackson who introduced him to the leaders of Newburyport society and so, of course, to the pick of legal clients. In due time they shared in the construction of a double house, as was then the fashion on High Street, the town's choicest avenue. They raised their sons and daughters with the expectation that marriage would unite their families.

Jonathan Jackson married once, and well, to Hannah, the daughter of Patrick Tracy, who was the wealthiest of Newburyport's merchants at the time of the War of Independence. John Lowell married three times, and each time to the daughter of a merchant, Higginson and Cabot and Russell, though when he met Rebecca Russell she was already the widow Tyng of Dunstable. Their expectations from their children were not disappointed, as Patrick Tracy Jackson and Francis Cabot Lowell became brothers-in-law. By 1813 the Jackson-Lowell connection rested on two generations and multiple marriages, on the memory of secure alliances of affection and wealth. No enterprise like the Boston Manufacturing Company, revolutionary in so many ways, would be undertaken without some recognized tie to the past. If the departure from shipping to factory was a wrenching one for these two cronies, the wrench was soothed by the securities they took with them. Patrick Tracy Jackson bought 20 of the 100 shares in the BMC, more than any other investor and five more, in fact, than Francis Cabot Lowell.

and 20, and train them to operate the frames and looms of his mills. These daughters of local farmers would be a transient labor force, for they were never intended to spend their whole lives in the mills. They were expected to return to the land, marry farmers, and allow their younger sisters and cousins to take their place in the factory. No one could be dead-ended in factory life and no male laborers need be

Even as shipping declined in the face of industrial investment, fishing continued to provide livelihood and sustenance for those living in towns near the mouth of the Merrimack. A fish market on the wharf at Newburyport, photographed in about 1860, bore a sign showing a larger-scale operation dating from somewhat earlier in the century, which perhaps had occupied the same site in better days. Courtesy, Society for the Preservation of New England Antiquities.

The Lowells by 1813 had moved from church to law to trade, resuming in themselves the most respected occupations their society had known for 200 years, a trinity of gain able to snatch a pound or a dollar from the devil's own hand. With the Jacksons, they were common proprietors of a tradition of confidence, the experience of success. That tradition had carried their fathers through the political revolution and war with England, and the same tradition carried the sons, new Americans, through an economic revolution.

Jackson and Lowell sought out other investors only within their families and among the merchants of Boston they knew and trusted. Two Jackson brothers joined in the venture, as did Warren Dutton, a lawyer and a Lowell in-law. The Israel Thorndikes, father and son, each subscribed for 10 shares. Others followed with more modest amounts: Benjamin Gorham, Uriah Cotting, John Gore. Then Jackson and Lowell came to the name of Nathan Appleton, in some ways their most difficult case. Appleton was a student of

the new social science of economics, having read the works of Adam Smith, David Ricardo, John Ramsay McCulloch, and others. Still he was not attached to the values of any one particular writer. "I have always made my system conform to facts," he wrote. So he waited for facts: he was able to recognize new conditions but unwilling to make them. His pleasure and his talent lay in careful calculations and well-chosen risks. This business sense was cultivated from the experience of generations of cautious Appleton enterprise. His ancestor, Samuel, the first Appleton to settle in the New World, left England for Ipswich in Massachusetts only after demanding and getting the personal assurance of John Winthrop that there would be enough cattle to support his large family.

Nathan Appleton was well read in the science of his day, but he trusted only what he saw. Timing was the basis of sound business decisions, and for at least three years Appleton waited for the signs that cotton manufacturing was a sound investment. He had long conversations with Lowell about the subject in 1810, when it happened that both were at Edinburgh, Scotland. Appleton was interested enough to visit New Lanark, near Edinburgh, where Robert Owen had built a factory on the Clyde River so considerate of its workers that even American Virtue was not shocked at seeing it. It was proof that factories need not degrade the workers who labored in them.

Appleton monitored Lowell's progress and was duly impressed with the mechanical magic of the power loom. More appreciative of business skills, Appleton may have been even more impressed by the performance of Patrick Tracy Jackson, who came dangerously close to bankruptcy in 1811 and yet recovered his fortune. Finally, Appleton was impressed when war began with England in 1812 and the flood of English cotton imports came to an abrupt stop: domestic cotton manufacturing promised high profits for prompt investors. Still, Appleton hesitated. When Jackson and Lowell offered him 10 shares of the BMC, Appleton accepted five "until the experiment was fairly tried."

With the technology and the labor and the capital assembled at Waltham, the BMC built the first factory in any country where all the cotton processes were done by machine under one roof. This "integrated factory" was a resounding success. Even after British imports were readmitted to the American market in 1815, the Boston Manufacturing Company proved itself a type for survival. By 1817 there were two more mills at Waltham, but by 1817 all the power available from the Charles River had been used; further expansion forced the search that brought Appleton and his friends to Pawtucket Falls. Many of the individuals important to the triumph of the Boston Manufacturing had living roots in the Merrimack Valley: Lowell, Jackson, Moody, Appleton, Perkins, Dutton were all recent transplants. The move from Waltham to

Chelmsford appears then as a kind of homecoming. So it seems. But there is the career of Nathan Appleton to tell a different story. The Souhegan was his native river, and if home was the object, he twice passed up the opportunity to invest in that: the first time at New Ipswich and the second at Amherst in September 1821. Appleton doubted until the Boston Manufacturing had proved itself, and if he shared with his colleagues an instant approval of Pawtucket Falls, it was because the choice was obvious. In choosing Pawtucket Falls it was power they came to, not place.

Waterpower was measured in the ratio of volume to drop and since Pawtucket Falls offered a drop of some 30 feet over the entire breadth of the Merrimack it was clear that the site was a major resource. The Boston Associates, as the Waltham group came to be called, obtained a charter from the General Court in February 1822, incorporating them as the Merrimack Manufacturing Company. This corporation set out immediately to buy the land and water rights it would need at Chelmsford. Most of the land was acquired in three major blocks, the three farms of the area owned by the Fletcher, the Tyler, and the Cheever families. The rights to the power were bought from the owners of the Pawtucket Canal, who had owned them since 1792 under their legal title, the Proprietors of Locks and Canals on Merrimack River.

The Pawtucket was built as a transportation canal, merely a loop, to get river traffic around the falls when the falls were more a hazard and a nuisance in the business of commerce than a manageable source of industrial power. Now that technology had caught up to the prospect, the Merrimack Manufacturing Company intended to use the Pawtucket as a feeder canal. It would carry a volume of water maintained at the level above Pawtucket Falls, where the entrance to the canal was located, to the site of their mills so that, there, it could be dropped back into the Merrimack at a point below the falls. The water was diverted a total distance of perhaps a mile and a half on the horizontal line, and then dropped a total of 30 feet on the vertical where it reached the Merrimack Mills. The wheels were located beneath the mills, and, as was the rule, their diameter was equal to the distance of the fall. Gravity did the rest. Once the water was set loose at the top of the wheel it dropped in a direct vertical line, but the wheel translated that into a rotary motion, and it was this motion—transmitted up in a system of belts, pulleys, and shafts through the stories of the mill—that *each* machine again translated into all the motions it was designed to perform.

Like all the corporations of the Boston Associates, Merrimack Manufacturing followed a pattern of structure inherited from the merchant background of the principals. Its chief executive was the treasurer (Patrick Tracy Jackson), while full authority on the site was vested in an agent (Kirk Boott). Until his death in 1837, it was Boott

who supervised the construction of mills and canals and the manufacturing of cloth. He was suited to the task by temperament and training. Some said he was far too suited, since his experience as a British officer had left him with the disposition of a tyrant.

Born in Boston of a British mercantile family, Anglophile Kirk Boott (1790-1837) was the resident agent of the Merrimack Manufacturing Company who had primary responsibility for planning and executing the development of Lowell. Although rigid he was respected, and this portrait by Chester Harding was commissioned by the Middlesex Mechanics Association and paid for in subscriptions democratically limited to no more than five dollars each. Begun from life, it was completed after his death. Courtesy, Pollard Memorial Library, Lowell.

Preparations were completed on schedule. The first cloth made by the Merrimack Mills came off a power loom operated by Deborah Skinner, whom Moody had brought from Waltham to train the labor force at the new mills. That was in November 1823. Only the previous May, however, the directors of Merrimack Manufacturing had met at

Chelmsford and begun the process of reorganizing its resources, retaining only the land and power needed for its own operation, and transferring all that remained of both to the Proprietors of Locks and Canals on Merrimack River. Familiarly called the Locks and Canals, this former commercial enterprise became the developer and power broker of the site, selling land to other textile corporations as these were chartered by the General Court, and leasing to them the mill powers of the Merrimack in a most exact accounting. The Locks and Canals was reconstituted in 1825, and with these financial and organizational issues resolved, the site was ready for the intense industrial activity that characterized the place for a quarter of a century.

In 1826, as if to affirm the beginning of a new era in the story of the lower Merrimack, the site of the mills at

Both neighbors and the nation were curious to see the mills that had grown up in the meadow, and several views of Lowell were made. This 1848 engraving showing the town from the Dracut shore appeared on sample folders of cloth printed by the Merrimack Manufacturing Company, and the mills depicted are (from left to right) the Massachusetts, the Boott, the Merrimack, and the Lawrence corporations. (MVTM)

Chelmsford was separated, given independent political existence, by the General Court. The new town was named in honor of Francis Cabot Lowell, who had died in 1817; it seemed fitting, at least to Appleton, to commemorate his part in the coming of age of America. Lowell was literally on the map. By coincidence, 1826 was the 50th anniversary of the Declaration of Independence. By a more arresting coincidence, it was the year that John Adams and Thomas Jefferson died, both on the Fourth of July, removing the last living tie to America's Revolution.

Textile corporations now sprang up like mushrooms. The Hamilton (1825), the Appleton (1828), the Lowell (1828), the Middlesex (1830), the Suffolk and Tremont (1832), the Lawrence (1833), the Boott (1835), and the Massachusetts (1839) were added to Merrimack Manufacturing, and these together were the Big 10 among a host of other, smaller and ancillary, operations. It was a scale that impressed contemporaries, and it's easy to see why. By 1840 these corporations controlled a capitalization of $10.5 million, while in 1813 at the same place, Fletcher and Whiting had built their cotton "manufactory" for a mere $2,500. By 1840 the Big 10 were producing over 1.1 million yards of cloth each week, most of that in cotton goods. (The Middlesex Mills, the only

MERRIMACK PRINTS

LOWELL MASS.

one of the Big 10 that drew power from the Concord River, was the only major Lowell corporation that produced woolens.) It was also the pace that impressed contemporaries. In 1836 Lowell was given a city charter, only the third such charter in Massachusetts, and four years later Lowell was the second-largest city in the Commonwealth. This physical burgeoning, this explosion of population and concentration of mills, was regulated by the capacities of the engineers at the Locks and Canals to exploit every means they could devise to wring power from the Merrimack; that is where the throttle of the operation lay. Until 1845 the Locks and Canals was also the parent corporation of the Lowell Machine Shop, so that it had for those 20 years (1825-1845) a very good claim to being the most important technological firm in the nation. In addition to being a symbol of American social innovation, Lowell also was a shrine of American engineering.

To be sure, it was hydraulics, the engineering of water,

that dominated at Lowell at the time. In the first decade or so it was Kirk Boott as agent of Merrimack Manufacturing, and Paul Moody as superintendent of the machine shop, who directed the design and construction of Lowell's power system. For a brief time (1834-1837), George Washington Whistler was in charge as chief engineer at the Locks and Canals. Whistler was a graduate of the military academy at West Point, which was then by far the best, and very nearly the only, school for engineers in the United States. To replace him the directors of the Locks and Canals chose his assistant, a very young man and yet another British immigrant. James B. Francis was 22 in 1837, having learned what he could of engineering from his father while in England, and from Whistler in the four years since coming to America in 1833. He followed his mentor from assignment to assignment, but at Lowell they parted. Whistler moved on, pursuing a career that took him to czarist Russia, where he died in 1849. Francis had found his career: he was chief engineer at the Locks and Canals from

George Washington Whistler (1800-1849), the son of a British soldier, became an officer in the U.S. Army and trained as an engineer at West Point. After working as a surveyor for several early railroads, Whistler became chief engineer of Lowell's Locks and Canals corporation, where from 1834-1837 he ran the machine shop and designed locomotives. His skill in civil and mechanical engineering took him to Russia, where he served as a consultant for the building of the railroad between St. Petersburg and Moscow, and where he died of cholera. Courtesy, Lowell Historical Society.

James Bicheno Francis (1815-1892), a British immigrant, succeeded Whistler as chief engineer at Locks and Canals and devoted his extraordinary talents to improving the canal system and water turbines. His book, Lowell Hydraulic Experiments, *published in 1855, made Lowell's technological advances known among engineers worldwide. (MVTM)*

1837 until his retirement in 1882.

Francis was among a handful of mathematicians and engineers—Swiss, French, and English—who developed the water turbine, a device more efficient at taking power from falling water; these began to replace the older water-wheels in the wheel pits of the Lowell mills during the later 1840s. Francis also made important improvements in the city's canal system, the system that delivered the fall of water to the turbines. In 1837 five power canals were completed at Lowell. The Hamilton (1826), the Lowell (1828), the Western (1832), and the Eastern (1835) had been added to the first power canal at Lowell, the Merrimack, completed in 1823.

However, by 1840 these "ditches" were distributing the waters of the Merrimack to 32 mills, and delivering the volume needed for this scale of things had become a strain on the capacity of the Pawtucket Canal, the only feeder bringing water into those six power canals. Moreover, in the years from 1840 to 1845 there were several seasons of drought, and that created real anxiety about the future of the mills at Lowell. Two ways were found to repair these soft points in the power system. First, Francis supervised the construction of a second feeder, the Northern Canal. The work was difficult and expensive, involving the construction of a river wall to keep the waters in the Northern separate from, and 30 feet above, the waters of the Merrimack. In conjunction with this, Francis also built the Moody Street Feeder, an underground conduit moving water directly from the Western into the Merrimack Canal. Both of these were finished in 1848, after 18 months of arduous effort and an expenditure of half a million dollars.

But marvelous as this work was, it was useless without the assurance that there would be enough water flowing down the Merrimack to maintain the canal system at capacity. And to do this the Locks and Canals took its second step to improve the system. In 1845 the corporation bought the outlets of several bays and lakes in New Hampshire and also bought the rights to control the flow of water through these outlets. In times of low water, then, the Locks and Canals was able to release the reserves in New Hampshire and so meet its contractual obligations to the textile corporations at Lowell, its legal promise to deliver a stated volume of water to their penstocks. This reserve system was regulated from Lowell on information transmitted to the city by observers reporting on rainfalls and on water levels from their locations in New Hampshire.

Impressive as these achievements were, it was his "Folly" that earned Francis the gratitude of the people of Lowell. He saw that the canal system was a physical invitation to disaster, inasmuch as it brought the waters of the Merrimack into the heart of the city. When the Merrimack reached flood stage, as it did periodically, the city would be inundated. To prevent this, Francis built a massive gate across the Pawtucket Canal shortly past the point where it leaves the river; the gate was suspended above the canal against the possibility of the rising of the Merrimack. Contemporaries were ill-advised to call it the Francis Folly, since the gate was let down once in 1852 and again in 1936 to prevent major flooding of Lowell.

In his lifetime James B. Francis wrote more than 200 papers for the learned societies of the world; in 1855 he published *The Lowell Hydraulic Experiments*. Whatever this publicity did for him, it also put the development of the lower Merrimack among the leaders of world-class engineering. Indeed, the development of human capacity to control and exploit the power of the Merrimack had been nothing short of a wonder in the half century since 1800. Then it was possible only to use the falls on the river's tributaries, and the major source of power, the Pawtucket Falls, had been an obstacle to avoid. However, in the 30 years after 1820, the falls themselves had been the site of prodigious learning, a veritable explosion of knowledge. The falls had in fact become the keystone in a vast system of power, covering hundreds of square miles of reserves in New Hampshire, and all of it focused on the need to drive the machines of textile production. Nevertheless, there was yet another step to take in this progress toward mastery of the river. After avoiding the falls in 1792, after exploiting the falls since 1820, engineers and manufacturers now moved to fabricate a falls by damming the river. That was done at the New City on the Merrimack, now Lawrence, Massachusetts, in the years from 1845 to 1848.

The site was Bodwell's Falls, a drop of some four feet that lay in the Merrimack nearly 11 miles below Lowell, at a spot where a bridge connected Andover on the southern side with Methuen on the northern. The idea for a dam on this site originated among some local entrepreneurs, notably Daniel Saunders, a man who had been involved one way or another in the manufacture of woolens since deciding, in 1817, that farming held no future for him. Local manufacturers, however, did not have the capital resources to finish anything like a project of this magnitude. So, it was again the Boston Associates, this time incorporated as the Essex Company in 1845, that undertook to finance the development of this site. The Lawrence brothers, Abbott and Amos, were most directly involved. Since organizing the Middlesex Mills at Lowell in 1830, these two late joiners had worked themselves into full membership in the Associates, and like most of these industrialists they had made their original fortune in commerce. The Essex Company included a machine shop in the plans for their New City, and though that firm never prospered financially, the building that housed it remains today perhaps the finest example of industrial architecture from that era still standing in the Valley of the lower Merrimack.

Of course, the Essex Campany also built a canal, which it located on the northern side of the Merrimack. Compared to the complex of canals at Lowell, distributed as these were and operating at two levels, the Northern Canal at Lawrence was a tame affair, finely designed but basically a straightforward trench describing a power island between itself and the river. The Great Stone Dam, however, was an epic construction. It ran the breadth of the Merrimack for more than 900 feet and rose from the bedrock of the river to a height of 36 feet. And it was built with no example in the world to follow. It was invented at the site.

Charles Storrow was the engineer in charge of construction, and it takes nothing from his task and his achievement to note that he was able to find a group of men distinguished for their talent and experience to assist and advise him. He had the services of Joseph Bennett to survey the site and locate the dam. The noted Uriah A. Boyden served as consulting engineer in the early stages of construction, while after 1846 Storrow's principal assistant was Charles Bigelow. A graduate of West Point (class of 1835), Bigelow had gained valuable experience while working with Colonel Sylvanus Thayer in building fortifications in Boston Harbor. Storrow also benefited from the advice of James B. Francis, though to what extent it is difficult to tell. But many of those experiments reported by Francis in *The Lowell Hydraulic Experiments* were done during the designing and construction of the Great Stone Dam. There were other, lesser lights who left the Locks and Canals to join Storrow in his magnificent project. There is the individual known only as Mr. Folsom, master stonecutter. And there was George Russy, who described himself as a self-trained engineer, having worked at various sites in New York State and as a draftsman for the corporation at Lowell.

Storrow himself had the benefit of opportunities that together made him one of the best-educated engineers in the country. While still an undergraduate at Harvard during the later 1820s, he had access to the books collected by the Loammi Baldwins, senior and junior, when theirs was the best engineering library in the United States outside West Point. Afterward Storrow studied at the French National School of Bridges and Roads at Paris, and made an extended tour of France and England to see for himself the engineering achievements of Europe. When he returned to America in 1833, he served as assistant to Loammi Baldwin, Jr., in building the Lowell-Boston railroad, which, as it happened, was often laid out on a line following the Middlesex Canal that Loammi Baldwin, Sr., had engineered some 40 years before. Storrow stayed with the Lowell and Boston line as general manager for 10 years after its completion in 1835. In undertaking the construction of the Great Stone Dam at Lawrence, Storrow drew on the resources of generations of experience, collected from his own study

Lawrence is shown while still under construction in the spring of 1848 in this lithograph by A. Conant of Providence. Much of Essex Street (center left) is lined with temporary wooden buildings, but the brick Mechanics Block (center right) stands completed in its square. Only the Machine Shop (left foreground) and one mill each of the Bay State and Atlantic corporations have been completed. More construction would follow until the mill island became a wall of brick. (MVTM)

and from those around him.

The dam was completed in three years to the day: the first stone was set down on September 19, 1845, and the last on September 19, 1848. The other components of the Essex Company's grand design, the Northern Canal and the machine shop, were also completed by 1848, so the place was made a going concern in rather a short time. Meanwhile, in 1847, the General Court of Massachusetts had set off seven square miles taken in equal portion from Andover and Methuen. Over the next decade the new town, Lawrence, saw the erection of several textile corporations designed to follow the Lowell model, each with its row of boardinghouses for the young women who were expected to labor in its mills. The Duck Mill, the impressive, nine-story Bay State Mills, the Atlantic and the Pacific, and the ill-fated Pemberton were in production before 1860. None of them, however, enjoyed the early prosperity that had marked the Lowell experience in the 1820s and 1830s. For the town of Lawrence the timing was unfortunate. The Essex Company began its project in 1845 under the sunshine of prosperity, but by the time cloth production had begun, a depression was at work in the national economy, which, then as now, seemed to operate beyond the reach of anyone's engineering.

To note that all the vast projects of power on the lower Merrimack were under the management of the Boston Associates, in its several corporate guises, is to note that a real change had come in the relations of the republic's citizens. Wealth and power were concentrated in 1860 as they had not been in 1800. Moreover, the power of the Merrimack belonged to no community on the Merrimack. It belonged rather to a new variety of community, with no particular loyalties to place and committed primarily to survival. Francis Cabot Lowell set a precedent in 1816 when he went to Washington to argue the case for a tariff to protect the new cotton industry. If there was not always a member of the Boston Associates in Congress during the succeeding years, the company was able to rely on the abilities of Daniel Webster, whose infinite appetite for money put him all too clearly in the pocket of those who provided him with "sweetners." And unlike the Federalists of the Essex Junto, the industrialists of the Boston Associates knew how to manage sectional alliances. They were called the lords of the loom, and, together with the slave-owning aristocracy of the Southern states, they were the central axis of the national Whig Party. But that party could not indefinitely contain the rising sentiment against slavery; that issue finally destroyed the Whigs as it divided the Union.

The revolution begun at Pawtucket Falls in November 1821 is so majestic in its scope that we are tempted from our vantage to see the hand of destiny at work, moving with a secret purpose to force the discovery. But that is not the story as Nathan Appleton tells it. This is what he says:

> I was at Waltham one day, when I was informed that Mr. Moody had lately been at Salisbury, when Mr. Ezra Worthen, his former partner, said to him, "I hear Messrs. Jackson and Appleton are looking out for water-power; why don't they buy up the Pawtucket Canal? That would give them the whole power of the Merrimack with a fall of over thirty feet."

His language skips along like a stone on the surface of the water, leaving behind a trail of widening circles until finally the circles touch and form a chain. This is how Appleton gets across to us, by adding segment to segment, each with the name of a person or a place and each with a verb to carry the name to the next connection. In his sentences, information comes at us in the making, the way events do. That is the reason it strikes us true: like Worthen and Moody and Appleton, we live in a network where information becomes event and event becomes information.

The process is constant and nearly invisible, as when we are at a gas station where we have been countless times before, and we meet an acquaintance who tells us his cousin is in town and his cousin has a friend whose father wants to sell his '54 T-bird. In fact, the car had been in his garage for 20 years, and it's at this point that it almost seems that the car has been waiting for us because that's how long we've been looking for it. So are events and information connected at an infinite number of points, and at each point of connection is a person. Most of these connec-

tions produce results that affect few people only, and only for a week or a month. At most they may last a lifetime. However, there are persons, and Appleton was among them, who operate in a different class of network when the information and events being swapped and sold and converted affect many people, whole regions of them and generations of them. These get more attention. These we drag out and call history.

Appleton is telling about events so successful at changing his world into ours that the events themselves come up like a wall when we try to see behind them. But here is the language of Appleton, with its construction of truth, to bring us the testimony of one who was there. It is experience and chance and attention, not Genius and not Fate, that move us across the surface of time.

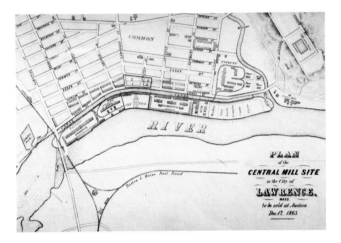

In 1863 one last mill site remained to be developed on the island along the North Canal. Sold at auction in December 1863, the central mill site became the worsted division of Pacific Mills, known as the Lower Pacific to distinguish it from the Upper Pacific located just below the dam. Because it occupied the central mill site on the island, this mill was also sometimes called the Central Pacific. The plan also shows land across the canal available for boardinghouses. (MVTM)

VI

NEW AMERICANS,
OLD DREAMS

The effective work of patriotic soldiers and sailors in the
war of the Rebellion and the war of the Revolution not only
saved the nation but made this Merrimack Valley in which we
live and labor a place where the workers of the world can
congregate in security and in peace.
> — Robert Tewksbury, *Memorial Day address to a*
> *group of schoolchildren at Lawrence,* circa 1905. Essex
> Company Collection, MVTM.

In 1646 Andrew Greeley sailed up the Merrimack on a sloop that
took him as far as the head of navigation, where he was left on the sandy
banks of the river with his ''store goods,'' farm tools, and farm supplies.
Andrew Greeley also carried leatherworking tools and presented himself
as an itinerant shoemaker. He had come some distance to the frontier of
Massachusetts, toting his goods and his skills, nursing a hope. Before him
was Haverhill, what there was of it: half a dozen log houses, each with a
clearing. Behind him, could he have seen them, were thousands like himself, tens of thousands, who reached landfall perhaps at Boston, likely at
New York, and traveled overland to the towns and cities on the

Immigrants entered the retail trade and commercial pursuits as well as performing
factory labor. The Portugese owner and staff of Ostroff and Sousa Company's clothing
and millinery establishment on Gorham Street in Lowell pose in about 1910.
Courtesy, Lowell Historical Society.

Two hundred years after Andrew Greeley's landing at Haver-hill, the hard work of generations of immigrants had built a prosperous city. Gustavus Pfau's 1850 lithograph, taken from Silver Hill looking down Washington Street, shows a place that was home to nearly 6,000 people, a large percentage of them employed in the shoe trade. Both the railroad bridge (fore-ground) and the highway bridge were covered at this time. Courtesy, Boston Athenaeum.

Merrimack. For more than three centuries since 1646, now through 12 generations, a typical American has been a newcomer looking for work and ready to accept what there is of it. If one move was not enough, if conditions were not favorable or if the place became crowded—whenever success was illusive—it was possible to go elsewhere. So were the towns on the Merrimack planted, as corporate enterprises, groups of families on the move and assuming new collective names, christened by the authority of the General Court. So the Appletons, allied with others, moved from Lincolnshire to Massachusetts to New Hampshire.

A century later, when individuals were less restricted by communal control, mobility became a turbulent stream of individual ambitions. The father of Moses Hale moved his family from Newbury to Dracut, where he operated a full-ing mill on Beaver Brook. In the next generation, Moses moved across the Merrimack to Chelmsford to locate his textile operation, and brother Ezekiel moved up the Mer-rimack to Haverhill to locate his. So, too, Oliver Whipple walked from his native Vermont to Southboro, Massachusetts, in 1815, and there he earned a capital of some several hundred dollars, which he then invested in a powder mill on the Concord at Chelmsford. Americans were made on the move and bred with the conviction that there would always be another chance. In the American experience the reality of Eden lay in the future, once a road to it was cleared. Black Africans, brought here by force to

labor for someone else, were excluded from this American dream, but the mass of arrivals, even the indentured ser-vants of the 17th century, hoped that labor would earn them a "sufficiency," economic independence. In labor was freedom. It was a dream worth moving for.

From the time of settlement in the 1630s to the rise of Lowell two centuries later, farming dominated the economy of the Valley, and while this was true the family was the prevalent unit of labor. When nearly everything had to be done on site, it needed all the waking hours of a large family to make the farm a successful enterprise. Self-reliance was not a part-time job, nor for that matter did it ever rely exclusively on self. Driven by the Yankee virtues of thrift and industry and allowed only the enforced leisure of Sabbath, family labor was not regulated by any clock but by the rising and setting of the sun, moving within the longer rhythms of the seasons. From November to March, when New England winters put an end to nearly all work on the land, the family retreated indoors, to kitchens and barns, and filled many dreary snowbound hours making products for market. These "domestic industries" provided a significant portion of a family's support and would often mark the difference between bare survival and the addition of a small surplus, the family's profit at the end of a year's work. Normally, domestic industries centered on a product of everyday use, something of clothing or dress for in-stance. Considered ideal for domestic manufacture was some product, then, that had a mass market but did not require farm families to make a large investment in tools or large investments of time in learning skills they would not otherwise need in their daily and seasonal farm chores. And it helped if it was small and light enough for a child's hands, for none was left idle in the domestic labor force.

Though this tradition of manufacture can be traced near-ly to the origins of Massachusetts Bay, it was in that first generation after Independence, from 1790 to 1820, that it

Newburyport's Market Square, shown here about 1870, was the scene of economic transactions throughout the 19th century. Local farmers brought produce to the market building (at right, with white awning), which also housed town offices and fire engines. (MVTM)

Farm chores didn't change with the coming of the factory, but markets for farm products expanded to include the new factory towns. This wooden pantry box for holding butter or other food protected Farmer Gray's product on its way to the point of sale or in the pantry. Similar in design to Shaker boxes, it measures eight and three-quarters inches in diameter and four inches high. Courtesy, North Andover Historical Society.

Recreational activities occupied the young of the 19th century just as they do today, although sports equipment was more primitive. Ice skates fashioned from wood with iron runners were attached to the skater's leg with leather straps. Iron spikes held the shoe firmly in place, but must have made new heels a frequent necessity. Courtesy, North Andover Historical Society.

reached its zenith. The towns on the lower Merrimack lie at the northern end of Middlesex and Essex counties, and in both counties the domestic industries of farm families were tied to the butcheries and tanneries concentrated at the southern end. A census of "American Manufactures," taken in 1810, reveals the importance of leather in the domestic manufactures on the lower Merrimack. Products and their dollar value were tabulated by county, and this makes it difficult to know the level of production attained in regions such as the Valley. Still, domestic industry produced about 2.2 million shoes in Massachusetts that year, and 86.11 percent of them were made by the households of Essex and Middlesex. Essex County alone accounted for more than 1.5 million shoes, and shoe production in Essex was in fact the only enterprise in the entire Commonwealth in 1810 with a product value of more than a million dollars.

In a textbook example of the vigor and ingenuity of Yankee economy, the census of 1810 also counted some 105,000 combs made in Essex County, carved from the horns of the same animals whose hides were stiched into shoes—or gloves. Domestic manufacture of combs of every description and quality survived in the Newburys down to the second and third decade of this century, but it was shoemaking that occupied by far the largest number of individuals and families in the towns of the lower Merrimack. In 1810 Haverhill and Bradford were already established as centers of shoemaking. The leadership of Haverhill as a shoe city in the 20th century rested securely on a knowing labor force created during the era of domestic manufacture.

Isaac Watts Merrill (1803-1878) kept a diary for nearly 50 years in which he recorded the activities of his life as a shoemaker, farmer, and ordinary citizen. His Haverhill home, built in 1828 of locally made bricks, was photographed in 1878, the year Merrill died. The men at the left are probably his nephews James and Moses Merrill, who inherited the place, and the women may be their wives or sisters. Courtesy, Trustees of the Haverhill Public Library.

Three cordwainers work at their benches in a typical shoemaker's shop. A town meeting notice is on the right wall. Known for their active political participation and often radical views, shoemakers elected a strong socialist government in Haverhill in the 1890s. (MVTM)

Economics was by no means the only dimension of family relations, no more in 1782 than in 1982, but in that dimension family had the structure of a labor exchange where there was very little cash, if there was any at all, and where the books were kept in terms of service. It was service, too, that knit scattered farmsteads into a neighborhood, for each family depended from time to time on the like economy of its neighbors so that each accepted the conditions that made cooperation necessary. Scarcity of labor made cooperation the virtue of place. Each one day would likely help a neighbor dig a well or raise a well crotch because he was certain on the next day, or the one after that, to need help himself, and this regular exchange of time and energy—not cash—made the character of their relations obvious. This may indeed be part of what Thoreau meant in his *Week on the Concord and Merrimack Rivers* when he praised labor as "carrying into practice certain essential information." It was certainly part of what Emerson acknowledged in December 1838 when he began a lecture by declaring, "a household is the school of power."

Emerson was in the lecture business, and he knew his audience would understand and accept that sort of overture because the larger part of the populations at Concord or Haverhill was still living in a mixed economy, one in which cash transactions were only a portion of the larger process of production and consumption. No doubt gain was the object and ambition a force. There are enough recorded insults given and taken, enough lawsuits over property, to keep us from idealizing these Valley residents and their economic relations. Emerson did not try to tell them that a household was the school of the feckless. The point remains that during the 1820s and 1830s, even through the 1840s, the American economy was within the comprehension of the average citizen and so put the average citizen within the possibility of effective control over some portion of it. Until the eve of the Civil War, a significant part of the Valley's population lived in an economy that offered multiple relations in getting and spending, and a series of dealings that made many persons participants in the transactions deciding their economic well-being.

There is the case of Isaac Merrill. He was born at Haverhill in 1803 and died there in 1878, making him a contemporary of Emerson, who died some four years later in 1882. Effectively, they were witness to the same America. Merrill traveled a fair amount in his long life but never very far and not for long, and he always returned to Haverhill. For his amusement Merrill kept a diary from 1828 until shortly before his death, and fortunately for us it recently was brought back to light. He was a shoemaker all his life and worked at his home, located very literally within a stone's throw of the sovereign state of New Hampshire. He earned a good living at his work, but his diary shows him spending a considerable amount of time caring for his

The shoe trade brought prosperity to Haverhill, but it suffered from the ups and downs caused by overproduction and competition, as did the textile industry. This view of Water Street, looking east from White's Corner in about 1868, shows a commercial center of some liveliness despite the snow. Many of the sleighs were probably made in and around Amesbury, famous for its carriage-building trade. Courtesy, Trustees of the Haverhill Public Library.

crops and livestock, and sometimes helping his father and occasionally a neighbor in caring for theirs. In April 1859, Merrill notes having "settled with father," that after 14 years of open account the total cash value of his indebtedness was $192.91. A part at least of his gainful employ happened outside the cash connection. By contrast, his brother Gyles, who was visiting in April 1859 was a superintendent of the Vermont Central Railway at a yearly salary of $3,000.

On the shoemaking side of Merrill's economy, he operated in a situation that allowed some choice of the dealer he would sell his shoes to and on what terms. Like all "shoemakers" Merrill did not market his own product, leaving that to the "manufacturers" who collected shoes from several makers and packed them off to markets in Philadelphia and Baltimore. In March 1832 there were 28 shoe "manufacturers" at Haverhill, and of these, 16 were also dealers in "English and West Indies Goods." It is easy to see how the dealers of shoes would often pay the makers of shoes in goods as well as cash; cash was generally at this period a small part of the price paid for making shoes. The

coming of the railroad to Haverhill in 1841 began the process of consolidating the business of marketing shoes, so that shoe "manufacturers" began to see the advantage of consolidating the business of making shoes—under their control. By April 1859 shoemakers of the Merrill type were numbering their days, poised at the beginning of a frightening decade when the market economy would turn the character of their labor inside out. An editorial published in the (Haverhill) *Gazette*, June 26, 1858, explains how reasonable the change was:

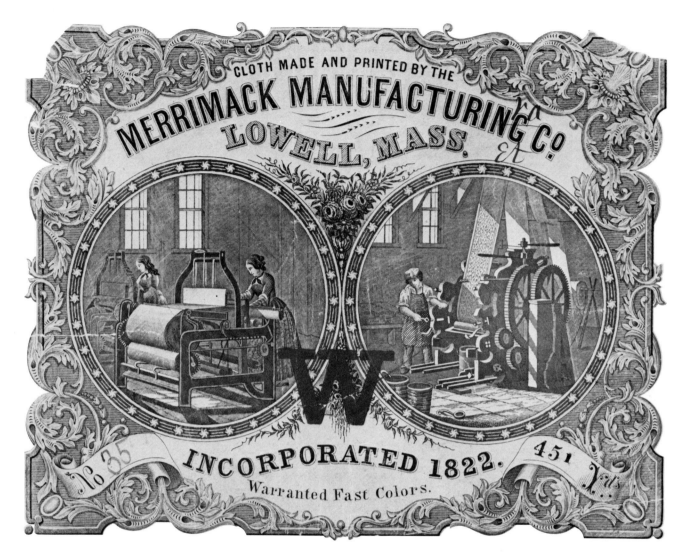

We recently had a conversation with one of our largest and most enterprising shoe manufacturers, in which he urged the necessity of holding out inducements to shoemakers in New Hampshire and the various towns in this state, who are engaged in the business to remove into town, where they can get more pay and be more sure of work than those who live at a distance, etc., etc. Manufacturers would pay 20% more and the expense of transport would be saved &c. If manufacturers would present this subject to their workmen showing them the advantages of being located here, and pay them a little extra for their labor, when they remove we should soon have a desirable change in this respect.

For 20 percent more in cash, shoemakers would be persuaded to become shoeworkers: instead of a product to sell for a price, they would have labor to sell for wage. For 20

A bolt label for cloth made and printed by the Merrimack Manufacturing Company in Lowell pictures women weaving at their looms and a man adjusting a cylinder printing machine. Cloth labels marked piece lot and yardage consigned to the selling agent. Interior views of factories from this period (1840-1850) are rare, and it is unusual for a label to show the process of goods being made. Lowell was an object of nearly universal curiosity, however, which this marketing device was designed to satisfy. (MVTM)

percent more in cash, they would entrust their economic well-being exclusively to one manufacturer's ability to follow a market of a million shoes, with no real assurance that this person had 10 times more capacity to do this than any one smaller manufacturer had used in following a market of 100,000 shoes. For cash he was asked to eliminate competition among shoe manufacturers, when that competition was the field of option where his choice was accepted as a value. So, at the time of the Civil War (1861) the shoemakers of the Merrimack Valley were about to notice what the textile workers had noticed 20 or 30 years before: labor had become an activity done for cash, and one that offered no hope of ever reaching the point of control. The control belonged to the person who bought the labor. The textile workers at Lowell were among the first Americans to make that observation, because they were among the first to be given the prospect to see it. The female mill operatives assembled on the Merrimack during the 1820s and 1830s were at the vanguard where labor in America began its transformation into American Labor, the point where the story of American working classes begins.

The technology perfected at Lowell had a long history of development, but the Lowell mill girls were almost without precedent, and by their numbers and example they were something entirely new. Before Lowell, textile mills in the Valley were small and so drew their laborers from the immediate vicinity. The physical setting of these early mills, neither country nor city, has been described as a middle landscape, and this was also an early image of Lowell advertised by friendly critics. As places of labor these mills were, again, a middle way. Much of the relations among workers and mill owners during this early period from 1790 to 1820 remains obscure, and it will take more research before the picture is clarified. However, there is no doubt that it was an intermediary stage in the evolution of the American workingman and -woman, and the introduction of the power loom was vital in ending that stage. As long as weaving was done on hand looms (until the century's second decade for cottons and the 1820s for woolens), it was necessary for mill owners to hire handweavers, men and women, who practiced an ancient trade, one with virtually no ceiling on the level of skill it could provoke. Machine-spun yarn was often "put out" to local weavers, and weaving done this way was a part of domestic manufactures. Otherwise, handweavers might be set up in a room or attic of a mill in a sort of shop. Wherever they were put, they were a bottleneck in the production of cloth, for no handweaver could hope to keep up with the supply of yarn spun by machine.

Paul Moody, trained first in handweaving by James Scholfield and trained later by Jacob Perkins as a machinist, was able to enjoy the practice of his abilities in both. But there were few so fortunate. The power loom eliminated the bottleneck in cloth production, and it also eliminated a degree of skill in the weaver. The skill in weaving was now shared by the skill of the machinist in making the loom, and the weaver became to some degree a machine tender. Managers and overseers were happy with this mechanization of clothmaking because it served their purpose of rationalizing the work process and brought them that much closer to total domination of the workplace. All the

labor of making cloth was recast to fit the mold of their system, in which productivity and profit were the only recognized objectives and management the supreme skill.

So, in 1837, Abbott Lawrence was delighted to find William Crompton, yet another immigrant English machinist, who said he could find a way to quick-change the pattern program of a power loom. Without such a device American manufacturers could not compete in the fashion market of fancy woolens against the high quality of English imports. The power loom worked well enough with sturdy cotton yarns in 1813, and it had been improved since then to make satinet, which mixed a cotton warp with a woolen weft, and plain woolens. But the weaving of fancy woolens remained in the preserve of handweavers and constituted one of the last pockets of personal skill holding forth amid the machine technology of textiles. By 1840, Crompton delivered his invention, and the improved looms were installed in the Middlesex Mills, owned by Abbott Lawrence and his brothers. The fancy woolens made at Lowell were not quite so fine as the English product, still made by hand, but they were cheaper and that made them

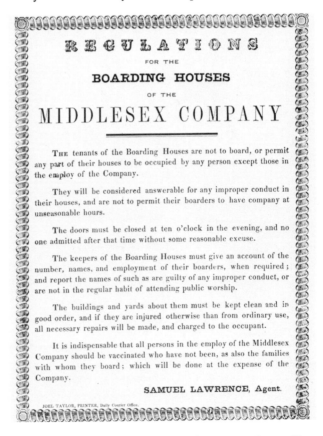

Corporation housing provided a convenient means of controlling the morality of the working population. The boardinghouse matron, acting "in loco parentis," made sure that the young women in her charge followed the regulations of curfew, good conduct, and church attendance. (MVTM)

preferable to the growing appetite of American consumers. The market economy had worked its magic, and another cluster of skilled laborers evaporated under its wand.

The loss and transfer of skills in the making of cloth was a long process and of course it was part of another process, the technological revolution. And from a beginning, say in 1790, to an end, say in 1840, the workingmen and working-women of the Valley lived between two economic systems. On the one hand was the failing economy of domestic manufactures, where products were made by households as part of the economy of family labor. On the other hand, there was the emerging economy centered on the fiscal structure of the corporation, bent on shaping and kneading a labor force to its image and likeness. In the half-century of adjustment the workers of the Valley were given a choice between them, like the Pennacooks who had preferred to bivouac where ecotonal zones offered alternate food chains on which to prey. Many men and women chose the new economy, they chose the Lowell system. However, by the decade of the 1840s it became clear to an increasing number of Lowell workers that the market economy made demands

The boardinghouse system of factory labor, as introduced at Lowell, was continued at Lawrence. It employed large numbers of single women housed together under the supervision of a resident matron who acted on behalf of the corporation. This stereograph of Lawrence in the mid-1870s affords a fine view of the Atlantic Cotton Mills at the right, and across the canal, the double rows of corporation boardinghouses along Canal and Methuen streets. The Moseley truss bridge in the center of the picture still spans the North Canal, but only a section of the mill building and one boardinghouse remain standing. (MVTM)

of them that they were not willing to meet. They rebelled and they fled, but they failed to make the voice of labor an integral part of the directorate now taking command of production at the industrial centers of the Valley.

Of all the stories told about the Merrimack Valley, none is more famous than the story of the Lowell mill girls. Poets sang about them and dignitaries came from Europe and from the far corners of America to see for themselves whether it was true that people could work in factories and still be contented and moral. The French economist Michel Chevalier, on an official visit of inspection for his government in June 1834, compared Lowell's mill girls to nuns in the neatness and femininity of their work habits. Others have preferred to compare them to students, together for a time in dormitory-like boardinghouses, laboring toward similar futures and leaving after three or four years to take with them a host of sweet and dear memories. And there was more than one minister to invoke the discipline of labor—the rod of the ancient Puritan God—to explain that Lowell was in fact both a church and a school.

But for the mill girls themselves, living through the Lowell experiment was work, long hours of it at a stretch, before they could take the time to comprehend what else it might be. In November 1823, when the Merrimack Manufacturing Company began cloth production, and for a decade after, Lowell kept the promises it made, those it needed to make, to attract farm women to labor in its mills. They were housed and fed reasonably according to the standards of the time, and the long hours of their work were no longer than they would have faced at home, on the land. Their wages were generous when compared to the alternatives open to women in the 1820s. They were paid from $2.25 to $3.50 for a 60-hour week, from which they paid their own board of one dollar a week. These figures are appalling to us, but they were then quite attractive to a girl in the farming towns of New Hampshire and Vermont. Even at 14 or 15 years of age, such a girl was quite aware what her future would be like if she rejected the opportunity of work at Lowell. She might stay at Nelson or Claremont or Woodstock and marry a farmer like her father. She might even be lucky enough to rouse the attention of a man whose land was sufficient to support a household. In any case, it would be days and seasons of work and no more freedom than her father had allowed her.

She could choose instead, or have it chosen for her, to migrate to the West. Thousands of farm families did leave New Hampshire and Vermont after 1810, happy to exchange the difficult soil of upcountry farms for the larger, flatter, and stone-free soil of the Ohio Valley. There were other thousands, however, who interpreted the American tradition of moving-on to counsel another course. These migrated to Lowell and other industrial cities then growing on the banks of the Merrimack and elsewhere. So in addition to the pull of Lowell there was the push of the land, which offered a difficult life for all in the best of economies and made it pointless for many, since the Embargo of 1807 separated them from the lucrative markets of Europe.

Lowell promised freedom from these doubts and pressures as it promised work and an income, so that arriving at Lowell must have been part relief and part exhilaration. After this came the slow discovery, delivered through a network of kin and friend, that Lowell was not only a new town but also a haven of the young where a girl might find thousands like herself to share interests common to young women through the years from 1820 to 1840: clothes, marriage, books of devotion and fiction, sound preaching from a good minister and, under it all, "self-improvement." Their motives for work were less altruistic, less centered on family, than they once were thought to have been. Still, there was more than one Lowell girl who gave part of her wages to help with a father's mortgage or a brother's education. Ties to family were not severed when it was at all possible to keep them, and this fact was significant in making Lowell's labor force a transient one. Mill girls would work for two or three years, than leave Lowell to return home, perhaps simply for the change of it but more likely for a rest from the pace and confinement of mill work. Though these women were used to long hours of labor, they were not accustomed to working with machines that set the pace of work and demanded that human partners keep up. And like their menfolk the farm women were not used to the clatter of the textile mill, and the heat and moisture needed to make carding and spinning feasible.

The Lowell mills were to these women a place to join or leave as circumstance or decision might say, but never a place to find lifelong employment. Even as late as 1845 the average length of stay at Lowell was four and a half years. Those who were tied permanently to mill work by necessity were the object of concern and pity by their sisters, and too often the object of their own curse. The Lowell experience was helpful to a majority of its workers during that first decade, but soon enough there was trouble in this paradise of labor.

The first "turnout" (strike) in the Valley occurred in 1834, when the corporations lowered wages by 12 to 25 percent. There was another turnout in 1836 when the amount withheld for room and board was increased to $1.37½ a week, an increase of $.12½. But these strikes, and others, were not effective against the textile corporations. Workers could refuse to work, but the solidarity needed to make the refusal effective was sabotaged by the fact that the strikers were also boarders in corporate housing, and by the fact as well that so many of them had no means of support during the strike. Some left the city. Yet if a woman

Working hours in mill towns were regulated by the factory bells, and corporations in Lowell resisted installation of church and city bells in order to control even the time of day. Hours were staggered to make best use of available light, but winter evening work required the use of oil and, later, gas lamps. The Saturdays closest to March 20th and September 20th were celebrated (respectively) with "Blowing Out" and "Lighting Up" balls. (MVTM)

thought she might need or want to work at a textile mill the future, she was well advised to be quiet about anything she disliked or found unjust in the Lowell system. A troublemaker was blacklisted and the list was circulated to other mill towns from Dover, New Hampshire, to Chicopee, Massachusetts, where the mills often were owned by the same men who owned the mills at Lowell.

There was no surer way to blacklisting and dismissal than for a woman to attempt to organize her fellow operatives, but the Lowell women organized nevertheless. There was a short-lived Factory Girls' Association formed during the turnout of 1836. The more durable Lowell Female Labor Reform Association was founded in January 1845 by 15 women, including the tireless Sarah Bagley. Lowell women also joined with others, male and female, to participate in the New England Workingmen's Association, which held a convention at Lowell in March 1845. The sense that workers were able to get of their situation was expressed by Josephine Baker, who signed herself J.L.B. when she wrote for the *Lowell Offering* (April 1845):

There is a class, of whom I would speak, that work in the mills, and will while they continue in operation. Namely, the many who have no home, and who come here to seek, in this busy, bustling "City of Spindles," a competency that shall enable them in after life, to live without being a burden to society, — the many who toil on, without a murmur, for the support of an aged mother or orphaned brother and sister. For the sake of them, we earnestly hope labor may be reformed; that the miserable, selfish spirit of competition, now in our midst, may be thrust from us and consigned to eternal oblivion.

The thrust is obviously set against the argument used by the Lowell corporations when faced with worker demands, that conditions of the marketplace forced them to compete with other like corporations and that productivity had to be increased or the company would fail, and the workers would lose their income. So when weavers were "stretched out"—asked to tend three looms instead of two, or four instead of three—they were given to understand that it was necessary for their own self-interest. The same reasoning explained the "speed-up," when machines were made to run faster, or the "bonus system," which rewarded overseers for their skill at managing workers to produce at a piece rate. And indeed productivity did rise. According to figures "compiled from authentic sources"—from the corporations, that is—Lowell's 10 large corporations together produced 125 yards per worker per week in 1836, while in 1860 they produced 188 yards per worker per week. Yet, somehow, that rise of productivity never appeared in the laborers' pay envelopes. The average wage in 1860 was exactly the average in 1836: $2 a week clear of board for females and 80 cents a day clear of board for males.

There is no need to seek the hidden hand of God or the perverse will of any devil for what followed. With the best wills in the world, corporate directors were overwhelmed by the demands of leadership, which, nevertheless, they insisted was theirs alone. Panics and recessions appeared and vanished at will, and the appeal to the Natural Laws of economics made by Abbott Lawrence during the crisis of 1837 had no effect whatever except to calm his nerves. The truth is that corporate leaders were puzzled by the forces of the market and so were powerless to control them. Naturally, they lay hands on what they could control, the productive system, provided only that the productive system could be shaped to give the handles they thought should be there.

Prophecies have a way of becoming self-fulfilling, and the directors of corporate industry on the Merrimack prophesied that the end of production is profit.

Some of the women who protested the system of labor at Lowell spoke of themselves as the "daughters of freemen" and saw their struggle against the power of money as a continuation of their grandfathers' struggle against the English crown. They pleaded, threatened, explained, testified without outcome. Nothing they said or did had any consequence on the terms of their labor. It's fitting perhaps that the grave of Sarah Bagley is unknown, invisible as well as mute to us, if only because it forces us finally to hear her words published in the *Voice of Industry* as the true monument to so many lives like her own. By 1850 the same network of kin and friend that had praised labor at Lowell in the past now carried the message that despite marvels of engineering and feats of productivity, Lowell as

Sarah G. Bagley, a New Hampshire-born weaver, also worked in the warp dressing room. She may have been a drawing-in girl, like the one pictured here, drawing warp ends through the reed in preparation for setting up the loom to weave. No known likeness exists of Bagley, an articulate writer and speaker on behalf of labor reform. Founder and first president of the Female Labor Reform Association of Lowell, she worked in the mills for more than a decade between 1837-1849. (MVTM)

Winslow Homer's New England Factory Life—Bell Time, *engraved for* Harper's Weekly, *portrays the rush hour of 1868, when crowds of working people left the mills to walk home along the tree-lined canals. Carrying their lunch pails, old and young, Yankee and immigrant, they swelled the ranks of every town in the Valley after the Civil War. This scene illustrates the Washington Mills at Lawrence, where Homer's brother worked. (MVTM)*

an experiment in labor had failed. Thousands left the city and there was one, at least, who moved on and pursued elsewhere the American dream of free labor that had eluded her at Lowell.

Mary Paul had come to Lowell in November 1845, at the age of 15, and worked there, off and on, for about four years. When she left in 1849, she returned to live for a time with her father, described as a shoemaker at Claremont, New Hampshire. In the early 1850s she worked as a seamstress at Brattleboro, Vermont, but in May 1854 she arrived at the North American Phalanx (Redbank, New Jersey). It seems a strange career but it was not uncommon of its generation, sharing as that generation did the migrating habits of American workers, and wedded to a mission all its own to fabricate a better community out of self-improvement and labor reform.

There were many such communities in the 1840s and later, from Brook Farm to Salt Lake, some of them claiming descent from Christ and some of them not. The community chosen by Mary Paul followed the teachings of Charles Fourier, whose blueprint for the Phalanx promised to integrate individual ambition with the common wealth of all. Mary Paul stayed a full year at the North American Phalanx, and its failure in the summer of 1855 did not dim the vision she had found in it. For her the failure was neither conclusive nor permanent. After all, she told her father in her letters, because the Phalanx was "but an

experiment of itself there must be many failures, since man is not perfect." The community, she explained, was a joint stock corporation with the workers holding the stock and exercising authority together. There was only one member, a man, who was too poor to own even the smallest share of the venture, but she doubted that even he was denied the right to vote, "for although he is poor he is very useful & probably that balances his deficiency in *money*." Her conclusion after one year's observation was that "imperfect as it is I have already seen enough to convince me that Association is the true life."

The daughter of a shoemaker from Claremont, "common schooled" in a farming village like most of the women who worked in the mills at Lowell, was able enough to judge for herself the character of republics as she joined and left. She did not need James Madison to tell her that man is not perfect, or that society must take notice of that. Nor did she need Emerson to tell her that, "political economy is as good a book wherein to read the life of man and the ascendency of laws over all private and hostile influences, as any Bible, which had come down to us." However, it was very different with the workers who came to replace the dispersed female workers native to New England and its traditions. By 1850 fully half of the labor force at Lowell was Irish and immigrant, and these were only the first of many Europeans who arrived, wave on wave, until the second decade of the 20th century. They arrived when the American dream of free labor already had been seriously compromised in the textile cities on the lower Merrimack. And they shared no community except the future, where independence meant having a job and economic freedom meant the opportunity to compete with other families to insure that their children would have a better one. In only one generation, the corporate ethic of competition had contradicted precisely Emerson's sense that a household is the school of power.

A number of immigrant groups that came to the Valley carried with them the memories of violence suffered for religion's sake, or persecutions that threatened the extinction of ethnic minorities by more powerful ruling castes. Such were the Jews who had lived under the German, the Austrian, or the Russian state, the three dynastic empires that divided among them the rule of eastern and central Europe at that time. Similarly, the Lebanese and Armenians had suffered for their Christian faith under the rule of the Turkish sultan at Constantinople, if the rule is the right word for such a brutal system. For these, and perhaps to a lesser degree for the Italians and Greeks, reaching the cities on the Merrimack promised the freedom to pursue unmolested their own course to God and community. They were well educated to understand Milton's counsel that "our country is where we can live as we ought," and primed to expect that its tradition of tolerance would make

Right: *Skilled workers formed an important component of the Valley's industrial work force. These women weavers and the two male loom fixers of the Merrimack Mill in Dracut posed proudly in their best clothes protected by aprons and coveralls at the turn of the century. Each worker was armed with his or her tools, wrenches or shuttles, scissors, and reed hooks. (MVTM)*

Below: *As principal landowner and developer of Lawrence, the Essex Company maintained control over land use and sales. This "descriptive plan of shanties," prepared in 1857 when lots were being divided and sold, shows the location of Irish families in temporary dwellings in South Lawrence. Company housing was not provided for Irish construction workers, only for Yankee factory hands. (MVTM)*

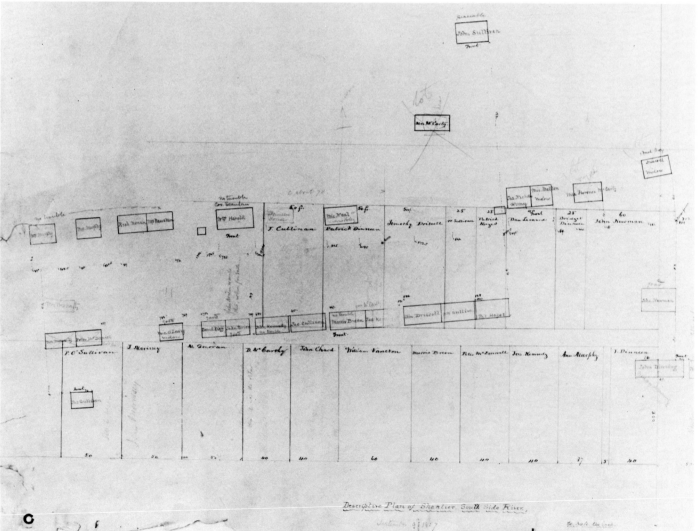

America a home for them all.

Also, of course, all the immigrant groups of the period between the Civil War (1861) and the First World War (1914) were driven by the same economic needs that had pushed and pulled the original millworkers from the farms of New England. The Irish, the French-Canadians, the Greeks, the Germans and Poles, Lithuanians and Russians, the Portugese, Italians, and Lebanese came from agricultural economies no longer able to support their explosive populations. If the immigrants to the Merrimack Valley had to adjust to a new system of laws and social convention, if they had to learn a new language, this was still not the end of the adjustments they faced. For the bulk of them, a move to the Merrimack was also a move from farm to city.

The percentage of Massachusetts people living on the lower Merrimack remained virtually unchanged between 1865 (8.51 percent) and 1915 (8.39 percent), but the concentration of those populations into cities already begun before the Civil War continued at an accelerated pace in the 50 years after it. The population of the entire lower Valley in 1865 was counted at 107,966, the population of Lowell alone was exactly one dozen persons more than that (107,978) in 1915. Two percentage values, the first from the high end and the second from the low end of the spectrum, may express most clearly this concentration of the Valley's people. The first tells us that its three largest cities (Lowell, Lawrence, Haverhill), which held 58.71 percent of the lower Valley's population in 1865, had mushroomed to contain 79.84 percent 50 years later. The second reveals that there were six Valley towns of fewer than 2,000 persons in 1865 and that they counted 8.22 percent of the population, while in 1915 there were four such towns with a like value of 1.87 percent. It will help to focus this demographic picture to add that the four towns of less than 2,000 in 1915 were at either end of the Valley, with Tyngsborough and its population of 967 on the state boundary with New Hampshire, and Newbury (1,590), West Newbury (1,529), and Salisbury (1,717) at the seacoast end. Finally, the numbers that tell about concentration of people also give the reverse image of physical space, or the lack of it. Tyngsborough in 1915 held 57.2 persons per square mile and Dracut 192.9, while Lowell, in between, held 8,058 persons per square mile. And at Lawrence a fearsome 13,381 persons were jammed into 1,491 habitations on each of its 6.7 square miles.

Though the people of the Valley were unevenly distributed among its cities and towns, only Amesbury, Newburyport, and the four smallest towns reported less than a quarter of their populations as foreign born. The others counted from a quarter (Chelmsford, 25.80 percent) to a third (North Andover, 33.36 percent) to nearly a half (Tewksbury, 46.98 percent) of their residents in that classification. The state census of 1915 does not relate "gainful occupations" of these foreign groups by town, but the statewide tabulation makes it understood that most males of foreign birth were employed as semiskilled workers in the "manufacturing and mechanical industries." Nevertheless, there was a surprising number working as farm laborers, blacksmiths, glaziers and painters,

South Lawrence was slower to develop than the commercial center north of the river. Amidst the neat frame residences, this shanty on Kingston Street survived until the 1890s when it was recorded by Richard Hale for the Essex Company. No longer used as a dwelling, it did serve as a reminder of the difficult conditions faced by the first residents, when Lawrence was the "New City" on the Merrimack. (MVTM)

To provide a good "head" for waterpower, flashboards held the river water above the dam. Maintaining the flashboards was a regular job of the Essex Company workmen in Lawrence, pictured here in 1898. The privy allowed the crew to remain on the barge all day without offending passers-by on the nearby Broadway bridge. (MVTM)

"Professor Bill Artist Bootblack" was William R. Mobley, second from right in this circa 1900 photo of his Haverhill shop. Born in Kentucky in the 1870s, Professor Bill came to Haverhill in the late 1880s and established himself as a bootblack, tailor, and dry cleaner in 1893. One of the Valley's few black businessmen, Professor Bill was a friend and confidant of politicians and sportsmen before his death in 1948. Charles Diggs, his son-in-law, still operates the business on Merrimack Street. Courtesy, Trustees of the Haverhill Public Library.

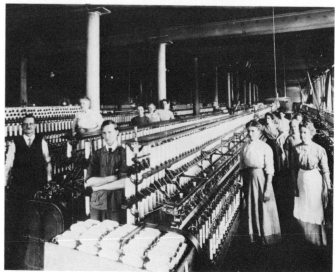

Cotton-spinning operatives of northern European descent were photographed in December 1913 and January 1914 as part of a series of pictures made for the Pacific Mills depicting all aspects of that large corporation's activities. (MVTM)

Surrounded by their stock of furniture, the sales force of C.C. Morse and Son in Haverhill awaits the arrival of customers in the late-19th century. Traditional retail businesses flourished with the influx of population to the Valley's industrial cities. Courtesy, Trustees of the Haverhill Public Library.

plumbers and steamfitters. And there was a substantial number, particularly among the Northern Europeans, who entered the more skilled crafts as machinists, millwrights, and toolmakers. The females of all groups, for the most part, went into "domestic and personal service," when they did not work along with their children in the mills of the larger cities.

The state census of 1915 shows that, taken as a whole, fully a third of the people living on the lower Merrimack were foreign born, and in all the communities of the region their numbers became an enormous reality in the minds of the American born. There were only 203 foreign born counted at Tyngsborough that year, yet even those few made an impression when there were only 764 native-born residents in town to mingle among. The result was culture shock for both the residents established in the place and for the newcomers. Both withdrew from encounter, and for a generation or two unofficial ethnic boundaries of language and culture were at least as real as the authorized political boundaries established by the General Court. However, the native and foreign born could not avoid each other at the workplace, and labor was the steadiest contact each had with the other. Labor is the base of all community, but division was found here and even encouraged nevertheless.

Alien workers were unsure about their nationality and the workplace exposed these feelings of insecurity to exploitation and manipulation, for any protest over hours or wages or conditions of work was likely to brand them as un-American.

Like native New England farm girls half a century before who were told that protest was not ladylike, foreign-born workers had their own feelings held hostage against them. Rather than argue the demands of workers on the grounds of economic need or social justice, employers were willing and sometimes able to make a political issue of the conflict and so enlist the support of native-born voters anxious to have their votes make a positive statement, at least about themselves. And so, besides undermining with doubt the determination of the immigrant workers, the tactic had the added advantage of separating the native workers from the actual issue at hand. With so large a labor force to command, labeling all resistance as un-American was too convenient, too potent a lever of control, to let lie unused. The issue helped enliven politics at Haverhill in the last years of the past century.

Shortly after the Haverhill municipal elections of 1894 had shown that the entrenched Republican party was losing its hold on the voters of the city, the shoe manufacturers initiated a bitter controversy with their workers by requiring that part of each week's pay be left with them until $50 had accumulated on deposit. This was to insure, they said, that workers not leave their jobs without notice, but workers also suspected that the money—another hostage—would be confiscated in the event of a strike. Fifty dollars was in the neighborhood of seven percent of the average shoeworker's yearly earnings, and the hardship this deduction brought was compounded by a wage reduction earlier in the year. Also, the manufacturers had imposed production quotas on the workers in the form of mandatory contracts. When the workers struck against these exactions in December (1894), the manufacturers retaliated with a lockout: they would not give up even the appearance of control. They did not give up the substance either. When the strikers returned to their work in the spring (1895), none of the issues had been resolved in their favor. Yet despite its failure, the strike began a curious evolution in the politics of the city.

In the winter of 1895, when some strikers had been brought into police court on charges of assault, the judge in making his decision lectured the defendants, warning that their leaders were Socialists, by which he meant "men who hate the flag." As often happens with name-calling, especially when it originates in learned places like the bench, the name was accepted as a banner of truth. James Carey and John C. Chase, among some others who had been involved with a populist coalition in the first half of the 1890s, took the initiative and formed a local branch of the Socialist Labor Party. Their purpose was to run candidates for municipal office. After some impressive but failed attempts, James Carey was elected to the Haverhill city council in November 1897, which made him the first municipal official in the nation elected as a Socialist. The odd thing is that the victory upset Carey's own party more than any of his opponents. The leader of the Socialist Labor Party, Daniel DeLeon, was more than disappointed; he was scandalized by Carey's lack of fidelity to doctrine. By making allies of labor unions, by addressing local issues and worker opinion, by trying reform, in other words, when DeLeon wanted revolution, Carey had fallen away from the purity of Socialist dogma. So while the new councilman was praised by the *Gazette*, the Republican party newspaper published at Haverhill, he was denounced in the pages of *People*, the Socialist Labor organ published at New York. Carey concerned himself with unguarded railroad crossings and clothes for children who would otherwise be un-

able to go to school: this was not the stuff of revolution. "Weeping James" he was called by his party, stung by what they took to be his betrayal. Carey and Chase in February 1898 returned the charter that bound them to DeLeon's party and allied with the less dogmatic Eugene Debs and his Social Democracy Party. The elections that fall showed that party labels counted for nothing when up against leadership. In November 1898 Carey and Louis Scates were elected to the Massachusetts General Court, while in a separate election some weeks later, John C. Chase became the first Socialist elected mayor of an American city.

Haverhill elections were drawing national attention, and the elections of 1899 provided political lessons fit for the audience. The *Gazette* thought those elections "the most memorable within the recollection of the oldest inhabitants." To meet the electoral challenge of the Socialists, the local leaders of the Republican and Democratic parties combined to make up what they called the Citizens ticket headed by Mellen Pingree, a corporation lawyer, as candidate for mayor. The Citizens candidates ignored the referendums, also on the upcoming ballot, for an eight-hour day for municipal workers and for the elimination of unguarded railroad crossings, still an issue. Instead, Pingree warned the voters of Haverhill that Socialists met on Sundays and that they favored free love, and so were a threat to the traditions of New England. Socialism in fact was not American, but "imported from foreign countries" where kings ruled. This electoral strategy by Pingree and other Citizens candidates failed to excite terror or revulsion in the voters of Haverhill. Socialism at Haverhill was manifestly not what Pingree said it was. Honesty may have been the solitary joy of Weeping James, but the making of his political career was that voters could tell he was honest and they could tell because he addressed issues within their vision and grasp. To these voters the Socialist Carey in 1899 was the same person as the Populist Carey who in 1893 had demanded a "money system of the people, by the people, and for the people." Besides, who at Haverhill could confuse anything foreign with the name Chase? Anyone familiar with the place was familiar with the name, at least with the history of Haverhill published 30 years before by George Wingate Chase. In the election of 1899, John C. Chase as candidate for mayor gained 1,200 votes on his winning plurality in the previous year. Three councilmen and three aldermen also were elected on the Social Democracy ticket.

In the confused currents of Haverhill politics that crossed party lines and even made fellow Citizens of Democrats and Republicans, the followers of DeLeon managed to pick up the tactics of their ideological opponents. In the course of reporting on the elections of 1898, one of them remarked that Carey's followers were not true Socialists but rather "some few New England 'Yanks,' more anarchist Jews . . .

Socialist politician James F. Carey of Haverhill, called "Weeping James" by his party, was elected to the city council and the state legislature. His attention to local issues and gradual reform offended the more militant branch of the Socialist Labor Party. After 1898, Carey and John Chase allied Haverhill's socialists with the less dogmatic Eugene V. Debs and his Social Democracy Party. Courtesy, Trustees of the Haverhill Public Library.

John C. Chase, active in the formation of Haverhill's socialist parties, served as the city's mayor from 1899 to 1900. He was the first socialist to be elected mayor of an American city, and three councilmen and three aldermen were elected with him on the Social Democracy ticket. This portrait of Chase, based on a photograph, hangs in City Hall. Courtesy, City of Haverhill.

and still more French Canadians.'' But the tactic was more effective for DeLeon than for Pingree. The workers at Haverhill were able to assimilate the issue of being un-American by their happy coincidence of a populist tradition alive with honest leadership of local constituents. At Lawrence in 1912 the currents were so large, so concentrated, that they nearly made for the revolution DeLeon had wished for at Haverhill.

The strike at Lawrence in 1912 became a world event, and that has made it hard for us to see it as the local story that it is. Also, it has suffered from familiarity. The actions of the strikers have been recited so well, as they are still by the few witnesses who remain, and they have been celebrated so often by radicals from London to Los Angeles, that now they have become outsized. So the events of the

strike come to us like the report of a foreign place called history where saints and heroes discuss fate in a white supernatural light. The story is rooted in the region nevertheless. It tells how workers new to Lawrence, immigrants from Eastern and Northern Europe, were able to combine against the corporate will of the Valley's largest textile manufacturer. Strangers to the place, the workers were also strangers to one another, but they found in the conditions of their labor the common bond between them.

The issue was wages. The legislature of Massachusetts had mandated a reduction in the number of hours worked in the textile factories of the Commonwealth. This was done over the objections of the manufacturers, who predicted that it would harm their ability to compete with the manufacturers of textiles in the nation's Southern states and with manufacturers abroad. As they were not able on this occasion to make their view prevail at the General

The Massachusetts National Guard was called up for strike duty at Lawrence. The Second Batallion of the Fifth Infantry Division was photographed in February 1912 with a panoramic "Cirkut" camera. Operated with a swinging motion, camera and film rotated independently. This camera could photograph large groups, which if posed in a semicircle appeared as a straight line in the finished picture. Buildings were not as malleable, so the Pacific Mills in the background appear distorted and curved. (MVTM)

Court, the manufacturers felt justified in cutting the wages of the workers to match the cut in hours. That would protect the fiscal health of the corporations and that, they said, was the bedrock of industry on the Merrimack. Without that, where would the workers be? The workers for their part could not afford to speculate in probable futures. It may say all there is to say about the strike of 1912 to add that this haggle over money amounted to a reduction of 30 cents a week for the average laborer at Lawrence; in the tenement districts of the city, 30 cents a week was the difference between the acceptance of a difficult life and the point of desperate resistance.

That movement of resistance began on Wednesday, January 10, with a meeting of the Italian branch of the Industrial Workers of the World, Local 20. The meeting was timed to precede the first payday of the new rates on the 11th, and the decision of the branch was that all Italian workers should refuse to work. The Lawrence Local also appealed to its parent body, asking Joseph Ettor, a professional organizer, to come and help the strikers. But the initiative had been taken at Lawrence, and on Friday the 12th workers at the Wood Worsted Mill abandoned their machines and moved through that enormous structure damaging machines, cutting drive belts, and making threats, some in Italian, to those workers who refused to join them. The next day, Saturday, was quiet on the streets of Lawrence. But Ettor had arrived and was indoors, beginning to organize the workers. Addressing the Italians of Local 20, he focused on their feelings about the owners of the mills. The owners, he said, accepted the Italians as long as they lived quietly, "next door to a dog and work for $4.20 a week. But when they want a little more...they are foreigners, then Socialists and anarchists." Ettor

saw, however, that he could not expect to organize a successful strike while ignoring the other ethnic communities at Lawrence.

Besides the Italian branch, the IWW had, before the strike, a Polish and a Franco-Belgian branch in the city. And indeed it was these three local branches that provided the core of leadership for the strike over the next eight

Serious overcrowding in the central district of Lawrence prompted a survey published in 1911. Unlike the Sanitary Survey of 1850, which found a model town, the 20th-century investigation disclosed the wretched living conditions of Lawrence's immigrant population. It was said that occupants hung their pots and pans on the outside walls of adjacent buildings and reached them through the windows. (MVTM)

weeks. Yet there were scores of other immigrant minorities at Lawrence, and the strike committee, which ruled the strikers for its duration, put together the efforts of representatives from all of them wishing to be included. The presence of such well-known agitators as Ettor and Bill Haywood, the activities of Socialist poet Arturo Giovannitti and the "red flame" Elizabeth Gurley Flynn, gave the strike at Lawrence the image of being a major front on the worldwide struggle of labor against capital. Owners of the mills at Lawrence pointed out that the workers were being used by the dark will of international communism, and that it was dangerous to bring such a godless force into the city. (Leaving us to infer that the only "safe" outside force at Lawrence was the money carted in from the banks of Boston and New York and which mortgaged the city's future production to the nameless face of American capital.) It is true that Ettor used the temper of workers at Lawrence in 1912 to recruit more members for the IWW and so push his organization ahead of its rival union, the American Federation of Labor. Yet the effort and the victory was a local event.

State militia as well as the National Guard patrolled the streets of Lawrence during the strike of 1912. Horsemen of Battery A of the state militia ride along Canal Street in front of the Washington Mills boardinghouses. In an attempt to keep the peace, the city government allowed only English-speaking people on the streets near the mills. (MVTM)

Mill Work in Lawrence

In 1913-1914, just a year after the strike, a series of almost 1,000 photographs were made of the Pacific Mills in Lawrence that recorded the numerous steps in the manufacture of printed cotton cloth and worsteds. Produced as albums for management and as stereographs with an accompanying booklet for use in the schools, these photographs document the work of thousands of individuals who labored at the Pacific. Differences in jobs and status of the workers according to nationality can also be discerned from these pictures.

Right: *Child labor was employed, if the children were over 14 and had certificates proving school attendance and literacy. Both parents and overseers bent or ignored the rules, however; many children entered the mills at 11 or 12 to help support their families. This girl empties the bins of full cops of spun yarn. (MVTM)*

Below: *The operatives working at the cotton drawing frames appear to be southern European. Lower-paying, dirtier jobs were held by the most recently arrived immigrants who shoveled coal in the yard gangs or breathed lint in the fiber preparation rooms. (MVTM)*

In the scene of the measuring and folding room for cotton cloth, one gains a sense of the production capacity of such a large operation. Pacific percales and lawns, shirting and serges, poured from the mills at the rate of more than a million yards per day. Mills at Dover, New Hampshire, and later in the South, lured the Pacific's capital investment away from Lawrence. Absorbed by Burlington Industries, the Pacific Mills ceased operation in Lawrence in the mid-1950's, just one hundred years after they began. (MVTM)

The strike at Lawrence in 1912 is a milestone of American industrial history and the only major victory that labor was able to organize against the textile manufacturers of the Merrimack Valley. The success was grounded on the cohesion of the workers around their ethnic communities, and on the ability of some of these communities to collaborate on an issue affecting them all. Not only was the wage reduction canceled, but the manufacturers now agreed to raise wages, some by as much as 20 percent. Textile manufacturers in other cities of New England felt compelled to follow the example and raised the wages of their workers. For these workers, for a while, Lawrence became the emblem of labor's emancipation.

After such a struggle, even victory is traumatic. Though there had been surprisingly little violence, given the size of

NOTICE.

The Mule Spinners of Lowell having combined together with a foreign association to coerce their employers to raise their wages, and having made a peremptory demand therefor, and to carry out their purpose having voted to "bring out the Lawrence and Massachusetts Corporations on a strike," and those of them employed by these Companies having given notice that they should quit work on the 12th instant,

NOTICE

Is hereby given that if said Spinners shall execute their threat by quitting work accordingly, the services of the Mule Spinners in the employment of this Company will not be required on and after the 14th instant.

MERRIMACK MANUFACTURING Co.,

J. S. LUDLUM, Sup't.

LOWELL, Mass., April 5th, 1875.

In 1875 the Mule Spinners Association of the United States ordered a test strike at Lowell. The mill owners responded with a lock out, a tactic often used in Lowell, and then substituted ring spinning frames for mules. In this way they reduced the level of skill involved in the spinning operation and exchanged less skilled, more tractable labor for the troublesome mule spinners. This notice records the managers' reaction to the threatened strike. (MVTM)

Lowell's "Mile of Mills" along the Merrimack employed about 17,000 people, who earned only 10 cents an hour on the average for a 62-hour week in 1900. Problems such as low water and high inventories closed the mills for several weeks each year, and no unemployment benefits were available. (MVTM)

the crowds and the presence of thousands of armed police and militiamen, the strike pursued the memories of everyone involved, whatever role they had played, whichever side they had favored. However, the reaction of Laurentians to the strike was part of the story of their cultural life in the Valley, distinct from the economic center of the strike itself.

The principal opponent to the victory of the strikers was William Wood, and that puts yet another face on the experience of immigrant labor in the Valley, and on the strike of 1912, because William Wood was born on Martha's Vineyard in 1858 to the wife of a Portuguese seaman. There were very many thousands of Portuguese immigrants at work in the textile mills of Massachusetts, especially at New Bedford and Fall River, and he had his experience of that. But Billy found his way to the fast lane in American society, where he accepted as fact that he could not change the rules but only play by them. He had a will of iron, forged, it seems, in a determination not to divide it. He bent his education to learn the skills that American society rewarded. He learned to manage men and money. He learned how to sell textiles. He learned, before they were written, the words of the Massachusetts Labor Census (1894): "Indeed, it is essential to the success of industrial operations, as at present conducted, that

Lowell Daily Courier.

12 Pages.

FINANCIAL NEWS

ON PAGE SEVEN.

4 O'Clock.

ESTABLISHED 1845.   LOWELL, MASS., SATURDAY, MARCH 28, 1903.   PRICE ONE CENT.

FIGURES OF LOWELL FACTORIES

MILL GATES SHUT

Closed at Noon for Indefinite Time.

NOTICE GIVEN AT MILLS

Employes Notified That It Is Impossible to Run During Strike, as Intended.

---

capital should be massed, controlled, and directed in few hands.'' His work was directed to insure that his hands would be among the few in control.

The American Woolen Company, which he organized in 1899, became in time the largest manufacturer of woolen and worsted cloth in the world. He based that corporation at Lawrence, partly because he was already treasurer of the Washington Mills there, and partly because Lawrence had the reputation of having a nonmilitant labor force. There's no doubt that his effort began the spectacular growth of the city that doubled the number of workers in little more than a decade. The speed of that change was no doubt one factor that unsettled the people and labor relations at Lawrence. The independent giants in the city, the Pacific Mills and the Arlington Mills, were enlarged, and a new Everett Mill (1909) was constructed. To these were added the two large

In 1903 Lowell experienced its first city-wide strike, called by the skilled workers of the Lowell Textile Council. The strikers demanded a wage increase. Foiled by several months without work or income and the strike-breaking activities of unskilled workers, the skilled craft unions lost not only the strike but also their positions and cohesive strength. In 1912 following events in Lawrence, Lowell workers struck again and gained the wage increases granted industry-wide as a result of collective action and IWW support. Courtesy, Lowell Historical Society.

---

mills of Wood's American Woolen Company: the Wood Mill (1906) and the Ayer Mill (1909), each built on the southern bank of the Merrimack and powered by its own steam-generating plant. There is some measure of the drive of William Wood in the fact that the mill that bore his name, providing 68 acres of space in two parallel struc-

tures, was built and put in production between August 1905 and April 1906. Yet, in another sense, there is no measure of his ambition, because William Wood, American, refused to see the future close. There were never enough mills, never enough profits. Eventually, the American Woolen Company operated 60 mills throughout New England, in New York, and in Tennessee.

The meeting of William Wood and the strike in 1912 present such a telling circumstance that we are inclined to put a drama at the center of it. "Immigrant labors to distance himself" might fit the marquee. But it is a drama only he might have given us, and it is well that we respect his silence. In the face of that silence, no amount of evidence seems able to resolve the conflict over his memory. There are those who see in Billy Wood the typical American industrialist of his age, grasping and ambitious in his purpose, ruthless in his methods. There are those, on the other hand, who read in his career the great American success story. Even for the thousands who failed he is proof that

Above: *Masons erect a wall for the new Pacific worsted mill on Hampshire Street, Lawrence, in 1910. In the decade preceding World War I, production capacity among New England woolen and worsted mills enlarged enormously. Lawrence experienced a great building boom, the Wood and Ayer mills of American Woolen Company were constructed, and significant additions to the Arlington, Everett, and Pacific mills appeared. (MVTM)*

Facing page: *In the 1915 city directory, the Chamber of Commerce advertised Lawrence's prosperity, which reached an all-time high during the World War I period. Uniform cloth and blankets rolled off the production line to meet the high wartime demand. Despite 20th-century modifications such as coal-powered steam and electricity, this ad pointed to the waters of the Merrimack—"the river that turns more spindles than any stream on earth." (MVTM)*

LAWRENCE, MASSACHUSETTS, U. S. A.

It has a population including its suburbs of about 125,000.

It is a manufacturing centre, by reason of its location on the Merrimack River—the River that turns more spindles than any stream on earth.

It is here that is located the largest Cotton Print works and the largest Woolen mill in the United States.

It has an annual Pay Roll of over 15 millions of dollars distributed to over 40,000 operatives.

It has 11 Banks and Trust Companies with resources of $32,000,000.

It has 40 Schools, training 14,000 pupils. It has 52 Churches. A Public Library.

It has 76 Societies and Clubs, including a Y. M. C. A., a Y. W. C. A., a C. Y. M. A., a Y. M. H. A., a Country Club and Canoe Club, also 213 Fraternal and Charitable Societies.

It is governed by a Commission Form of Government.

Right: *William Madison Wood (1858-1926), son of Portuguese immigrants who settled on Martha's Vineyard, rose by his wits and abilities to become wealthy and powerful. He created the American Woolen Company, which included about 50 woolen and worsted mills in New England and New York and became the largest producer of woolen cloth in the world. Despite his success as an aggressive entrepreneur, Wood's world crumbled after the death of his favorite son in 1922, and he took his own life in 1926. (MVTM)*

Below: *"Brick Shawsheen" and "White Shawsheen" housed two levels of American Woolen Company management. The more prestigious brick homes were separated by village shops and the office building from middle management's white frame dwellings. Individual garages were not constructed for either sector, however. Wood insisted on large common garages in the center to keep the feeling of a small town where executives walked to work. In this way he hoped to foster an interchange of ideas and a community spirit to benefit the corporation. (MVTM)*

they were not wrong to attempt the American dream, here, on the Merrimack.

Nor did the strike deflate his ambition. Between 1912 and 1926, when he took his own life, William Wood directed the creation of Shawsheen Village. It is located just south of the Lawrence city line in a part of Andover formerly called Frye Village. There he built an impressive structure of concrete and red brick as the headquarters of his American Woolen Company. Recently, the office building has been converted to a condominium, with the workmanship of its paneling to recommend it to its market. What is remarkable about Shawsheen Village is the attempt to give the place a totally American appearance, or at least the appearance of

residents of Shawsheen. Besides its even tone of ersatz colonial Americana, the other feature of the Village was its segregation of labor. There was a woolen mill built at Shawsheen, but unlike the manufacturers in the 1820s Wood provided no housing for the workers. What he gave was a streetcar line to take them back to Lawrence when their day's labor was done. Instead of housing for the workers, Wood directed the erection of "Red Shawsheen," brick homes for those in upper management, and "White Shawsheen," frame clapboard houses for the middle-level managers. By preferring a style of architecture that was make-believe, by shunting off most of its workers and separating the others into a hierarchy, above all in its over-

what Wood fancied as American. What we have is a homogenized rendition of preindustrial American buildings. The Village is colonial revival in its persuasion; the 19th and 20th centuries—where Wood was living his life—are pushed into the background and camouflaged. Wood did not allow the houses at Shawsheen to have garages for the residents' cars. Cars were garaged in common and residents were advised to enjoy the weather whatever it might be as they walked to or walked from.

There is the story of how William Wood, on seeing the fieldstone headquarters of Washington at Valley Forge, barked over his shoulder to one of his entourage, "Get that!" It was got and reproduced as the polling place for the

The bustle of "bell time" 20th-century style is reflected in this drawing of Lowell workers in about 1905. They came from every corner in the Old World to contribute their labor and customs in forming the New World. They found work and exploitation, kindness and prejudice, prosperity and poverty in unequal measure. (MVTM)

bearing concern with appearance, Shawsheen reflects the textile corporation of the Merrimack Valley as it entered its second century. It is a place where management becomes contrivance. Whatever else we cannot say about William Wood, we can say that he knew to which America he had come home.

VII

CULTURE, HIGH AND LOW

I heard the merry grasshopper then sing,
The black clad Cricket, bear a second part,
They kept one tune, and plaid on the same string,
Seeming to glory in their little Art.
Shall Creatures abject, thus their voices raise?
And in their kind resound their makers praise:
Whilst I as mute, can warble forth no higher layes.
　　　　　　　　　— Anne Bradstreet, *Contemplations*
　　　　　　　　　　　　(Number 9), circa 1640.

How could it be that you lived, for as long as you did, so
near to this living water and not have been overcome with
words aching to be written welling up within you?
　　　　　　　　　— Andrew D. Gray, *To Robert Frost,*
　　　　　　　　　　　　*Laurentian,*1981.

Anthropologists, who say they know about these things, often
measure the level of culture by the distance a people have put between
themselves and nature. According to this standard, the Pennacooks are

*Members of a Newburyport bicycle club pose with their vehicles on June 29, 1891. In
the 1880s and 1890s, cycling became popular in the Valley. Bicycle clubs appeared
everywhere, and cycling women and men toured the countryside, taking picnics and
enjoying the scenery. Photo by Osgood & Foss. Courtesy, Historical Society of Old
Newbury.*

called primitive because they developed neither metals nor sources of energy to alter significantly their natural environment, and so they could not see a very clear difference between themselves and the place. They had no idols, because idols demand a certain level of craft. The Puritan English, on the other hand, were intensely anxious to "rise above" nature, and their observance of the work ethic was very much a part of their need to see, before them, the farms and the industries of the Valley towns as proof of success. The towns themselves might be called their material culture, made of the labor of their bodies. The Puritans also produced a culture of the mind; indeed, there have been few communities more intent on that. However, in this as in everything, the Puritan mind was deep from want of being broad so that the stamp of the culture was its

Despite the Puritan culture's disapproval of pageantry and secular music, some sacred music survived. By the 18th century hymns were part of the church service, and by the 19th century community members participated actively in church choirs. The choir of the First Parish in Newbury sings in December 1861, as the impressive organ towers as evidence that this congregation took its music seriously. Courtesy, Society for the Preservation of New England Antiquities.

Harriet West (1798-1889) is seated in this 1870s photo before a portrait of her grandfather, a physician who introduced small-pox innoculation to Haverhill and to whom she bears a strong resemblance. Courtesy, Trustees of the Haverhill Public Library.

utter concentration on the word, written and spoken, and the neglect of picture making, of sculpture and theater—the neglect, in fact, of nearly all other ways of capturing and expressing thought. This may be why, for lack of a better explanation, language and narrative have had a larger place than the plastic and performing arts in the towns on the lower Merrimack.

In the first and second generations of European settlement in the Valley, perhaps even to the eve of the War of Independence (1775), it was the preacher who bore the major part of this culture of words. At the meetinghouses from Salisbury to Dunstable it was the spoken word that went among its public, each Sabbath. Even the printed word at this time was likely as not a sermon or a collection of sermons rather than some other form into which words are cast. Few of these would reward any attention we know how to give. The purpose, the images and devices, the vocabulary of these sermons are lost on us, and except for the passion that obviously motivated their quest for meaning, there is little in them to convince us that anyone could take this sort of expression seriously. Yet the townsfolk on the Merrimack not only accepted them seriously, they also sought them out earnestly.

It is somewhat easier for us to read the secular verse of the age, just barely, and it is true that the first book of verse published by an American was written by Anne Bradstreet, who for a time was resident at Andover, "by Cochichewick." However, it is also true that her early verse was written before 1644 when she left Ipswich with her husband and settled close to the river. Some reservation, then, must be made in claiming Mistress Bradstreet as genetrix of writing in the Valley, though the reservation is no greater than is needed to make an American of any English Puritan born, as she was, in 1612. Besides, we have the poems, and they tell us that she was very much part of her generation in this place. Her work constantly returns to questions that her community defined as vital: the history of the world, which is to say the story of God's wonder-working Providence, themes of filial piety and obedience, the struggle to accept herself as a creature, and a constant need to keep a watch on herself, to alert herself, and warn herself of evil tendencies. Her mental life was a constant round of scrutiny, judgment, and resolution. She wrote a short story of her life, to instruct her children, typically, and there is enough of that left to give us a glimpse of how this poet was made:

> In my young years about 6 or 7, as I take it, I began to make conscience of my wayes, and what I new was sinfull, as lying, disobedience to Parents, etc., I avoided it. If at any time I was overtaken with the like evils, it was a great Trouble. I could not be at rest 'till by prayer I had confest it unto God. . . . also found much comfort in reading the Scriptures, especially those places I thought most concerned my Condition, and as I grew to have more understanding, so the more solace I took in them.

The "Condition" she speaks of was her illness, frequent companion of her youth, so that she spent much time confined to bed. It makes a touching picture of so young a girl looking to find herself in the words of aged men, wondering whether so long an affliction of her body might bespeak a corruption of the soul. Finding her own voice in a din of Hebraic proverbs and Greek philosophy was an act of valor, so true and patient was her womanly heart. Victories, then as now, were few and fleeting, but one of her *Contemplations*, written sometime between 1666 and her death six years later, shows her by the river in a brief clearing of freedom:

Under the cooling shadow of the stately Elm
Close sate I by a goodly Rivers side,

Anne Bradstreet (1612-1672), born in Lincolnshire, England, came to America with her husband Simon in 1630 in the company of Governor Winthrop and other prominent colonists. The Bradstreets lived at Salem, Cambridge, and Ipswich before joining the first band of Andover settlers in the 1640s. Often ill, Mistress Bradstreet recorded her trials in poems, where she also related the joys of her life: "Upon my Daughter Hannah Wiggin her recovery from a dangerous fever" and "On my sons Return out of England, July 17, 1662." One volume in her own hand survives. Courtesy, Trustees of the Stevens Memorial Library, North Andover, Massachusetts.

Where gliding streams the Rocks did overwhelm;
A lonely place, with pleasures dignifi'd.
I once that lov'd the shady woods so well,
Now thought the rivers did the trees excel,
And if the sun would ever shine, there would I dwell.

Even when the religious tone had been left behind, language was used still as a tool to hone down the edges of character. Only now the command to name the evil Self and call it out became a cult of "self-improvement," which was so evident in the life of New England down to the middle of the last century. On the Merrimack, the most conspicuous example of that was undoubtedly in the much publicized cultural activity of the Lowell Girls. There is evidence to show that a number of these women went to

Lowell principally because it gave them a choice of religious congregations, just as the diary of Isaac Merrill shows him willing to travel to Atkinson, New Hampshire, and to the churches of Andover to hear a good preacher. Even Sarah Bagley, who was no friend of the Lowell system of labor, counted in its favor that the city gave her the Good News well spoken. By the 1820s, however, the spoken word was becoming secular, and there was in the Lowell Lyceum a more worldly congregation where Emerson and other famous lecturers came to talk about society and politics, about geology and minerals.

The audience of workers at Lowell also pursued the printed word. The famous *Lowell Offering* published a range of literature for and by the city's female labor force, and it was their most distinguished badge of breeding and gentility at this time when other women made a display of both exactly to distinguish themselves from the factory girls. The textile mills on the Merrimack were making a class of factory workers and that was something entirely new in the American experience, but both the women who

Operatives in top hats and hoop skirts play cribbage outside one of the factory houses at Stevens Mill, North Andover, in about 1865. Working people in the Valley's mill towns and factory villages experienced the new discipline of work regulated by the clock while still recalling the preindustrial rhythm of seasonal tasks. Some pleasures, however, did develop from the companionship found in the boardinghouse and work place. (MVTM)

were in that labor force and those who were not used language to deny what was happening. The *Offering* was first printed in October 1840, but it originated earlier that year at the so-called Improvement Circle at Lowell, where young women met after their hours of work in the mills to read aloud to one another from their own writings or from those of others that they fancied.

The notion to print these works instead of speaking them was intended to "improve" a larger circle. In a sense the magazine attempted to make the cultural community open to the entire laboring community, because for two centuries that had been the purpose of culture in the towns on the lower Merrimack. On everyone's part, the *Offering* was an attempt to deny that the mills had changed anything in this generation of New England's children. Those workers who were alarmed at the divisions and strife that factory labor brought to their communities were naturally repulsed by what they took to be a charade to hide the truth. *The Voice of Industry* was published in the later 1840s and was one attempt to use language to expose the shenanigans of the *Offering*. By its nature, however, the *Voice* and other publications like it were critical and negative, and the larger reading public tended to reject what they had to say as un-American. After all, there were the mills, and these were the production figures to show that progress was real and right.

Nostalgia for what they had left behind was a theme often expressed by the women of the *Offering*. In 1841 the magazine published "A Weaver's Reverie: No Fiction," which was signed by Ella, one of the pseudonyms used by Harriet Farley, a frequent contributor to the *Offering* and also one of its editors. She thinks on nature, Ella said, as famine victims think of food: it was the lack of it that gave her the need to seek a place to be alone. "I should love to be *alone*. Alone! where *could* I be alone?" With the hours at the mill and the slapping of belts against pulleys or the throwing of shuttles in the loom, with the activity of the boardinghouse and the hours at this meeting or that, where *indeed* could she be alone? And so, at the end of her Reverie, this weaver stands by a window of the weaveroom, having left her work to admire the blue sky. Suddenly the charm is broken: "'Your looms are going without filling,' said a loud voice at my elbow; so I ran as fast as possible, and changed my shuttles."

Farley's "Reverie" was followed by something called "A New Society," and that neglects the past to turn toward the future. It was written by Betsey Chamberlin, who followed the affectation of her peers and used a pen name, Tabitha. She recounts that once while reading quietly in her room a boy entered and handed her a newspaper. Then the boy left, never speaking a word. Her eye fell at once to an article headed "Annual Meeting of the Society for the promotion of Industry, Virtue and Knowledge." She read on. The

Society had enacted several "resolves," all of them unanimously. Some of these demand equality between the sexes in the "advantages" of education and in wages. Another resolve changes focus somewhat and puts all workers together to define a right common to all. It states that "as the laborer is worthy of his hire the price for labor shall be sufficient to enable the working-people to pay a proper attention to scientific and literary pursuits." It demands an eight-hour workday that will leave all the members of the Society with the time and energy to read and to write. Yet, if each is given the chance to use language for self-expression, none is allowed to do that only. For Tabitha reads, the Society resolves that they "will not patronize the writings of any person who does not spend at least three hours in each day, when health will permit, either in manual labor, or in some employment which will be a public benefit, and shall not appertain to literary pursuits." This New Society has her full approval, because work in the mills at Lowell has put her in a position to see the improvement in what it resolves to do. Still this news left her with a puzzle: sitting in a room reading, she knew it to be 1841, but the newspaper was dated April 1, 1860. The puzzle was quickly solved for her when, on her way up the stairs to tell the other girls, she "stumbled, and awoke."

Putting these two articles back to back may have been the inspiration of a good editor or it may have been the inspiration of chance. Whichever it was still leaves us now with the delight of finding them nestled against each other, one head dreaming of the past and the other dreaming of the future, while both are dreaming *out* of Lowell in 1841. Both writers do with words what dreams do with waking reality, and that seems appropriate; language and dreams are a precious yoke, since both are subversive and break through the denial of social change that the *Offering* was peddling to the "waking" populations of the Valley. Miss Chamberlin introduced her New Society with a verse that makes the point.

Dreams are but interludes which fancy makes;
When monarch reason sleeps, this mimic wakes;
Compounds a medley of disjointed things,
A court of cobblers, a mob of kings.

Lowell was the subject of much national interest, and international visitors added their comments to our written picture of its development. Novels, stories, and plays depicted its daily events. The women workers, known for their magazines and their militancy, created a market for cultural events, lectures, and recitals. A play conceived in 1849, "A new local drama. . . written for this Theatre," the Mill Girls of Lowell *included local scenery, mechanical effects, and a moralistic ending: "Virtue and Industry Rewarded; The Mill Girls of Lowell Triumphant." Courtesy, Lowell Historical Society.*

The pace of life at Lowell, the stepped-up pitch of labor regulated by the mechanical works of the clock and the loom, the noise of the city and the close isolation of living within sight of thousands of strangers, all of these were new to nearly everyone who came to the factory towns on the Merrimack. Like Harriet Farley and Betsey Chamberlin, all of them owned the living memory of a previous life, and for them it was a struggle to find ways of expressing the shock of the city. Language, then, exploded with breathy reports of what they found, as though a prudent and careful observer of country livestock fairs had suddenly been called on to write home about these beasts called camels and giraffes. Novels came pouring out of the presses, each with a stock description of what a factory girl, hybrid creature, might be.

There was the breathy sentiment of *The Factory Girls: or, Gardez la Coeur* by A.I. Cummings, MD, published at Lowell in 1847, a novel that tells the story of the trials and triumphs of Calliste Barton. Some dozen years later there was the heavier breathing of *Flora Montgomerie, The Factory Girl: Tale of the Lowell Factories* in which "kisses and caresses were submitted to by females, and enjoyed by males." The author of this novel called himself Charles Paul de Kock for some clearly commercial reason and used the transparent device of putting his heroine naked in front

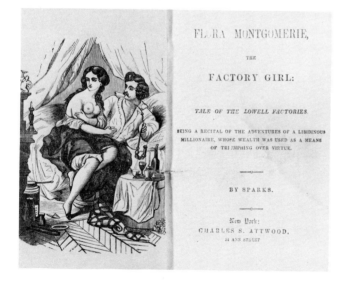

Factory fiction described life in the factory as imagined by novelists who had never worked there, yet it appealed to the audience of working women who no doubt enjoyed the fantasy of figuring as heroines of these tales. Some novels were more lurid than others; Flora Montgomerie shows a hookah being introduced to a topless, hapless, operative. Very little of the plot and action actually concerned the making of cloth, but the mills served as a convenient setting to reach the market of factory girls and to warn young women against the potential dangers of strange men and city ways. (MVTM)

of a mirror so that she could describe herself to herself. Meanwhile, the reader is modestly kept outside, watching, "but not with LUSTFUL eyes." Heaven forbid! Private is private after all, and so we get the visible ***** to displace the invisible sexual gymnastics in these gilded sinks of iniquity. Sex is presented as a reasonably elaborate if somewhat clumsy fan dance: now it's there, now it's not. On the other hand, one murder and one case of embezzlement are given in full frontal view.

These pulp novels not only described factory life on the Merrimack, they also were a thing gone out into the nation, a commodity like the other commodities pouring out of the factories of America. The story was often a coarse package perhaps, but good enough to satisfy the growing habit of thoughtless consumption. Yet all the fiction using the mill-town for a setting was neither sentimental nor so erotic. For instance, *Merrimack: or, Life at the Loom* (1854) is moderate in expression and thoughtful in content. Written by Day Kellogg Lee, this novel makes the attempt to describe characters of complete human dimension, using the model of the immensely popular Dickens.

While much of a certain brand of fiction was written by hacks and published out of back rooms in New York, some observers living on the lower Merrimack were trying to fashion something better than gossip from their culture of words. They made the most exact demands on their craft and shared an immediate concern with this place. Five in particular found the language that the reading public in America, at one time or another, was ready to accept as its own: Henry Thoreau and John Greenleaf Whittier in the last century; John Marquand and Jack Kerouac to match them in the 20th and Robert Frost in between. These writers among the many who have lived and worked in the Valley received the attention of a national—and international—audience.

Of the five, Thoreau was most attached to locale. His writing attempts the closest observation of the dynamics and spectacles of nature. Equally important to Thoreau, however, is the platform from which he makes those observations. For the circumference that is nature is described from the center, which can only be the mind of the individual; there is not one universe but many, as many as there are observers. Calling Thoreau a nature writer, then, is only a half-truth that has confused and misled readers since his work was first published. Late in 1849 James Russell Lowell reviewed Thoreau's *Week on the Concord and Merrimack Rivers* for the *Atlantic Monthly*. Lowell was perplexed in a generous sort of way; he complained that after accepting what he thought was an invitation to a boating party, he was sat down at the bow and preached at by the helmsman. Lowell could not accept finding long, extended digressions on religion, on friendship, on poetry, in a book he thought should be about the fishes and the

Top: *Although not a native of the Valley, Robert Frost was the son of two native Laurentians and moved to Lawrence in 1885 at the age of 12. This photo was taken when he graduated from Lawrence High School in 1892. Although Frost's life as a farmer in Derry, New Hampshire, had more influence on his poetry than his Lawrence experiences, certain poems recall his past in the Valley, such as "A Brook in the City" and "A Lone Striker." Courtesy, Jones Library, Amherst, Massachusetts.*

Above: *Andover children enjoy the sandy shore of Haggett's Pond in the 1890s. The several church services and prohibition of activity on the Puritan Sabbath gave way two centuries later to the pursuit of nature and the perfect Sunday picnic spot. Courtesy, Andover Historical Society.*

fowl. In fact, *A Week on the Concord and Merrimack Rivers* reports a voyage Thoreau made with his brother John during the last week of August and the first week of September, that time when high summer is about to turn and give a show of choice even when we know there is none. That was in 1839, but Thoreau did not write his *Week* until that famous retreat he took at Walden Pond from 1845 to 1847. In those years when the Essex Company was building its Great Stone Dam across the river, Thoreau, alone for a good part of his days and nights, was busy calibrating a different sort of energy from the Merrimack. The mills on the river were then a powerful symbol of a new society, an open society in which individuals were free to compete for distinction and wealth. The American way promised that persons would earn, not inherit, what they got. Nearly always out of step with the business of his time, Thoreau gave in his *Week* his own definition of the self-made man. It is solitary confrontation with nature, not culture, that generates the full stature of personality. We are all self-made men, he seems to be saying, only some of us pay attention.

It's significant that Thoreau was nearly totally free of our national obsession with time, free that is from the need to find what history "means." The Great Seal of the Republic proclaimed "a new order of the ages" (*novus ordo seclorum*) and after 1800, as if on cue, there appeared an endless number of schemes to make the "new order" materialize in this promised land. Between the time of his birth in 1817 and his death in 1862, Thoreau's America was alive with an enormous variety of social experiments and movements of reform, all with the purpose of self-improvement and some hoping to assist in the birth of the Millennium, that thousand years of peace and justice that Scripture promises will follow the second coming of Christ. In this cultural fever, some writers used language very much as the Puritan preacher had, very much, that is, like the pharmacist uses chemistry to formulate nostrums and cures that reach well beyond chemistry. In moments of power or bravura, they also claimed to be the doctor.

One of these was William Lloyd Garrison, born at Newburyport in 1805. At 13, Garrison began a seven-year apprenticeship with Ephraim W. Allen, editor of the Newburyport *Herald*, and during these years, young Garrison used his skills at the printing press to make war on drink, Sabbath-breaking, and a number of other vices. But it was not until he heard the Quaker abolitionist Benjamin Lundy speak against the slavery of blacks that Garrison knew he had found the cause worthy of his editorials. He became an influential journalist, founder and editor of the *Liberator* in 1830. This combination of journalism, poetry, and reform typified the culture of words in antebellum America. It marked the career of another Newburyporter, George Lunt (1803-1885), and of John Greenleaf Whittier, born at haverhill in 1807. We remember Whittier now as a

John Greenleaf Whittier's poem, "The Barefoot Boy," evoked his own boyhood on the family farm in Haverhill and symbolized the typical American rural experience at that time. The Whittier homestead, painted by Thomas Hill in 1868, came to represent this way of life to many, and the painting was reproduced as a chromolithograph that was hung in thousands of parlors around the country. Courtesy, Trustees of the Haverhill Public Library.

talented poet, some of whose works are genuine masterpieces of regional poetry. "The Barefoot Boy" retains some of the charm of his early years and the moments of freedom stolen from the hours of labor on the family farm. Yet, in his own day, Whittier was known as well for his prose writing; he was editor of newspapers at Boston, Hartford, Philadelphia, and Lowell. Whittier published his first poem in Garrison's *Free Press* in 1826, and the two men were associated in one way or another until Garrison's death in 1879. Yet the moral tone Whittier brought to his work was more restrained and in a sense wider. Whittier protested the slavery of blacks, but on one occasion he also joined the protest of factory labor, here on the lower Merrimack. In 1852 he took the side of the workers against management during a strike at the Amesbury/Salisbury woolen mills. Whittier was born in the Valley before industry made its startling transformations of the place, and in the end he was not convinced that Lowell—or any other factory town on the river—was the birthplace of the "Millennium of Mechanism." When he was a young man, the factory system on the Merrimack promised to free Humanity from toil, to lift Mankind into a radically improved way of life, but as both Whittier and the system matured he noticed that it did not

end toil so much as make a new distribution of labor among the populations of the textile cities. It was not machines that would disclose the meaning of the American experience of freedom.

Writers in this century have been less obvious about awaiting or abetting the opening of the American millennium. Yet both John Marquand and Jack Kerouac, who had not very much in common, set out to explain America; both were inspired by John Galsworthy's *Forsythe Saga* to produce a family chronicle in fiction as a symbol of the American story in fact. John P. Marquand spent half a century at Curzon's Mill in West Newbury, and he was a sort of Merrimack industry in himself, earning about $10 million as a wordsmith in just under 40 years. Some of that was found in the Hollywood market by the popular stories of the instructable Mr. Moto. Many of his other novels, however, show us a character in the process of discovering that the American success story—money and the "women of the upper brackets" who come with it—is at heart a tragedy, for the futility of the prize is hidden until the game is played out. The novels are, on reflection, the story of Marquand's own life, cautionary tales that perhaps indicate the traps of culture without indicating an escape.

Kerouac's story, although beginning so differently from Marquand's, nevertheless finds a similar end. Like the older writer, Kerouac knew the influence of Galsworthy, but being of the generation next after Marquand's he also knew the work of Thomas Wolfe, closer to home. Both Kerouac's parents were children of French-speaking Canadians and Jack's first look at America was from the inside of the working class in a textile city past its prime. Despite that, and because of it as well, he was devoted to the power of words,

Descended from French-Canadian mill workers, Jack Kerouac graduated from Lowell High School in 1939, when this photo was taken. While attending Columbia University on a football scholarship, an injury interrupted his career, and he turned to writing adventures with himself as the central character. His 1957 novel, On the Road, *caught the imagination of the Beat generation and inspired the flower children of the 1960s, but Kerouac also wrote five novels about Lowell that are less famous. Courtesy, University of Lowell Collection.*

using language to dramatize himself in stories of mythic proportions, epics of spiritual emancipation and beatitude. He was born at Lowell in 1922 and left the city in 1939, and he later wrote five novels set in that locale. However, those novels have never commanded the kind of response given to *On the Road,* published in 1957. All his work is autobiographical but it was in this book that America recognized itself. So, the saga of the town on the river goes unread while Kerouac, "King of the Beats," still races time across the whole of the American continent, a trajectory without a center, as one of his cronies said of him. In the right place at the right time, Kerouac helped the next generation accept speed as the latest commodity in our national cycles of discovery and consumption.

Any attempt at reading the culture of a people and of a generation in the career and work of one individual is risky at best. Given the entire range of the performance and presence of these writers, however, it is difficult to ignore the lack of care and grace that Americans have shown for this place in their anxiety to discover the secrets of the future.

The word "culture"—so the dictionary tells us—derives from the same root and stem as the word "cult"; both originate in the Latin verb *colere,* meaning to attend to, to

respect. The sense of experience behind that is flexible enough to describe mental things—respect for Apollo, attending to the oracle at Delphi—and to describe as well some very earthbound things like the culture of tulips or pinto beans or maize. But nowadays the word nearly always has the sense given to it here, the sense of human culture that comprises the ways and forms of expression we use to attend to ourselves, to reflect on what we do and find what there is to respect in that. There has been human culture on the lower Merrimack for several thousands of years but it has been for less than two centuries that culture has reflected so many human forms and images that no one has been able to attend to them all. The Pennacook sense of respect for this Strong Place was eradicated, consumed in the burning need the Puritans had to tell God's Time in their beating out of the measure and cadence of Scripture. The experience of the past 200 years has multiplied the things we ought or might attend to and left us not very certain which of them to respect. We are left, now, with many cultures separated from one another by language, customs, and religious ideas and rites, as well as by education and income, so that while we are here at the same time we do not share really the same place.

One sign of that is our material culture, for instance in the separation of the workplace from the living place. That was begun by tying production to a machine and the machine to a central source of power, and it was completed when the automobile made so many of us independently mobile. Or, again, the styles of domestic architecture also bespeak cultural fragmentation and hints at cultural conflict. Until the 1820s there was a remarkable degree of simplicity and uniformity in the style of dwelling of the residents on the lower Merrimack. There was cohesion, therefore, in the appearance of the towns. But between 1820 and 1860, four styles of building gave a choice to those with the means to choose how they wanted to represent themselves to their neighbors, or distinguish themselves from the common lot of those around them. Greek Revival, Gothic Revival, Italianate, and Empire all made their appearance in one generation, and it is emblematic of how material culture changed and continues to change in this region, as in the nation at large. So rapidly, in fact, that the way of life of one generation is not readily accessible, perhaps hardly plausible, to the next; the tools and the place of labor of the fathers no longer apprentice the sons to a way of life common to both. What we have now, in our architectural heritage, is a bewildering collection of heirlooms and hybrids, a built-up environment that reflects a persistent confusion about what time it is in the Valley.

The varieties in material culture fostered by the revolution in production and mobility were overlayed, and not a little camouflaged, by the arrival of spectacular cultural varieties from Europe.

Architectural Culture

One readily apparent facet of culture is architecture. In the Merrimack Valley a multiplicity of styles remains to show the affluence and taste developed by the middle and upper classes during the 19th century. Architectural studies of individual communities and the region as a whole document both surviving structures and those lost to "progress." Two books in particular are worth noting. John Mead Howell's *The Architectural Heritage of the Merrimack: Early Houses and Gardens* (1941; reprinted 1980) treats the 18th- and early 19th-century legacy, with particular attention to Newburyport. John Coolidge, in *Mill and Mansion: A Study of Architecture and Society in Lowell, Massachusetts, 1820-1865* (1942; reprinted 1967), discusses the relationship of factory buildings and housing in the evolution of the city.

Below: *John Coolidge described the influential square, solid Italianate style with its inevitable tower as "rich and substantial, although varied and not stuffy." Built in 1852 the William Livingstone house, located on Thorndike Street at Chelmsford Street in Lowell, had lost some of its pairs of brackets and other details by the time Coolidge took this photo in the late 1930s, but it still displayed the overall plan of the Italianate style: a great cube with a wing, porches, and balconies, topped by bracketed eaves and a cupola. (MVTM)*

Above: *Built in about 1839, this house on Howard Street displays the common combination of Gothic and Classical elements. The pointed windows and decorative bargeboards are Gothic details above the doorway's Ionic columns. The flush-boarded facade and recessed doorway are Classical . (MVTM)*

Above: *Near the Livingstone house, a Highland Street neighbor imitated its forms—cupola, porches, quoins—in a compressed format later in the 1850s. Bow windows replaced open porches and balconies, but the builder kept the cupola and loggia in nearly exact replication on a smaller scale. The mansard roofs of its neighbors are the most prevalent characteristic of the French Second Empire style of architecture, also frequently found in Lowell and throughout the Valley. (MVTM)*

Right: *By the 1830s the basic New England frame house had been embellished with details such as the Greek Revival pedimented portico and Ionic columns built as part of Kirk Boott's Lowell mansion in about 1825. Its pillared portico bears a strong resemblance to those of Southern plantation mansions, recalling the close link between the economic interests of the manufacturers and planters of cotton. After Boott's death in 1837, the house was moved and served as the Corporation Hospital. When later incorporated into St. Joseph's Hospital, run by the Sisters of Charity of Quebec province, it bore a sign in French: "Hôpital." (MVTM)*

In 1892 the Hale family of Lawrence enjoys an outing to a farm and Haggett's Pond in Andover's West Parish. The decorated wagon represents a Mediterranean agricultural tradition reminiscent of the Old World. Andover's West Parish contained rich farmlands along the Merrimack, and Armenian families joined the Yankee, Scottish, and English families who had settled there earlier. (MVTM)

Foreign-born laborers began arriving in numbers at the textile cities on the lower Merrimack during the 1840s—Irish immigrants looking for work and escaping the horrors of famine at home. These strangers and those who came after were taken by the native American for an ominous sign with no clear intention but with certain obscure dangers for the traditions of the Merrimack towns. The foreign born themselves reacted to the Anglo majority by closing circle, unaware as yet of the irony that put them inside the wagons while the natives whooped and hollered around them. This siege mentality drove scores of ethnic groups and made citadels of their neighborhoods, whose boundaries were defended on more than one occasion with brawn and bricks. These ethnic enclaves, small cultural republics, might be crowded and unsanitary like the tenement districts of Lowell and Lawrence, or they might be more healthy and spacious like the farms of Pleasant Valley in Methuen or those in Andover's West Parish.

Always, however, the enclave served to buffer the transition from the old country to this one, to surround the immigrant with the assurance of the familiar in dress, food, and language. In this way, and in many others, the Polish and Russian immigrant or the Italian and Greek coming to these towns behaved just like the English who founded them two centuries before. Always, the church—as a building and as a community—was the center of these ethnic groups, and worship in the traditional language was often an issue of intense feelings among new and later arrivals. The use of Lithuanian in Lithuanian Catholic churches, the

use of French among the French-speaking Canadians, was a matter charged not only with the conditions that immigrants found on the Merrimack, but also by the conditions in the country of origin, where language was often a badge of solidarity with the past. Schools were only slightly less important than the church to these ethnic groups, and often they were tied to the parish in funding, administration, and curriculum.

Aside from providing psychological security, the ethnic communities also gave some measure of social insurance, a real fiscal safety net to individuals and to families. In those years before the first term of Franklin Roosevelt when the New Deal owned up to the economic and social costs of a market economy, charitable organizations and mutual-assistance societies were the last resort for the jobless or the destitute, or for anyone who seemed stranded in a bleak and hopeless present. Each club or society was organized to serve one particular ethnic group, and in the decades that began this century there were hundreds of them in the cities and towns on the lower Merrimack. They paid for food and shelter, for drugs and health care, and for burial in consecrated ground. The sense of community included the dead.

Observing these ethnic communities from the outside and seldom with a friendly eye, native Americans failed to notice the points of similarity among them as they almost willfully neglected the points of similarity between themselves and the newcomers in the Valley. Because these newcomers were ignorant of the English language, they were too often counted illiterate when in fact language, spoken and written, was highly prized as a pledge of survival, a vessel in transit from past to future. It was in the nature of the place and the process that this regard for language was most often put to liturgical uses. The *Librarie Biron*, for example, doing business in the heart of Lowell's Little Canada, was a kind of literary arsenal, selling and circulating books printed in Quebec and Montreal as so many arms in the ongoing experience of struggle and survival. At Lawrence, on the other hand, the Lebanese community printed a book of grammar codifying the rules of that language and making it more accessible to more people. The book found a market outside the Valley. Lawrence, in fact, was something of a center of foreign-language press in the nation, turning out books in Lithuanian, Polish, Italian, German, French, and other "native tongues." Finally, the towns and cities on the lower Merrimack were active centers of foreign-language journalism. Dailies and weeklies brought news from the Old Country and news of what was happening within the readers' own ethnic community. Also, these newspapers were often the only alternative to the priest or rabbi for information about the wider world outside the Valley and its many communities. This was often important, though it led to tugs of war between priest

Not all of the supporters of the 1912 strike were radical anarchists. The strikers did have a just cause, vindicated by their victory and the national support shown at Congressional hearings and in reports by progressive journalists. In order to commemorate the strike without the tinge of anarchy, Pleasant Valley Citizens Club, a German social organization, records its solidarity with the positive aspect of reform: "For the struggle of the Strike of 1912." Courtesy, Immigrant City Archives.

and editor for leadership of this or that group.

The barrier of language was real. Sometimes the misunderstanding was not intended, sometimes it was humorous. The French-speaking Canadians at Lowell tended to pronounce Moody Street as though they were saying "Maudit" Street, that is, Cursed or Damned Street. So subtle is the alchemy of language in the relation of word to its context, that mere sound can transform the name of a respected mechanic into a cuss word. However, the humor in the trick depended on a knowledge of two languages and a certain distance from both, in the same way that visual depth is perceived. Other misunderstandings were not so innocent and involved bitter contest over the meaning of English words, words "translated" from one group's experience by another group's memory of it.

In September 1912 a public meeting was held at Lawrence by some of the strikers of the previous winter; they called themselves Anarchists and displayed banners advocating "No God, No Country." And as they *were* anarchists and they *were* immigrants, those banners proclaimed their conviction that this place fit the description of things they had learned to recognize before seeing them put before them in the Valley. Those at the meeting in September meant that both God and Country had become the idols

of another clan, that they were names used by their corporate employers only to cover with decency the indecent fragmentation brought into the lives of workers by what employers liked to call the "organization" of production. Those words—God and Country—struck their souls with the same chilling effect as the water from the hoses turned on their bodies during the demonstrations of the previous winter. Each side in this war of words was so sure of its own rendition of the facts that the other side's view of it was put down to bad faith rather than bad vision. The workers themselves were divided on the question and large segments of them had kept away from strike activity, partly at least because so much of the propaganda of the strikers was red and communist and godless. So, when Father O'Reilly of St. Mary's church organized a parade "For God and Country" on Columbus Day (1912), there were 32,000 marchers behind him to give witness that God and Country were well wedded at Lawrence. Most of these marchers were workers, of course, and some of them no doubt had been among the strikers who demonstrated in the earlier months of the year for what they had called "bread and roses."

There can only be one public language of course, and it was inevitable and necessary that the public language of these cities and towns should be English. Teaching the English language to the foreign born was one motive that prompted some women of the upper classes from the Lawrence area to found the International Institute of that city in 1913. This was one response to the strike of the previous year, resting on the faith that all conflict is the result of ignorance and misunderstanding. The institute continues

Americanization as an institutionalized process developed wherever the native-born population felt threatened or overwhelmed by the customs, language, and numbers of immigrants. Throughout the Merrimack Valley, classes in English language and American citizenship competed with ethnic clubs and churches. Instruction for women included domestic duties, nutrition, health, and child care. A cooking class for immigrant women at Lowell's girls' vocational school on Lee Street follows the directions read by instructor Miss Soroka, circa 1920. Courtesy, Lowell Historical Society.

Education in the Valley

The culture of the word on the lower Merrimack was manifest in the concern the founders of its towns showed for educating the young and the dependent. Paramount in this early concern was to teach "children and apprentices so much learning as may enable them perfectly to read the English tongue." The effort at public education in the Valley began in 1639 when the town of Newbury voted 10 acres of land to Anthony Somerby, "for his encouragement to keep schoole for one year." Gradually, improving conditions of security and economy allowed for common schools at Bradford in 1701 and at Andover the year before, at Methuen in 1735 and at Dunstable not until 1748.

Private academies were also founded. The first of these was the Dummer school at South Byfield (Newbury), established in March 1763 following the will and bequest of the late Lieutenant Governor William Dummer. Still flourishing as Dummer Academy, it was the first independent boarding school in the Commonwealth. Somewhat later, Samuel Phillips of Andover, with the help of brothers John and William, founded the academy that still bears their name. Phillips Academy began offering courses of instruction in 1778, but it was not until October 1780 that it was legally incorporated by the General Court "for the purpose of instructing youth, not only in english & latin grammar, writing, arithmetic, and those Sciences wherein they are commonly taught, but more especially to learn them the *great end and real business of living.*"

A similar institution in the town's North Parish was the first incorporated academy in the Commonwealth to admit girls; named the Franklin Academy, it survived until the middle of the past century. Another educational institution for young women founded in 1803 survives to this day as Bradford College, though it is now coeducational. Yet another, Abbot Academy, founded in 1828 at Andover, has in recent years been merged with Phillips.

Andover was also the site of a theological seminary opened in 1808 to combat what some took to be a growing laxity in the teaching of Calvinism at Harvard College. Although located at Andover, the seminary was begun with the support, spiritual and financial, of William Bartlett and Moses Brown, both wealthy merchants of Newburyport. The seminary was a regional effort at recalling the true purpose and real business of the communities on the lower Merrimack. In 1908 it was moved to Cambridge by special agreement with the Harvard Divinity School. Similar sentiments led the Augustinian Fathers to found Merrimack College in 1947, so that Catholic households in the area of greater Lawrence might have a place of higher education to send their children. The region is served also by the Northern Essex Community College at Haverhill and by the University of Lowell, organized recently by combining the Lowell State Teachers College and the former Lowell Textile Institute, which traced its origins to 1893.

Andover—a name synonomous with education—was home to the Theological Seminary, Phillips Academy, and Abbot Academy when this lithograph was published by local businessman W.F. Draper in 1857. The three portions of town, known in jest as the Mill, the Till, and the Hill, appear from left to right. The academy and seminary buildings occupy the lofty heights of the hill at right center. (MVTM)

Above: *The Haverhill High School class of 1935 included four sets of twins. Haverhill's first high school building was built in 1873 on the site of the first town schoolhouse. In the spirit of the 19th-century commitment to free public education, the advancement of learning was an early goal of Valley settlers, fulfilled by dame schools and private academies. Courtesy, Trustees of the Haverhill Public Library.*

Left: *Isaac Roberts became the first black graduate of Haverhill High School in 1895 and embarked upon an interesting career. Born in Liberia, he was brought to the United States as a boy. His father, a Baptist minister, served at Calvary Baptist Church in Haverhill as well as in Brooklyn, New York, and Connecticut churches. Always interested in science, Roberts studied soil chemistry and took the knowledge back to Africa, where he successfully owned and managed plantations. He served his country as a politician, ran a trading and exporting company, and was knighted by Liberia's President King. Courtesy, Trustees of the Haverhill Public Library.*

Phillip Coombs made a stereograph of people and carriages at the "Great Gathering," at sandy Salisbury Beach on September 17, 1861. (Private Collection)

to this day to help immigrant women and men adapt to the primary culture of the Valley, to find and to use the opportunities it holds for them.

One way to register and to calibrate the changes of culture, the innovations and crosscurrents of the past, is to look at our material culture, to learn to read our physical man-made environment as closely as archaeologists may learn to read the artifacts of cultures no longer living. And the beach at Salisbury is one place more convenient than most in the Valley to do this. The uses we have made of the seashore and the ways used to develop its commercial potential—certainly the design and purpose of the buildings erected there—all combine to reveal the transformation of our cultural values.

Up to the time of the Civil War, the seafront at Salisbury was very much as the wind and sea had shaped it in the centuries before the Europeans arrived on the Merrimack. Salisbury was incorporated in 1640, and for two centuries after that it was not different from most of the other towns on the river. Its economy was mainly agricultural, but with a district called The Mills at its western end where the waters of the Powow were put to textile production in the 1820s. The seafront end of the town, then, must have been very like what we see today at the wildlife reservation on

Plum Island, some few miles to the south. It is worth the mention that these seafront parcels were the very last pieces of Valley land to go from the estates of the descendants of the original proprietors. The Newbury lands on Plum Island were not finally divided until 1823, and the shares that held the beachfront at Salisbury were not sold by the common proprietors until 1911.

The diary of Isaac Merrill shows him on occasional excursions to Plum Island as early as the 1820s. Sometimes this was done by large parties in a festive mood, sometimes in more intimate groups suited to finding contemplation or to placing a confidence. In any case, it seems safe to say that his generation—born soon after 1800—was less restrained in its enjoyment of nature, less determined to maintain a strict frontier between the natural environment and human culture. We even find Merrill reaching for the word "transcendental" to describe the beauty he found in this place, a term very much in vogue in the higher circles of New England culture, the heady sphere inhabited by Thoreau and Emerson and their Concord friends.

We can suppose, then that the Beach at Salisbury was also a place of visitation even before the tradition of Tenting on the Beach that Whittier wrote about later in the century. Also, there were Great Gatherings, so called, held in late summer during the middle years of the century and mixing an abundance of food with a garnish of oratory such as once was provided by Caleb Cushing. There were no residents on the Beach until the first cottage was built in

Just as the river steamer became outmoded, the automobile replaced the trolley car as the primary means of transportation to Salisbury Beach. Reflecting America's love affair with the auto, the Dodg'em car ride was developed as an amusement at the beach. First introduced in 1921, the car was manufactured in Lawrence out of sheet metal provided by J.F. Bingham Company. Established in 1888 and still in business, the metal company has turned from making tea kettles and Dodg'em panels to parts for computers and electronics equipment. (Private Collection)

1864, but the growth of the place must have been very rapid, for the first plank road giving access to the Beach was laid down only two years later, in 1866. These dates mark the beginning of Salisbury as a resort, and for a half a century afterwards the story of that is more or less the story of the rise and fall of Edward Payson Shaw.

Shaw was born at Newburyport in 1841, a boy from a middling sort of family whose interest in the development of the Beach came in good measure from his venture in the manufacture of trolley cars and the operation of local transit lines. The fact that in one week in 1871, 1,158 carriages

rode over the plank road bearing nature-hungry visitors to the Beach no doubt helped Shaw to see the potential of the entertainment market in the residents on the lower Merrimack. Before he was through, Shaw owned the larger part of the action to be had in freighting people to the Beach and housing and feeding them once they got there. His most romantic enterprise perhaps, one that still is fondly recollected by some of the Valley's oldest residents, was the river steamer *Merrimac*. She was built in the shipyard of Lemuel Marquand at Ring's Island in 1892, and until 1915 she rode the waters of the river during season, carrying tourists from Haverhill or other ports along the way, to the Black Rocks at Salisbury. There, the passengers disembarked and found that Shaw's trolley cars were waiting to carry them to the resort center. The *Merrimac* carried its passengers from Haverhill to the Beach and back again for 25 cents, and that included a bowl of Colby's much-esteemed chowder.

In addition, Shaw owned and operated the Cushing Hotel at the Beach. Built in the manner of those large wooden-frame structures of the late 19th century, the Cushing served a class clientele and not the dailies who

Top: *Employees of the Brightwood Mills, North Andover, and their children enjoy an outing to Salisbury Beach in 1912. Despite the elaborate network of trolley lines, which brought workers from as far away as Lowell to the beach, this group traveled together in an early vehicle in the fleet of the Trombly Bus Company. (MVTM)*

Above: *Continuing the march of modernity, the streamlined design of the 1930s came to Salisbury Beach. The New Ocean Echo, revamped as the Frolics in a more modern style, became a nightclub offering dancing, big bands, and popular singing stars. By the 1950s fried clams, french fries, and pizza replaced the shore dinner of an earlier era. (Private Collection)*

made up the larger part of the passengers in the supply side of Shaw's operation. All of this came to a rather rude end for him in 1911, when heavy investment losses forced Shaw to sell his Beach properties to a group calling itself the Salisbury Beach Associates. Local residents resented this intrusion of developers who were based at Lawrence, and those common proprietors who still retained control over their shares of the Beach took legal action to prevent it. They failed, however, and their failure signaled the beginning of another era in the story of this resort on the Atlantic.

The break from the past is rather clean, marked clearly in September 1913 by a great fire that destroyed the Cushing Hotel and other structures at the Beach center. It also consumed some 100 cottages built along the oceanfront to the south of that. Instead of rebuilding the Cushing or another hotel like it, the Salisbury Beach Associates created a different sort of resort, offering faster-paced and more-transient entertainment. The physical center was now the Ocean Echo, a dance hall large enough to hold hundreds of spooning couples, who more and more often would arrive by auto rather than trolley. When this building was destroyed by fire in January 1920, a New Ocean Echo took its place. Several hotels were built during those years just before and just after the First World War, but none of them ever achieved the status or the success of the Cushing.

After 1913 the character of the Beach changed, and that was unmistakably apparent not only in the dance hall but also in the fun house, arcades, and rides, in the vending of food on the Beach, and in the live performers to entertain visitors. Salisbury Beach had lost the face of a somewhat genteel, if not thoroughly top-drawer, resort. During the Roaring Twenties, the Beach reflected instead the rather short-term expectation of flappers and their beaus. One novelty was the "Dodgem" which offered controlled mayhem and safe aggression. The Dodgem was developed and manufactured at Lawrence and introduced to the world during the 1921 season at Salisbury. A roller coaster was built also. Noise, speed, and crowds became the accepted ingredients of fun and entertainment. As an alternative to labor, it seemed badly designed to bring balance and refreshment to the environment of the textile workers who went there. Also, it was only after the fire of 1913 that buildings were put on the Beach itself. This of course created a street parallel to the shoreline, and the buildings along this street turned their backs to the Atlantic; they faced those happy throngs of paying tourists. The street is still called Oceanfront in flat denial of where it is and what it is.

It was during the period between the First World War and the Second World War that the southern end of the Beach was built up into ethnic neighborhoods, designed by imitation of the mill towns upriver and reflecting the cultural divisions of their labor force. This was yet another face put on the Beach, more quiet, less hectic, and oriented to the needs and pace of family vacations and outings. In 1936 this southern end was razed to make room for a public state reservation. Still there and still very popular, the reservation has in late years become a haven for recreational vehicles and the devotees of a seminomadic subculture.

Through the 1930s the Great Depression brought a scaled-down mix of entertainment to the beach. The New Ocean Echo was the site of more than one dance marathon and of Beano games only slightly less compulsive. Salisbury became so notorious for rum running that the local lifesaving station was transformed into a Coast Guard Station with a staff of some 30 persons. On the eve of the Second World War, the dance hall, the New Ocean Echo was transformed into something called the Frolics, which was a dinner club attracting customers with its reputation for tasty lobster and big-name entertainment. Getting there was as simple as owning a car and knowing the roads. The enterprise was a success through to the late 1950s, presenting star attractions of the time like Patti Page, Liberace, and the McGuire Sisters. Eventually, however, other and more highly capitalized places such as Las Vegas and Miami Beach could afford such staggering weekly engagement fees to these entertainers that Salisbury was forced out of the high end of the business. A decade ago the roller coaster and the Dodgem and the carousel were removed, and what Salisbury Beach has now are high-tech rides designed and made in France, and new arcades stocked with videogames designed and made in Japan.

The Beach has been called the industrial park of Salisbury in what may be an attempt to upgrade the image it has among its Merrimack neighbors, which once had world-reputed capacities for production. The shopping mall, however, is a better analogy, because the Beach is an environment saturated by the culture of consumption. Concessions and arcades and rides are now owned by local families—Irish, Lebanese, Jewish—who are in the second and third generation of enterprise at Salisbury. From that viewpoint, it remains local and native to the region of the lower Merrimack. But to its thousands of visitors during any one day of the summer months, it might as well be the Methuen Mall stocked with a constant flow of enticements designed, it seems, to prevent one moment from following another. Visitors at Salisbury, however, take away no product; what they consume is time.

VIII

FINDING THE FUTURE

Critical acumen is exerted in vain to uncover the past; the
past cannot be *presented;* we cannot know what we are not. But
one veil hangs over past, present, and future, and it is the
province of the historian to find out, not what was, but
what is.

— Henry David Thoreau, *A Week on the Concord and
Merrimack Rivers*, 1849.

Could we, indeed, say what we want, would we give a
description of the child that is lost, he would be found.

— Margaret Fuller, *The Dial*, July 1849.

Wilkes Allen, in his history of the town, betrayed no doubts in the
advice he gave the townsmen of Chelmsford, very likely because, in 1820,
he saw no reason to question how the world is made. He reported one
altar, one town, one community, deployed for a single purpose and all set
at play in "the" planetary system. When Isaac Newton disclosed the
clockwork of the planets in 1687, he confirmed the only piece of science
uniformly anticipated by every Christian, namely that the one living God

*Despite the Depression, Valley residents managed to find enjoyment at little or no
cost, such as swimming. This group cools off in Haverhill's Lake Saltonstall during
the summer of 1935. Courtesy, Trustees of the Haverhill Public Library.*

Haverhill's river front, shown in the early 20th century before construction of the Basilier Bridge in 1924-1925, was an important commercial and manufacturing district. The stern-wheeler at the wharf carried passengers to Newburyport and Salisbury Beach. Courtesy, Trustees of the Haverhill Public Library.

created only one universe, a harmony of magnitudes glorifying one motive. So, "the" planetary system he described looked familiar even when it was brand spanking new. It was a description of the universe both elementary and compelling; its mathematical formulas appealed to intellectuals, while the clockwork metaphor put it within the understanding of even the illiterate. Also, it was a description of the universe that expected and half invited the mechanics of industrial production. Newton's picture of how things are put together and how they work is clear, direct, certain. In 1820 it was evident to all the readers of *The History of Chelmsford*. Simply by reminding them of where they were—reminding them of their place in the system—Allen was asking the citizens of Chelmsford to find the future in their own convictions.

The Reverend Mr. Allen appealed for unity and harmony. The fabric of town life, he said, is made of its social and spiritual ends as well as the economic and political. All the ends of human life should come together as in the cloth, and they should work together as in the pattern. He wanted

A West Newbury farmhouse in winter forms a scene of stark but timeless beauty. Photo by Bill Lane.

human culture to imitate the design of Nature, and it is evident from his book that he expected Chelmsford—the town itself, the town together—would continue to be the most accessible and responsive tool in shaping culture. It was a hope natural enough for a minister of the Lord in this Valley where town had replaced church as the primary community. After all, in 1820 the towns on the lower Merrimack were nearly two centuries old, and their 200 years of tradition included the practice of economic regulation. However, in 1820 this traditional way of getting things done was old enough to be revered, old enough to be protected by its age alone. At town meeting on May 25, 1801, the voters of Dracut unanimously resolved against a petition then before the General Court of Massachusetts to allow "the erection of a dam across Merrimack River at Pawtucket Falls." They were against it, they said, because a dam would:

> totally destroy the fish in the said river and deprive the people [of Dracut] of the important privilege which they for a long time, even from time immemorial, have enjoyed without molestation; of taking neare theire doors the most delicate food and much of the real necessaries of Life.

The voters of the Merrimack towns had replaced the "saints" with their vested right and power to find the future, even if the voters trusted the omens of economic development rather more than the opaque directions of Holy Writ. But the voters at Dracut tended to find a future that looked very much like the past, and so, in 1801, they preferred the "necessaries" of fishing to the "necessaries" of manufacturing. From a strictly economic point of view their ideas were old-fashioned, and the towns had become agents of preservation rather than invention. They stood in the ways of "progress." Then, in February 1922, the General Court of Massachusetts began erecting manufacturing corporations, and these corporations came in time to rival the towns of the Valley in deciding the future.

The Merrimack Manufacturing Company was the first of them, but many textile corporations followed that one, and all of them together engineered a major revolution in the Valley. It was easy for these corporations, compared with the towns, to make a break with the past and find a new future—easier since all their decisions were economic ones, decisions cut loose from their social and political consequences for people and place. In the early years of industry on the Merrimack, the textile manufacturers had proven their social conscience and demonstrated a real concern for the well-being of everyone involved in production. By the time of the Civil War, however, that point of view was left behind by the large manufacturers at Lowell and Lawrence, and the republican model of production was replaced by the cult of the bottom line. The center of this new corporate universe existed in books, among production figures, cost-analysis figures, and the figures of profit margins—percentages and fractions of percentages. Imagining the process of production as a system of numbers gave it a complete and secure appearance; numbers validated conclusions and intentions the way mathematics had validated Newton's system of the planets.

The Merrimack Valley Militia trained each summer at Camp Dewey in Framingham. Notice the bed linen and wash stand, as well as the reclining chairs. Courtesy, Trustees of the Haverhill Public Library.

Essex County's Eighth Regiment mobilized at Camp Thomas, Chicamauga, Georgia, on the way to Cuba in 1898. Their model sanitary record saved them from the scourge of typhoid that killed more men than the Spanish-American War. Courtesy, Trustees of the Haverhill Public Library.

Figures, then, were set out in the boardrooms of Boston, where corporate directors used them to lay down odds on how the future would go. They were weighted with unnatural gravity and able to pull in their wake all the other factors of production, so that the well-being and job security of the laborers, the economic and ecological security of the region, became satellites of the system rather than partners of it. The great textile corporataions on the lower Merrimack did in fact invent a new future after 1820, but they did this by imposing a hierarchy of value rather than disclosing an increase of harmony.

Within a century, however, and even in less than a century, the textile manufacturers began making a grim discovery. They found that the towns on the lower Merrimack were aging, were "old" in fact. By the 1920s the opinion was firmly rooted that, like textile cities and towns throughout New England, Lowell and Lawrence had antiquated plants and obsolete machinery. They were cramped and congested, making traffic an added burden to organization. Some of the factories at Lowell and Lawrence even looked like "castles," towers and all. Anyone who looked for signs of age would find them, and eventually even a lover cannot ignore what is apparent. Age of course is relative, and if the Valley towns were old they had to be old in comparison to another place. That other place was in the Southern states of the Union, principally in the Carolinas and Georgia. Textile production in the Southern states was enormously increased in the years between the 1880s and the opening decades of this century. By the 1920s the Southern mills showed a clear competitive advantage over those of New England. One estimate made in 1923 claimed that Southern mills had a cost advantage of 14 percent, and that 85 percent of this advantage resulted from the lower wages paid to the Southern textile workers.

The Southern mills were also said to have a second advantage: the newest and most productive machinery. In the cotton industry, that technological superiority was centered on the so-called automatic loom, a loom equipped with an automatic bobbin changer that became available in 1894. That single device produced a tremendous leap in productivity and created a significant cost advantage for manufacturers using the automatic loom over those who did not. Northern manufacturers bought 104,955 of the looms in the years between 1909 and 1916, a figure comparing favorably with the 76,786 bought by Southern manufacturers during the same period. Sustained by the demands for cloth that came with the First World War, this expansion of productivity was the last undertaken by Northern textile corporations. It was in the postwar slump that manufacturers in New England judged, and judged correctly, that productivity of the industry *nationally* had outrun the market and that, other things being equal, the lower labor cost of Southern manufacturers would inevitably drive Northern products from the marketplace. Having made that determination, Northern manufacturers removed a considerable amount of machinery already installed in their mills and shipped it to locations in the South. One study made in 1934 estimated that 4.8 million spindles and 109,000 cotton looms had been transferred in this way during the previous decade. It is difficult to see in the move anything but an attempt by Northern manufacturers at fixing the odds to favor the wager they had already made on the future.

The relocation of Northern textile operations to Southern points was a complex process, involving social and political adjustments. From a fiscal point of view, textile manufacturers had no choice but to pursue survival according to the rules of the market economy. And in that they were merely following the values they had set themselves in the previous 100 years. Yet the economic and social consequences for Lowell and Lawrence—and for other Merrimack towns as well—were prolonged and severe. For those left behind in this "old" place, the transfer of operations looked more like a "runaway" than a "relocation." It seemed to them that the social costs of production, the taxes and the regulations imposed by state or local authority, were not separate from industrial manufacturing. Public authority did not invent social costs but merely added them after corporations had refused to take them into account in their anxious devotion to making the figures come out "right." Nevertheless, these social costs were far lower or totally absent in Southern locations, and that was another attraction drawing manufacturers to the South. Finally, the

By the 1930s, few clam shacks remained in Newburyport's Joppa Flats, and one had taken to cooking the clams. The ever-popular fried clam is said to have been invented on Massachusetts' North Shore. Courtesy, Historical Society of Old Newbury.

Above: *The automatic bobbin changer, developed for the cotton loom in 1894, was adapted for worsted weaving by the early 20th century. Shown here on worsted looms of the Pacific Mills, Lawrence, in 1912, the device is the cylindrical part filled with bobbins, visible at the center bottom of the photo and on each loom in the center rows. (MVTM)*

Left: *When the textile industry began to leave the Valley, houses as well as factory buildings were included on the auction block. Workers faced the double jeopardy of losing both jobs and company housing. Unemployed operatives couldn't buy their homes, and many were forced to relocate, following textile jobs south or learning a new trade, which was not easy during the Depression. (MVTM)*

A group of skiers await the Boston and Maine "snow train" in 1936. Courtesy, Trustees of the Haverhill Public Library.

abundance of waterpower that once had favored the textile cities on the lower Merrimack no longer prevailed against the cheaper, more efficient drive of steam or electricity.

In 1886 Charles T. Main, then assistant superintendent of the Lower Pacific Mills at Lawrence, calculated the cost of steam relative to waterpower and concluded that the saving per day for his firm was $27.73. That is a considerable amount counted over the life of this basic capital investment. Besides, Main said, even "were there no gain in actual money charged to running expenses, there is a great gain in having a steady power throughout the year . . . independent of the rise and fall of a river." There were unexpected benefits as well. Steady power meant steady employment, and that, according to Main, procured "the better class of operatives." Overall, he concluded:

> The many advantages which may be gained in the selection of the site, such as nearness to markets, low freights, cheap coal and favorable conditions for building, can be attained with steam as the motive power far more frequently than with water as the power.

All this was not news to the textile manufacturers on the Merrimack, not even in 1886. In the previous decade steam

had displaced water as the prime motive force in the mills at Lowell, overtaking the 10,000 horsepower generated by the Locks and Canals from Pawtucket Falls. However, the low cost and convenience of steam—and electricity—was not decisive until the other variables had been added to the equation.

Then, abruptly it seemed, in the early 1920s things began to fall apart. Labor cost, social cost, power cost were set to compete in the marketplace crowded by the overextension of productivity, and there, in that marketplace, Lowell and Lawrence no doubt gave an appearance of age. Abbott Lawrence told his constituents in March 1837 that those he called money holders "can transfer their persons and property to any given place in or out of the country, having means always about them to do so." Those with investments in the textile industries on the lower Merrimack, having always had the means, now found the reasons to withdraw their capital.

Relocation or runaway, both words contain a judgement; the choice between them is political and the choice reminds us that vocabulary is never neutral. But whatever it's called, the process was long and difficult and uneven. Cotton

manufacturers were the first to go, and because of that Lowell was most directly affected in the early years. Where the census of 1920 counted 29,693 wage earners at Lowell, 12,590 of those jobs had disappeared *before* the Great Depression added its impact in the fall of 1929. When hard times came to the rest of the country and to other industries, the residents of Lowell had already known the worse.

By 1940 only three of the Spindle City's original corporate giants were in operation. Two of these, the Merrimack Manufacturing Company and the Boott Mills, were closed in the mid-1950s. The third, the Lawrence Company, was acquired by the Ames Worsted Company in 1926, and the two were merged in 1955 as the Ames Textile Corporation. The woolen and worsted manufacturers on the Merrimack fared better than the cotton-goods industry, at least for a time. And so, Lawrence, a worsted center of the world, lost

A Newburyport High School mechanics class prepares students for war-related work in 1942. Courtesy, Historical Society of Old Newbury.

113

Etta and Fannie, the Kimel sisters, owned one of Haverhill's shoe manufacturing companies in the 1920s, a rare example of female entrepreneurship. Women operatives constituted an important part of the work force in boots and shoes, but they did not often own the operations. Courtesy, Trustees of the Haverhill Public Library.

Workmen stretch hides at the Hamel Leather Company in Haverhill, circa 1935. Tanneries, in addition to wooden-heel and last manufacturers, developed to serve Haverhill's important shoe industry. By 1930, the boot and shoe industry employed nearly 80 percent of Haverhill's manufacturing work force and accounted for more than 70 percent of the value of products manufactured. Courtesy, Trustees of the Haverhill Public Library.

only one-third of its workforce during those years from 1920 to 1940, compared to an attrition rate of more than 50 percent at Lowell. Production at Lawrence actually increased during the 1940s to meet the demand of the armed services during the Second World War. Prosperity survived the war but, as in the case of Lowell, the conclusion was swift once events were set in motion. Operating at near capacity in 1947, the Lawrence mills by 1952 had released 20,000 unemployed textile workers into the city. By the middle of the decade, all the city's major employers—the Pacific Mills, the Arlington Mill, the mills of the American Woolen Company—had ceased production. Walter Winchell predicted to his national audience that grass would soon grow in the streets of Lawrence, and Edward R. Murrow focused one of his television broadcasts on the plight of its residents.

Conditions in the shoe and leather industry were hardly better. When the labor statistics for Haverhill are added to those of Lowell and Lawrence, we find that the number of wage earners in these three cities were cut by more than half between 1920 and 1940. Not all the Merrimack towns were so seriously affected, of course. In those years Amesbury and North Andover retained their textile operations, and Andover was able to add to its stock of jobs. Yet those decades brought more hardship to more residents of the Valley than any before or since. Even when they were done with, those years survived as a legacy of bad feeling about the place itself.

A cloud of failure seemed to hang over Lowell and Lawrence and Haverhill. Psychologists say that individuals who are abandoned often react with guilt; they blame themselves for their predicament, if only because it is the nature of the problem that no one else is there to share the blame. In talking now with people who were left behind to deal with the thousands of unemployed and the acres of empty buildings, it is easy to conclude that communities react in much the same way. The textile and shoe industries had been powerful forces on the lower Merrimack, and their loss restored the full measure of responsibility to the cities for their own future. But finding a way through their legacy of negativism proved as difficult a task as solving the economic problems of the region for the two generations charting the way.

George Bower is a native of Lawrence and the author of *November . . . December,* a novel that pictures what life was like in that city in 1962. It is the story of B.D. Jordan and the relationship he enjoys with his father, and, in a sense, the action turns on the fact that B.D. discovers he can trust what his father has learned and use it to shape his own future. B.D. admires the strength of his grandparents, who "locked their egos in the mills" so that he could "develop as much as he wanted." And he is grateful that "they hadn't lived into the late forties when the woolen and worsted

While stumping for local Democrats in 1952, President Harry S. Truman visited Lawrence. Margaret Truman sat on the platform and listened with a youthful John F. Kennedy (at right). (Private Collection)

companies abandoned Lawrence for cheaper labor in the South.'' In the end, however, it is his father whom he admires and trusts. B.D. is a freshman at Tufts University but he returns to Lawrence for the usual academic holidays, and it is there that David Jordan advises his son to leave the city because, as he puts it, "just being a man here is a fight. . . . This city, mill cities like it, are dirty and Old World. . . . The truth is no one ever became anything by staying here and doing it." Harsh words, but David Jordan is talking from the bitterness of his own sense of defeat. Educated as a lawyer and elected to the state senate, he ran for Congress and lost.

If you really want to be a good lawyer [he tells his son] or mayor or public servant of any kind you've got to be able to breathe. If you strike too hard for excellence here you'll kill yourself because there's no atmosphere for excellence, the city doesn't understand it, what it is or what it means. You'll

finally be beaten by the people because they'll try to narrow you and condense you to what they are. And they will.

It is a tale of private virtue set against public indifference. It is a moral tale familiar in Valley fiction, at least since Flora Montgomery agonized over her future. Near the end of the book, David Jordan suffers a heart attack just as he has made important revelations about himself to his son. The drama of that scene seems contrived, set as it is on the banks of the Merrimack and within sight of the Great Stone Dam. Yet the point of the action remains true enough, that for both generations at Lawrence in 1962 there was no future to be found; not for those on the upside or for those on the downside of a life-plan. David Jordan is in fact killed by his heart, dying in the ambulance while it races death through the streets of "his wretched city." Consequently, B.D. accepts a football scholarship that will take him to sunny California, young California. He plans to be there in the very next month, January of a new year.

The man who *was* mayor of Lawrence in 1962 doesn't share the views of these fictional characters. John J. Buckley stayed in the city and was a prime mover in shaping policies for nearly 20 years. He was mayor of Lawrence from 1952 to 1966 and again from 1972 to 1978. John Buckley's recollection of events is that during those very bleak years of the early fifties, the city was left entirely to its own resources. Though given the extraordinary privilege of addressing the stockholders of the American Woolen Company, Buckley could not convince them of what he saw as their corporate responsibility to their employees and to the city, and so he could not affect the company's decision to divorce itself from both. The mayor also pleaded the case of Lawrence before public authority. He went to Washington soon after the 1952 election of Dwight Eisenhower, and he had a conference with the President together with Massachusetts Governor Christian Herder, Senator Henry Cabot Lodge, and Secretary Wilbur Weeks of the Commerce Department. Eisenhower, however, failed to recognize the promise he had made on the Lawrence Common during the campaign of 1952. Eisenhower the candidate had promised federal help, but now he thought better of that, and he defined the problem of Lawrence as local. The solution, he said, would have to be found by the city.

Since that time, state and federal authorities have become

very much involved in planning the future of Merrimack communities and have provided enormous amounts of money to help carry it off. The four cities on the lower Merrimack—Newburyport, Haverhill, Lawrence, Lowell—have all participated in projects of urban renewal and preservation and in programs of environmental control and rehabilitation. Since the 1960s, for instance, nearly a billion dollars has been spent in cleaning up the river, and 75 percent of that was provided by the federal government. In the area of urban planning, Lowell and Haverhill offer instructive contrasts on how to use the funds and how to combine federal and local government with the private sector of the region's economy as an effective coalition. From the early 1960s to the mid-1970s, millions of dollars were granted by federal agencies to renew Haverhill's center city.

Yet the number of "plans" written, the number of city planners, the variety of consultants—with offices in New York, Palo Alto, or Dallas—robbed all efforts of coordinated and cumulative results. The center of Haverhill was razed and turned over to the culture of the automobile. There is a shopping mall that reflects the most advanced thinking of the 1950s, though this one was built in the 1970s. And like most malls, this one is reached over a four-lane roadway, cut through the inner city and parallel to the river. This roadway, however, connects nothing with nothing and leads to nowhere, because federal policies about its funding changed before the connection could be made. One new result of all this was to alienate a fair part of

In 1925, Haverhill's Water Street, the heart of the commercial district, included numerous enterprises reflecting a variety of building styles, especially obvious in window treatments and cornices. The street is now flanked by a high-rise building on the right and a shopping mall on the left. Courtesy, Trustees of the Haverhill Public Library.

The Renaissance of Lowell

Lowell's renaissance, the result of grass-roots determination and solid organization at the local level, has benefited from federal and state support channeled through the Lowell Historic Preservation Commission. The Commission, a board composed of federal, state, and local officials, monitors the historic district and both initiates and supports programs in architectural preservation and rehabilitation, cutural events, and community projects. The turning point that spurred Lowell's dramatic rebirth was the demolition of the Dutton Street boardinghouses in 1966. Community response mobilized an effort that culminated in the Lowell Plan, the creation by Congress of the Lowell Historic Canal District Commission (1975), and the establishment of the Lowell Historical National Park (1978), the United States' first urban national park. A state heritage park, proposed in 1974 and mandated by the Massachusetts legislature in 1978, provides visitor services. Lowell's early years as a world-renowned industrial experiment are receiving new attention from both historians and tourists, the result of its increased visibility and variety of programs.

Left: *Built in the first half of the 19th century, these brick blocks on Dutton Street housed the operatives of Lowell's Merrimack Manufacturing Company. After a heated local debate that drew national attention from historians and concerned preservationists, the buildings were lost to the wrecking ball in 1966. (MVTM)*

Below: *Photographed immediately prior to their demolition in 1966, the Dutton Street boardinghouses sit serenely beside the Merrimack Canal, awaiting destruction. Their loss triggered a local response that ultimately led to Lowell's present commitment to its historic industrial past. (MVTM)*

the city's citizens from the city government. Like many clouds, however, this one has its silver lining. Enough citizens were put off by civic authorities to organize their own efforts at rehabilitating Haverhill. These local plans produced the Ward Hill industrial area and garnered a citation for Haverhill as an All-America City in 1978.

By contrast, the "Lowell Plan" included city, state, and federal participation from the time it was first put down on the back of a placemat at a local restaurant. The private business sector was included as well. Coordination comes in the Lowell Historic Preservation Commission, which seats representatives from all sectors involved in writing and executing the Lowell Plan. The commission is an agency of the Department of the Interior, which is also responsible for the operation of the Lowell National Historical Park. Lowell is the site of the first national urban park, and the park itself is an important part of the Lowell Plan. When Congress created the LHPC in 1978, it also committed 40 million federal dollars to fund its 10-year lease on life. It is, as Senator Paul Tsongas has called it, a $40-million "wager," and not a "bail-out." The wager is that the citizens of Lowell will continue to apply experience and attention to planning for the future, even after the commission dies its predetermined death in 1988. The organization and the structure are now being put in place, but, as the Senator indicates, the use of them is never guaranteed nor are the vagaries of chance and fortune ever entirely eliminated.

The attitude of industry has also changed considerably in the lower Valley since John Buckley met the unreceptive stockholders of the American Woolen Company. Today the largest employers of the region are the high-technology and communications industries that are located in many of its 16 cities and towns. Western Electric, Honeywell, the Raytheon Company, Digital Equipment Corporation, and Wang Laboratories conduct large operations on the lower Merrimack, and each of them has in recent years demonstrated some concern for the region and its future. Yet the painful lesson of the past is difficult to forget. The current era of good feelings comes easily in prosperity, while prosperity depends on politics and economics over which no one in the Valley has any control. Of these corporations, only Wang originated in the region and has displayed a vigorous attachment to the place. For the others, the lower Merrimack is not the center of production but one of its many outposts, and experience warns to make provision against the time when a "realistic" accounting of gain and loss might dictate a "relocation" for some.

There is one aspect of the high-tech and communications industries that surely will have its impact on the future. For, aside from the economics of the matter, those industries are generating a new language in a radical sense. They are generating new forms of picturing and understanding

Symbolic of Lawrence's new look, the Water Tower on Tower Hill recently underwent renovation with federal funds under the direction of Joseph P. Markey, alderman and director of engineering. The Water Tower is listed on the National Register of Historic Places. Photo by Gayton Osgood.

human activity, whether individual or social. This "language" will shape how we think of what we do, and so it will shape what provisions we make for the future we think we see. As surely as mathematics replaced the Holy Word for some as the prism of their focus on themselves, communications technology withholds another form of humanity for future revelation. It may be a picture so clear and so distinct that all previous peoples on the lower Merrimack look like strangers to the place, much as the certitudes of the Reverend Wilkes Allen prepared the ready acceptance of the industrial age.

For the moment, the signs of renaissance on the lower Merrimack are unmistakable. Theater, music, poetry flourish in the Merrimack Valley Regional Theatre

Collections and programs of the Lowell Museum record the past of every ethnic group and business enterprise, private citizen and municipal organization. This photo of the International Night competitors of 1925 is an example of the museum's rich documentary collection. Courtesy, Lowell Museum.

(Lowell) and the Merrimack Valley Philharmonic (Lawrence). Poets, such as those responsible for the publication of *Looms* at Lowell, are discovering again that the river is a unit of life and that the Valley is a locale. Also, Valley residents are beginning to recollect the region's industrial heritage with pride rather than embarrassment. State Heritage Parks at Lowell and Lawrence and the National Historical Park at Lowell draw attention to the accomplishments of the past and lend security to the future. Moreover, these establishments attract tourists, and tourism is a major consideration in the region's economy.

One further hopeful sign of things to come lies in the work of the Merrimack River Watershed Council, which was chartered in 1977. The council seeks to provide for the sensible and balanced use of the river and its watershed,

In the 1980s Newburyport's fishermen continue their work, mending nets and going out to sea. Photo by Bill Lane.

Concerned students and veterans protest against the Vietnam War in 1972. The energy of the 1960s generation pushed against traditional society in many ways. Courtesy, Trustees of the Haverhill Public Library.

bringing together the needs of farming, industry, and recreation. The council hopes as well to bring together the 16 political communities on the lower Merrimack to generate a truly regional approach to planning. For that reason the region has been divided into 56 units, and each of the units has been consulted in the writing of the council's Greenway Plan. At the very least, such a unified and regional plan will help prevent decisions about the future of the lower Merrimack Valley from going to others by

default, or simply because no one in the region has made the attempt to take a long view of the history of the Valley. Because the care of the river, and of all the life of which it is the site and source, is the only issue that surely lies in the future of all 16 communities on the lower Merrimack, it is as well the best issue on which to build the structures of regional cooperation. And, certainly, it will be the issue on which we decide how far culture may be allowed its will separate from nature. The council's undertaking is a timely venture in any case, now that the Commonwealth of Massachusetts has indicated that the waters of the Merrimack may be diverted for the needs of metropolitan Boston by the year 2020.

We find what we look for, Thoreau said, and that, no doubt, is why philosophers before and since have counseled care in choosing what we set our hearts on. Like the stone walls that mark its past, the design of the Valley's future lies already before us. But we see it vaguely, as a shadow, half forgetting it is there, we misplace the concentration that it takes to follow the shadow's track across the broken surface of the present. Mostly, we cannot see that the design will come of who we are rather than of what we do. So, the future haunts our restless present, like a song of childhood's imaginary playmate, as a prophecy.

The socially conscious spirit of the 1960s is evident in the concerned faces of these students at a peace rally in 1972. That spirit appeared to have been shorn along with hair and beards by the 1980s, but a resurgence shows that social responsibility is appearing once again in the Clamshell Alliance and other antinuclear organizations proliferating in the Valley. Courtesy, Trustees of the Haverhill Public Library.

Top: *Painted by an anonymous artist,* The Howard Farmhouse in 1830. Pond Hills, Amesbury *shows a prosperous Valley farm. The hay wagon at the right may be loaded with hay from nearby salt marshes or from the farm's own hay meadow. Courtesy, Historical Society of Old Newbury.*

Above: *Lowell was not yet fully grown when this view by E.A. Farrar was lithographed in 1834, but the row of brick mills already formed an impressive sight. At this date neither the Boott nor the Massachusetts mills had been started, so there is a clear view straight into the heart of the city. (MVTM)*

View on the Merrimack *from the Store House by Charles Hubbard shows the crude early bridge at the Pawtucket Falls and the village of Pawtucket in about 1833. Pawtucket, at first a part of Dracut, was annexed by Lowell in the 1870s. (Private Collection)*

Pennacook Indians in West Newbury mixed local deer hair and porcupine quills on hide with European trade goods, such as glass beads, to fashion this embroidered quill pouch, made about 1650-1675. Courtesy, Peabody Museum of Salem.

Painted by an unidentified artist in about 1845, this canvas portrays the Middlesex Company Woolen Mills of Lowell, the largest woolen mill in the country at that time. Women enter the mill to work at left, walking between rows of blue woolen cloth stretched on tenterhooks to dry. The Middlesex was famous for this fabric, which was used for uniforms and known as "police coatings." (MVTM)

Ballardvale, a section of Andover that drew waterpower from the Shawsheen River, had a fulling mill by the late-17th century. Woolen and worsted mills persisted there until the mid-20th century. Charles Sheeler (1883-1965) painted this dramatic view of a Ballardvale mill in 1946 following his tenure as artist-in-residence at Phillips Academy in Andover. Courtesy, Addison Gallery of American Art, Phillips Academy, Andover, Massachusetts.

New York artist Ralph Fasanella came to Lawrence in the mid-1970s, where he painted for several years. His Lawrence canvases portray the vitality of mill work and the legacy of labor struggles made famous by the 1912 strike. This 1977 canvas, Mill Workers—Lower Pacific Mills, *represents the mill as it might have appeared when occupied by the company's worsted division. The plant is now tenanted with nontextile industries. Courtesy, Ralph Fasanella.*

*Art in public places is part of the new spirit in Lowell. This
Worthen Street mural shows Lowell's pride in its industrial
past and the laborers who built the city, canals, and mills.
Photo by JoAnne B. Weisman.*

126

John Phillips Marquand achieved great success as a novelist, writing both serious, ironic fiction about American society and popular mysteries featuring Mr. Moto the detective. Marquand lived at Curzon's Mill, West Newbury, for much of his life. Portrait by Alexander James, 1944. Courtesy, Custom House Maritime Museum, Newburyport.

Salt-marsh hay grown as a cash crop on the marshes of Newbury and Salisbury was once a thriving and profitable industry. William Sherburne ''Sherb'' Eaton (1900-1982), the last of a line of Salisbury salt-marsh hay farmers, holds examples of three types of the hay: black grass, goose grass, and thatch grass. Photo by Betsy Woodman.

Facing page: Bert Fafard's painting, The Course of the Merrimack, provides an historical overview of the Valley's culture from 18th-century Newburyport, at bottom, to 20th-century Lowell, at center. Twenty famous persons born in the Valley are depicted at the top. John Greenleaf Whittier of Haverhill figures most prominently in the center, flanked by Bette Davis and James Abbott McNeil Whistler, both born in Lowell. Fafard's huge canvas hangs at Northern Essex Community College in Haverhill. Photo by Cliff Lawrence.

The Great Stone Dam at Lawrence, 30 feet of falling water, provided power for the textile industry and now produces 100 million kilowatt hours per year through the new hydroelectric station. Photo by Pat Thompson.

Methuen's Spicket River, one of the Merrimack's many tributaries, also powered mills. As seen here looking south from Hampshire Street, the Spicket flows into the mill pond of the former Methuen Company cotton mill, now a mixed warehouse, retail, and light-manufacturing complex. Photo by Joseph Feole.

The Lowell Dam and the Northern Canal wall hardly impinge on this tranquil autumn scene on the Merrimack at Pawtucket Falls, the site of the river's first major waterpower use. Photo by JoAnne B. Weisman.

Plum Island marsh, where the Merrimack meets the Atlantic, glows in the autumn sun. Photo by Peter Randall.

Facing page: *Waste water rushes from the Farnum family mill's tailrace after turning the turbine. The Farnum family sawmill has been in operation since the late-18th century. To saw wood for local farmers, it has utilized waterpower and, most recently, a small diesel engine. Photo by Gayton Osgood.*

Above: *North Andover's Parson Barnard House, built in 1715, is located in the original settlement area established in 1646. Restored by the North Andover Historical Society in 1957, its four period rooms reflect the styles of interior decoration befitting its four earliest owners of 1715-1815. Photo by Gayton Osgood.*

Above: *Rocks Village in the easternmost part of Haverhill is an historic district of great unspoiled charm. The Ingersoll-Johnson House, built in about 1740 at the corner of Wharf Lane, sits directly on the Merrimack River. Photo by Peter Randall.*

Right: *Children everywhere love to clown for the camera, and these youngsters at Methuen's Tenney Street Playground are no exception. Photo by Denise Goudreault.*

Facing page
Top: *Built in 1784, the mansion of North Andover's Doctor Thomas Kittredge is one of the high-style residences that were built even in the smaller Valley communities. Photo by Gayton Osgood.*

Bottom: *Historic homes line the training field in West Newbury, where militia men have trained since the 1730s. Photo by Peter Randall.*

Above: *Newburyport's warm, red brick and blue water provide the perfect backdrop for white sails, which evoke the merchant ships of yesterday amid the fishing and pleasure craft of today. Photo by Peter Randall.*

Right: *Renewed interest in cultural activities is evident in the number of people attending the free summer theater offerings each year in Lowell. An outdoor stage is part of the Heritage State Park's building and grounds on Shattuck Street, directly across from the headquarters of the Lowell Historic Preservation Commission. Photo by JoAnne B. Weisman.*

Facing page: *Old and new bridges spanning the river at sunset provide access across the Merrimack from Newburyport to Salisbury. A pier of the old Chain Bridge frames the modern arch of the interstate highway bridge. Photo by Frank Dalton.*

IX

PARTNERS
IN
PROGRESS

The institutions whose histories are recounted in the following pages are not a scientific cross-section of the Merrimack Valley's corporations. Yet their variety suggests an important truth about economic activity in the area today: No longer does a single industry dominate the scene. It is also apparent that a large number of men and women whose parents or grandparents came here as employees are now employers. Yesterday's immigrants have become today's establishment, joining the Yankees who once seemed to own everything in sight.

The task of gathering these histories was a rewarding one for the author. The opportunity to hear 40 institutional heads explain their origins and progress was, for the practicing historian, relatively unique. Interestingly enough, many of these business leaders were unwilling to attribute their success to causes more profound than pluck, luck, or father. Let future business historians with econometric models beware: Accident or familiarity may, as often as not, be the reason why something happened!

Perhaps the most common characteristic of the leaders of the corporations treated here is their strong commitment to community service. It is often remarked of the New England Yankee that typically he or she felt that serving the common weal was a moral responsibility. If that is true, then it seems clear that this healthy attitude has been transmitted to successive waves of immigrants of all persuasions.

Space does not permit a recitation of individual service but the record is clear: Area hospitals, schools, colleges, united fund agencies, churches, and communities have been and are today the beneficiaries of thousands of hours of volunteer service and millions of charitable dollars provided by generations of local residents. These traits continue to distinguish the Merrimack Valley's business community—employer and employee alike.

As the original watercolor design for the city seal of Lowell, this painting has strong symbolic meaning. The river, railroad, mill buildings, smokestacks, and cotton bales all represent the industrial "revolution" in manufacturing and transportation that transformed the farms of East Chelmsford into the city of Lowell. The cornucopia signifies prosperity. (Private Collection)

Alco Electronic Products

The founder of this small but prosperous firm is the son of Italian immigrants. Although Alfred Contarino's parents landed in New York City they had no luck in finding work there. Friends urged them to come to Lawrence, where Mr. Contarino soon established a successful construction business. His son, Alfred, was born and grew up in the Prospect Hill neighborhood and attended the public schools in the city. Like many others of his generation he took advantage of the availability of inexpensive public higher education by attending Lowell Technological Institute, where he studied electrical engineering. After graduation he worked for firms in Lawrence and Boston for a short time before launching his own business.

Alco Electronics Manufacturing Company opened for business about 1953 in a small building in Lawrence. The firm produced power supplies for the fledgling electronics industry. But young Contarino abandoned this line after a while, feeling the field was overcrowded. He also lacked the money and the technical skills he felt

would be necessary for success.

His second venture was to serve as a distributor of electronic components, providing other people's products to ham radio operators, to local industry, and to hi-fi buffs. He was making a modest living this way when a traveling salesman mentioned there was an unfilled demand for small switches in the commercial market. (At the time the U.S. military was the largest user of that technology.)

Seizing the opportunity, Alfred Contarino designed a series of small switches which were then

---

Some of the world's smallest switches are assembled at Alco's headquarters in North Andover.

Alfred Contarino, founder of Alco Electronic Products, is shown here relaxing in his office.

manufactured in Japan. His new enterprise marketed the product successfully in the United States. The firm moved twice before constructing its own plant on a wooded hillside in North Andover. Faced with a continuing need for capital to finance growth, Alco merged with Augat in 1974.

Today Alco Electronic Products serves the telecommunications, computer, and instrumentation industries in a worldwide market. Using 100 or more different parts, the firm's skilled workers can assemble over 30,000 different switches.

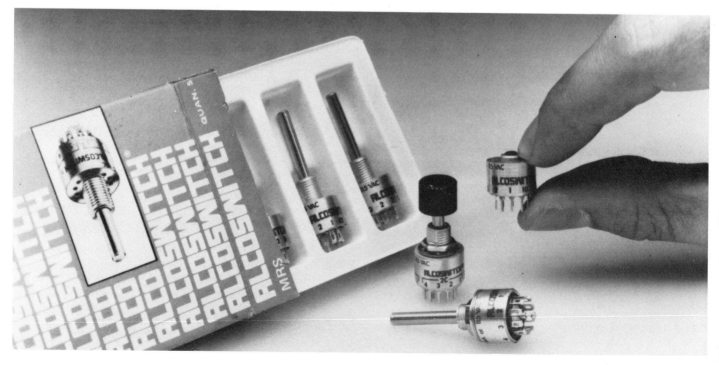

Alexander's Markets

Herman and Benjamin Gordon, the founders of this $100-million business, were the sons of European immigrants. They grew up in Nashua, New Hampshire, the mill town where their father owned and operated a small grocery store. The brothers decided to establish their own markets farther down the Merrimack River in Lowell. Although that old mill town was long past its peak, there was still room for good neighborhood groceries when the young men arrived in 1928. When their first two stores proved to be successful they were encouraged to open others; by 1945 they owned a "chain" of five corner groceries. Each boasted of a meat section with cuts to order, and each purchased its fresh produce from the local farmers' produce market.

But when Alexander Beaudry decided in 1946 to sell his self-service supermarket (it may have been the first one in Lowell) on Merrimack Street, the Gordon brothers decided to expand their local holdings by acquiring his property. In order to minimize the risk they took in two partners, their younger brother, Phillip, and William Soucy, one of their store managers. They discovered that by retaining Alexander's name they would be eligible to receive the sugar quota allotted to the former owner. Keeping the familiar name provided a second advantage—it encouraged the loyalty of the French-Canadian population that comprised the largest part of Alexander's customers.

Although its 5,000 square feet of space was small by today's standards, the new market was several times the size of any of the old stores. In order to free their energies for this more complicated operation, Herman and Benjamin sold all of the Gordon Brothers markets during the next year and a half. During the following decade they concentrated on maintaining a profitable business in a declining central business district.

By 1957 Benjamin and Herman Gordon were ready to retire. As they prepared to do so, they took on two new partners, M. Michael Weinberg, the owner of a small grocery, and Jason

Herman (left) and Phillip Gordon are shown here inside one of their grocery stores, about 1946.

Elias, Phillip Gordon's brother-in-law. At the same time Herman's son, Robert, was taken into the firm. Robert, who would ultimately become president and chief executive officer of Alexander's, was then finishing a tour of duty in the Army. Consequently, his father agreed to "work Robert's share" until he was discharged. He enjoyed it so much that he reentered the firm as a partner; even today he is only in semiretirement.

Robert Gordon had been born in Lowell and graduated from its public primary schools. He received his secondary education at Phillips Academy in Andover and earned his bachelor's degree at Brown University. An ambitious young man, he imposed a condition on his partners on entering the business—Alexander's was to be committed to a program of expansion.

The first of seven new stores to be opened during the next 20 years was built on Middlesex Street, Lowell, in 1958. It was such a success that it was expanded in 1962. In 1964 the Gordons returned to Nashua where—sensing the new mobility in the shopping

population—they built a store in the middle of a field, a quarter of a mile off the highway outside the central city. Subsequently, a mall grew up around it.

When the store on Merrimack Street burned in 1966, the partners decided to replace it with a new store about three miles away in the suburb of Dracut. Many former inner-city residents had moved to that area in the recent past and could be counted on to shop at a convenient Alexander's market. Here the corporate offices were also to be located.

The 1970s witnessed further frequent expansion: Manchester (1973), Hudson (1974), and Bedford (1976), New Hampshire; and Chelmsford, Massachusetts (1977), all became sites for Alexander's Markets. At that point the decision was made to pause for a few years. By 1982, however, plans for two more stores were well under way.

Ames Textile Corporation

This healthy company traces its roots back to Benjamin F. Butler (1818-1893), lawyer, politician, soldier, and businessman. Butler entered the textile business in the time-honored American way: As a congressman after the Civil War, he successfully proposed a law requiring that U.S. flags be cut from American rather than English fabric. He then organized the United States Bunting Company, which commenced operations in Lowell in 1865.

General Butler's daughter, Blanche, married General Adelbert Ames; their daughter, Edith, married Charles Brooks Stevens, grandson of the man who had founded the Stevens Mills in North Andover. Stevens and his brother, George, became active in the Bunting Company soon after Butler died. The future was with the Stevenses: C. Brooks' son, Ames, would succeed him, and today Ames' son, Edward B., runs the company.

In 1919 Ames Stevens received his bachelor's degree from Harvard College and went to work for his father in the U.S. Bunting Company. Within two years they began a process of expansion which has characterized the firm since. Not every acquisition was successful, nor was every product profitable, but over the years the good decisions have outnumbered the poor ones.

Even during the Depression, the Stevenses continued to look for opportunities. In 1935 they purchased the troubled Hamilton Woolen Company. In developing their assets by acquiring mills that otherwise would have closed, they benefited themselves and the communities in which these mills were located.

In 1946, after turning down an overture to merge with the family-related M.T. and J.P. Stevens Company, the Ames Textile Corporation (a selling company) was established in New York. This venture was merged with Ames Worsted in 1952 and with Lawrence Manufacturing Company in 1955 to form the present Massachusetts-based Ames Textile Corporation. Lawrence Manufacturing was formerly a Lowell-based knitted

Charles Brooks Stevens and his son, Ames, are shown here "racing" down a street near their Lowell home in 1906. The Northern automobile was new.

goods manufacturer that C. Brooks Stevens, in a calculated gamble, had acquired in 1926. A long and painful process of rehabilitation ensued, interrupted by the Merrimack River flood of 1936 and the demise of a market for cotton knitted stockings and union suits. By the late '40s, the company had successfully converted to the manufacture of industrial knits which were used as backings for vinyl, automotive, and furniture fabrics.

These mergers resulted in a strong corporation which in the '50s acquired an interest in several mills in New England and erected the company's first manufacturing plant outside New England, in Cleveland, Georgia. This was followed during the '60s and '70s by expansion overseas when plants in England, the Netherlands, Northern Ireland, and France were established.

Edward B. Stevens became president of the corporation in 1968. His father and uncle served as cochairmen. During the next two years the various Butler, Ames, and Stevens interests were sorted out, and the firm assumed the character it has today.

A number of other changes made during the past decade have further increased the diverse product line of the business. At age 117, it is one of the largest textile companies in New England and its prospects for passing safely into the hands of the fifth generation are excellent.

The Counting House, built in 1877 for the Lawrence Manufacturing Company, serves today as the office for the Ames Textile Corporation.

Avco

In March 1929 The Aviation Corporation was formed as a holding and development company in the air transportation industry. Surviving the stock market crash in its first year of existence, it went on to organize and centralize the management of its airline subsidiaries. Included among these was American Airways, the forerunner of today's American Airlines. In the early 1930s the new corporation began to concentrate on aircraft manufacturing and research, and soon added engine manufacturing and additional airframe manufacturing capabilities. Aircraft, engines, propellers, and naval vessels were mass produced for defense during World War II.

When the war ended Avco changed from an aviation and transportation firm to a diversified manufacturing concern. Freezers, refrigerators, ranges, washers, and farm machinery replaced much of the military hardware on Avco production lines. The beginning of the Cold War and the Korean War provided a market again for defense products. With the launching of Sputnik by the Soviet Union the space race was on; Avco organized the Research and Advanced Development Division to work on intercontinental ballistic missiles. By leasing space in the Wood mill in Lawrence, where as many as 2,000 people were employed, Avco played an

Inside the old mill building, modern equipment produces boron and silicon carbide filaments.

Avco's Specialty Materials Division's "permanent" home, however, is in Lowell, where it uses its space and missile technology in commercial as well as military applications. The company is situated in two facilities. important role in transforming the Lawrence economy to its current broad base. The firm built a facility in Wilmington which today is the home of Avco's Systems Division.

The historic Meyer thread mill in Lowell houses Avco's Materials Division's filament manufacturing equipment today.

One of these buildings still contains equipment that was used to fabricate the heat shield for Apollo's command module. Today the division concentrates on the thermal protection materials used in oil refineries, the space shuttle, electric cables, and other commercial and military applications. Also in this facility, high-strength graphite products are manufactured for use in structural reinforcement, replacement for asbestos, and many leisure-time products such as fishing rods. Ironically, some of these items are manufactured using traditional textile equipment. At the other site (a flourishing thread factory at the beginning of the century), boron and silicon carbide filaments are produced which, when joined with a plastic or metal matrix, form materials stronger than steel at half the weight.

Tomorrow's airplanes, missiles, and space vehicles will undoubtedly be composed in part of Avco materials; but so will fishing rods, tennis rackets, and golf clubs. The Avco Specialty Materials Division has as its mission the supplying of high-technology materials to worldwide markets. To this end Avco is dedicated to continued growth in the Merrimack Valley.

Bennett & Hodge Travel, Inc.

When Beverly A. Bennett took a summer job with the Barrows Travel Service in 1944, she had no inkling that she would one day own Lowell's premier travel agency. A native of Tewksbury, Miss Bennett had her mind set on a nursing career; however, when a family friend offered her the job with Barrows, she accepted. In June 1944 she began selling tickets for the agency at the Central Street Bus Terminal—48 hours per week for a salary of $17.

In September, when Miss Bennett began attending Bradshaw Business School in Lowell, she continued to work part time at Barrows. She finally joined the agency full time in 1946. Perhaps not quite the career she envisioned as a child, it was a decision she never regretted.

Barrows had been founded more than 12 years earlier by A.K. Barrows, who opened the business at 64 Central Street. Many travel agencies of that time were inevitably linked to bus transportation and Barrows was no exception. For a time the agency even operated out of the "Barrows and Parchert Motor Coach Terminal" at 63 John Street. In 1938, when Barrows returned to the Central Street location,

he sought to take the terminal with him by starting his own bus stop right outside the door. The new "terminal" inspired a major ruckus among city council members who saw only traffic congestion resulting from Barrows' "innovation."

Gradually the agency and the bus stop were accepted by the community—and just in time. When World War II broke out, the agency terminal was forced to stay open around the clock in order to handle the flood of soldiers and their families on their way to and from Camp Devens. Miss Bennett, of course, was one of the clerks selling those bus tickets.

But bus travel was not to be her forte for much longer. Something new called "air travel" was about to supplant it, and with its growth the travel industry would be changed forever.

During the postwar years Miss Bennett (who was called the "plane girl" by her colleagues and clients because she sold the agency's first airline tickets) gained valuable experience working her way up within the agency. As one of her duties, she flew Eastern Airlines' inaugural flight to Mexico City, which was hosted by World War I flying ace Eddie Rickenbacker.

Aboard and abroad in Mexico in 1955, this small group of tourists from the Lowell area surrounds their leader, Beverly A. Bennett (seated, center).

Beverly A. Bennett (seated, left) and the staff of Bennett & Hodge Travel, Inc.

By the late 1950s Miss Bennett had assumed active management of the firm, and in 1961, after purchasing part ownership, she was elected its president. Four years later Thomas T. Hodge, owner of his own accounting firm, replaced longtime staffer Elmer H. Davenport as treasurer of the agency. And in 1969 the agency officially changed its name to Bennett & Hodge Travel, Inc.

Today Bennett & Hodge is a specialist in international travel, utilizing the most modern, automated reservation systems available. The agency's well-trained, efficient staff can obtain instant confirmation for all major airline, hotel, and rental car reservations. Located in the Hildreth Building at 45 Merrimack Street since 1966, Bennett & Hodge is a member of the prestigious American Society of Travel Agents (ASTA).

The bus station is gone now and so are many of the trains and steamship lines that once composed the majority of the agency's bookings. But the loyal Bennett & Hodge clientele—some in their third generation—continue to be served by Lowell's oldest appointed travel agency.

Beverly A. Bennett may have logged thousands of miles for herself and her clients over the years, but the success of Bennett & Hodge proves that a local girl can find the greatest riches in her own backyard.

Berkshire Manufactured Products

The owner of this thriving business is a Connecticut native who began his career as an apprentice machine designer.

Edward G. Molin is the son of a tool and die maker. After graduating from high school in Waterbury, young Molin went to work for the U.S. Time Company. Before he left to join the Marines in World War II, he had become chief tool designer for the firm. Years later, after working for several other companies, he returned to become project manager for Timex's (the successor to U.S. Time) gyro division.

By 1958 Molin had decided the time was ripe to switch from being an employee to an employer. When an old friend with a small metal-stamping business in Peabody, Massachusetts, asked Molin to consider becoming his partner, he agreed to do so. Unfortunately, on the day they were to discuss their future relationship, Molin's prospective partner died. But his widow asked Molin to manage the business for her, and he agreed to do so.

Berkshire Metal Products was located at that time in a 2,000-square-foot building. Inside, 10 employees performed the metal stamping that was the firm's specialty. By the end of the year Molin had decided to buy the business. In order to purchase the assets he raised nearly $10,000, including $2,000 from his mother-in-law. The decision proved to be an auspicious one: Five years later he moved the firm to another location in Peabody, where he rented more than three times the amount of space.

In 1965 and 1967 the firm expanded

again. By 1972 Molin felt the company was stable enough to afford to construct its own building. Because Newburyport's business and political leaders were aggressively courting new business and because he found the old seaport community attractive, Molin decided to relocate there. The original 20,000-square-foot structure was expanded by 12,000 square feet in 1979. By 1982 the firm employed 80 men and women.

Berkshire Manufactured Products designs and builds its own tools, drawing on the skills of engineers who, like the owner, are students of the shop rather than a school. The company advertises itself as an operation "that thrives on tackling complex stamping problems at the highest level." Skilled

Located in Newburyport's industrial park, Berkshire Manufactured Products was still growing in 1980, when this photograph was taken.

Berkshire's first home was in this modest cement block structure in Peabody, shown here in 1958.

laborers do a great deal of work with high-temperature alloys for some 150 customers in the aircraft engine, aerospace, electronic, and instrument fields.

In 1959 gross sales totaled $150,000. During 1982 Molin expects to earn $4 million and he is optimistic about the future, anticipating that sales volume may double within the next two or three years.

Today sophisticated electronic equipment, such as the units shown here with president Edward G. Molin, is used to ensure quality in Berkshire's products.

Blue Cross and Blue Shield of Massachusetts

In June 1946 Blue Cross and Blue Shield of Massachusetts opened an office on Route 28 in Lawrence in order to provide health care coverage to residents of the lower Merrimack Valley. Massachusetts Blue Cross was then less than a decade old. Organized in 1937 as the Associated Hospital Service Corporation, it changed its name two years later to the now-familiar label. Blue Shield was even younger, having been organized in June 1942 as the Massachusetts Medical Service.

The idea for this kind of health insurance has been traced to Dallas, Texas, where a plan was introduced in 1929. Other plans followed until a nationwide system of private health insurance was available. In Massachusetts today more than 60 percent of the population is covered by Blue Cross and Blue Shield.

Until Blue Cross and Blue Shield arrived, almost none of the thousands of municipal, textile mill, and shoe factory employees in the valley had insurance protection with which to pay hospital and other medical bills. When the American Woolen Company, Boot Mills, Bixby Box Toe, and Ornsteen Shoe Company enrolled their employees in the Plan in the 1940s, a new era of access to health care arrived.

When the program was organized, only one set of benefits was available to subscribers; today more than 250 "benefit packages" are offered. The unique characteristics which distinguish Blue Cross and Blue Shield health care plans include providing coverage for all risks, accepting all membership applications, and automatic conversion privileges to persons leaving a group.

There are no stockbrokers in the two nonprofit corporations. Both are, however, closely regulated by the state's Division of Insurance and Rate Setting Commission. The Massachusetts regulatory system, in fact, is one of the most stringent in the nation.

Today the corporations also serve as Massachusetts' administrators for the federal medicare program and the state's Over-65 medicaid program, as well as offering senior citizens a medicare supplementary coverage called medex. In addition, the corporations are supporting the development of health maintenance organizations in Massachusetts and have undertaken a public health education program called "health thyself."

Customer-service representatives at Blue Cross and Blue Shield of Massachusetts' northeastern regional office at 499 Essex Street in Lawrence assist subscribers with their claims and membership questions. The office services the 4,000 group accounts and 200,000 subscribers in the area.

Bride, Grimes & Co., Inc.

This firm is one of the oldest businesses in Lawrence. It goes back to at least 1869, when W.F. Rutter & Co. advertised itself in the city directory as "steam and gas fitters." The proprietor also offered to sell wrought-iron pipe, chandeliers, brackets, and shades. William Rutter, the owner, was in fact a gas fitter by trade who had worked for the young Lawrence Gas Company before launching his own business.

By 1889 Rutter had added James H. Bride and Elias E. Grimes to his work force. Bride, a Lawrence native, had worked as a gas fitter since age 18. Grimes, a native of Andover, was a grocery clerk at age 20, but at 23 he had married Rutter's daughter, Carrie, and was listed in the city directory as a gas fitter.

Bride and Grimes found the business to their liking and in 1908 Bride, Grimes & Co. ("successors to W.F. Rutter & Co.") was providing plumbing, steam and water heating, automatic fire sprinklers, gas piping, and fixtures. The heating of buildings was described as a "specialty." By now the company had relocated to an office on Essex Street and a warehouse on nearby Franklin Street.

Grimes had no sons and on his death in 1941 the active role of the Grimes family ceased. By then James H. Bride's son, William T., had become the principal active partner in the firm. As a young man he had graduated from Lawrence High School. After attending Villanova University and the University of Pennsylvania he had applied his skills as a mechanical engineer to his father's company.

After more than a half-century in its central business district location, Bride, Grimes & Co. was forced to relocate during the course of a 1965 urban renewal project. The firm moved to North Andover. In 1970 the firm became two distinct corporations—one a wholesaler of industrial supplies which subsequently was sold, and the other a mechanical contractor which exists today. In 1971 Bride, Grimes & Co. moved back to Lawrence. By then William T. Bride, Jr., had worked for his father's organization for nearly a decade. The representative of the third generation of the Bride family had graduated from Andover's Phillips Academy and had earned a bachelor's degree at Brown University. He entered the armed forces, married, and became a father before he succeeded his father in the family business.

Today the company sells a variety of mechanical services, including heating and air conditioning, as well as serving in an advisory capacity for firms needing information about federal, state, and municipal building codes. Although the owner describes himself as a small businessman, the firm is currently being computerized, because he feels that the introduction of the latest computer technology will help ensure accurate estimates and cost analyses for the complex mechanical systems their skilled laborers install. In this fashion the firm plans to maintain and improve its reputation for reliability and quality.

James H. Bride, 1868-1952.

Elias E. Grimes, 1866-1941.

Cantor Insurance Agency

Since November 1, 1921, members of the Cantor family have been selling insurance from an office on Central Street in downtown Lowell.

Jacob Cantor (1871-1956), the founder, had worked previously as an agent for a life insurance company. It was his older son, William, a 1920 Harvard College graduate, who suggested that the two of them establish their own general agency. They were joined within a decade by William's brother, James, a 1929 graduate of Brown University.

During the Depression their agency sold fire, liability, and life insurance to residents of the greater Lowell area. Business was steady, but there was very little growth until after World War II. From gross premiums of less than $100,000 in 1943 the agency has expanded until it expects to do $6.5 million worth of gross premiums in 1982.

About 1950 William Cantor moved to Boston to open a second office, which was incorporated in 1951. Samuel Sokolsky, a Lowell insurance salesman, became president of what has become Cantor Insurance Agency, Inc., a position he held until his death in 1969. Meanwhile, James had become manager of the Lowell office, where in 1964 he was joined by his son-in-law, Neil M. Blume. A 1956 graduate of Harvard College, Blume is also an avid amateur photographer. Like his father-in-law, he has been active in civic affairs as well. Cantor and Company (Lowell) remained a partnership until 1969. The two corporations were merged on June 1, 1981, and Blume now serves as president and treasurer.

Today the agency prides itself on having "grown up with" individuals and corporations with whom it has done business for 60 years. The owners are also proud of the fact that their office employees are a loyal, stable group. Female employees often take leaves of absence to start or to raise a family and then return to work. They are so close that an "alumni" organization has been organized to provide an excuse for monthly social gatherings.

The two dozen men and women on the payroll of the agency today have mixed feelings about the future of the industry; they applaud the simplified forms, the trend toward "one-write" policies, and the time saved by computerized records, but they are less enthusiastic about increased government regulations and by the depersonalization that inevitably accompanies growth.

William Cantor (left) obtains a client's signature on a policy in the middle of a downtown Lowell street during the winter of 1924.

Central Industrial Laboratories, Inc.

Incorporated in 1977, Central Industrial Laboratories, Inc., is located in one of Andover's newer industrial parks close by the Shawsheen River on its northeasterly flow toward the Merrimack.

Today's company is the culmination of a shared business venture by two entrepreneurs, Charles T. Germain and Peter J. Richards. It was a dream which came to reality through a chance meeting in Boston in the early 1970s.

The meeting coincided with a change of direction in both their lives and spawned an idea in the "Great American Tradition" of "building your own business." Since that time they have worked to turn the dream into an everyday reality, and to become recognized in the area as a quality organization.

Germain, president, a native of Worcester, Massachusetts, studied at Clark and Boston universities and worked as a securities analyst. Richards, vice-president, a native of Derby, England, is a chemist who worked for Rolls-Royce in Montreal, Canada, and later immigrated to the United States. Their complementary talents have formed a financial and technical resource which has served well in making the company a success.

With one employee, the firm rented a small area in 1977 in Lawrence's Industrial Park. Central commenced to produce electro-plated metal coatings for local machine shops.

Involvement with the expanding Astro Division of New Hampshire Ball Bearings enabled Central to grow and develop a strong market in the aerospace industry. By 1980 it had become time to look for a larger facility to house the company's eight employees. Choosing an industrial park area in Andover, Central constructed a 6,000-square-foot facility to accommodate its process lines, which have increased from the original two to six.

Transferring the firm proved to be a hectic experience for everyone, with production in full swing and the

Peter J. Richards (left) and Charles T. Germain in front of the Central Industrial Laboratories display at the 1982 job shop show in Boston.

equipment being transported section by section to the new location. It took several weeks to complete the move.

Finally, all was in place in the newly painted and installed facility; everyone left to enjoy a beautiful summer weekend. Meanwhile, a faulty heater switch had allowed a 6,000W heater to continue to evaporate a solution in a plastic tank. The solution disappeared overnight and then the plastic began burning. From this point the fire spread along the processing line,

destroying equipment and filling the building with heavy black soot. Not even a locked drawer or file cabinet was free from the plague of soot, which passed through keyholes and cracks to leave its indelible calling card over every sheet of paper. The great clean-up was on, and it was weeks before the walls could be called white again.

By 1982 further expansion of metal-finishing process lines and inclusion of paint spraying had enabled the company to add four additional employees and begin servicing the growing local electronics industry.

Today the partners bill themselves as "Specialists in Metal Finishing" and produce work destined for Sikorsky Helicopter, Hughes Helicopter, McDonnell Douglas, Pratt & Whitney, Bell Helicopter, Bendix Aircraft, Menasco, and General Dynamics.

Continuing efforts in research and development, to increase the company's capabilities and adaptations to the changing technologies in the metal-finishing field, are expected to keep Central Industrial Laboratories, Inc., moving into the future.

Central Industrial Laboratories, Inc., is located at One Connector Road, Andover.

Courier Corporation

The Hamilton Mill on Jackson Street, which houses the Courier Corporation, was the second largest cotton mill to begin manufacturing in Lowell. It seems appropriate that a firm which utilizes the latest improvements in printing technology should locate its corporate offices at a historic site associated with the beginning of the Industrial Revolution in America.

William Baldwin, printer, was not a lucky man. The weekly newspaper he published in Chelmsford beginning in June 1824 had a life of less than a year. He started again with the *Phoenix,* which soon became the *Merrimack Journal.* When Lowell was incorporated the newspaper was retitled, merged with another weekly, and finally rechristened the *Lowell Courier.*

By 1840 the *Courier* was a daily paper. Two years later a new owner changed the newspaper from an afternoon to an evening publication. He also hired Washington and New York correspondents, a costly practice which ended when the paper changed hands once more.

Other owners kept the paper going during the 1850s, but on the eve of the Civil War a local printing firm purchased the daily. After the war it sold its interest to a reporter and an ironmonger. For years after the periodical espoused the principles of the Grand Old Party. By now, however, it was competing with several other local newspapers as well as a French-language daily. In 1894 the *Courier* merged with the *Citizen* (1856) and the *Lowell Courier-Citizen* was born. It included a directory division, which had begun to print telephone directories in 1878, just two years after Alexander Graham Bell's telephone was introduced in Boston. As thousands of telephones were installed in American businesses and homes, telephone directories had become big business.

In 1939 the owners of the company sold the *Courier-Citizen* to the *Lowell Sun* in order to concentrate exclusively on commercial printing. About a year later the organization purchased a specialized printing firm with plants in Illinois and New York. A forms division was then established, which was expanded significantly during the next 30 years.

In 1966 James F. Conway, Jr., was named president and chief executive officer of the *Courier-Citizen,* succeeding Peter W. Reilly, Jr. Reilly's tenure (1963-66) had been a brief one. His predecessor, Philip Marden, had reigned over the company fortunes from 1906 to 1963.

The year Conway was elected, the firm acquired the Murray Printing Company of Westford, Massachusetts, a major book manufacturer. Two years later *Courier* opened a new color printing plant which was equipped with the latest web-fed process color presses.

By 1972 the officers of the company felt the time had arrived to "go public." By reorganizing as the Courier Corporation they were able to raise the capital that was needed to finance further plant expansion. Reorganization left them with a directory division, a forms division, and the Murray Printing Company. The corporation acquired the National Publishing Company in 1975.

Today's corporation is quite different from the small business that was launched in 1824. The directory division prints more than 400 telephone directories annually on millions of pages of paper. For the purpose, hundreds of tons of lightweight low-grade paper is moved at high-speed through massive presses. Among the newest pieces of equipment is a computerized high-speed binder. With the addition of a new two-color offset press in 1982, the division's modernization plan will be complete.

Courier-Citizen employees lined up en masse on November 11, 1933, to demonstrate their support for the National Recovery Act.

The forms division made its reputation by producing the multitude of forms required by the property and casualty insurance industry. As the industry has standardized and simplified these forms, demand has decreased; consequently the division is now moving into more broadly based business in commercial forms.

The Murray Printing Company division, in nearby Westford, Massachusetts, completed construction of a new 75,000-square-foot warehouse in 1981. This additional space, coupled with the purchase of a high-speed automated casing-in machine, increased efficiency and capacity.

National Publishing Company (Philadelphia) makes its mark by producing the high-quality printed pages, gilt edging, and thumb-tag indexing that characterize many editions of the Bible. The printing of books on lightweight paper has been a distinctive feature of National's business for over a century.

In 1978 James Conway, Jr., became chairman of the corporation and Alden French, Jr., was elected president.

The home of the Courier-Citizen *can be seen in the background of this 1927 photograph. (Photo courtesy of the University of Lowell, Special Collections.)*

French, a resident of Acton, Massachusetts, had joined the Courier Corporation in 1964 and has served in a series of executive positions since then. Under his direction, he has said, the firm will "remain committed to the simple principle that successful printers are those that specialize and concentrate on specific, narrow segments of the market."

H.J. Doerr Painting, Inc.

Harold J. Doerr, the man after whom this painting company is named, went to work as an apprentice for his father in 1921. Although Harold was only 15 years old, he was needed in the new enterprise John Doerr had established. Moreover, in those days it was not unusual for boys and girls to enter the labor force at that age.

In the 1920s, although the task of mixing lead, linseed oil, and turpentine was laborious, the job of selecting colors was not complicated: The painter could only give the client about a dozen choices (today there are hundreds of possible combinations). But inexpensive wallpapers were becoming popular for residents of Lawrence's three-deckers, lending additional variety to interior spaces. Estimates of cost were agreed to verbally by both parties—and on a Saturday morning following completion of the work, the painter would drop by his client's home to collect. Theirs was a taxless, cash economy.

"During the '30s," Harold Doerr remembers, "it was all just plain. I don't care whether you were in Andover, Methuen, or Lawrence—the bathrooms were white, the bedrooms were ivory, and the parlor and dining rooms were stained." Today softer tones and infinite variety are demanded by clients who are "color educated," and by the interior decorators who sometime serve as middlemen between homeowners and the Doerr firm.

In the mid-1950s the third generation of the Doerr family in America reached adulthood and John J., named for his grandfather, entered the business. Beginning as an apprentice, he moved on to estimating jobs and then to managing them. Today he serves as president.

In the '60s the most important discovery of the decade for the paint industry was the link between lead poisoning and the paints traditionally used in American homes. Legislators reacted strongly and soon lead-based paints were outlawed.

The Doerr firm, meanwhile, continued to prosper. Known in the greater Lawrence area for quality painting, the firm gradually expanded its geographic coverage for clients with vacation homes and commercial property located throughout New England. In 1971, just 50 years after its founding, the company was incorporated.

Its customers today consist of residential, commercial, and industrial clients. Doerr continues, in this "ready-mix" society, to custom-mix large portions of the paints used on the job. Modestly headquartered in its original location in its neighborhood, H.J. Doerr Painting, Inc., puts little effort into advertising; the family believes that the quality of their work will speak for itself. They look backward with pride and forward with confidence.

Harold J. Doerr (pictured here) at 76 was still active in the painting industry; his son, John J., became the third generation to run the business.

Essex Company

The Essex Company created Lawrence, Massachusetts. When a group of Boston investors visited Bodwells Falls on the Merrimack River in 1845 they found the site surrounded by farmland and woodlots. Yet through the efforts of Abbott Lawrence, Samuel Lawrence, Nathan Appleton, Charles Storrow, and the other founders of the Essex Company, a "New City on the Merrimack" rose out of rural Methuen and Andover townships.

The entire venture was based on large-scale water power development. Essex's founders planned to sell water to mills, where it would be used to turn turbines and thereby power the industrial complexes. The firm not only provided power but also contracted to build mills and equip them with machinery from the Essex-owned Lawrence Machine Shop.

To fully develop the 11,000-horsepower available at this site the Essex Company constructed the Great Stone Dam, which raised the fall of Merrimack waters to a usable height of 30 feet. Completed in 1848, the dam stands unaltered today, a tribute to the engineering genius of Charles Storrow and Charles Bigelow.

Although it was seen primarily as a power supplier, a sizable portion of the firm's revenues came from land speculation. At the outset, company officials bought about 2,000 acres on each side of the Merrimack. Completion of the dam and North Canal in 1848, and the resulting transformation of marginal farmland into prime industrial space, brought about an explosion in the value of the company's land holdings.

Even after it sold parcels of land, the organization retained tight control over their use through restrictions and covenants written into each deed specifying the number and type of buildings that would be permitted. Similarly, control of public services such as sewer, water, and street paving helped Essex Company officials enforce their image of an ideal industrial community. Company influence in Lawrence's internal affairs waned as the city developed independent social and political communities.

By the mid-20th century the textile industry's migration out of New England and lower-priced alternatives to water power combined to threaten the firm's well-being. A radical increase in oil prices during the 1970s made water power, this time hydroelectric power, economically attractive once again. In 1975 Jacek Makowski, Eugene Patrick McCann, Gordon Marker, Geoffrey Mitchell, Richard Norman, and Barry Flynn formed the Lawrence Hydroelectric Associates, a partnership intent on a major redevelopment of the Merrimack's power potential. By 1979 the partners had purchased controlling interest in the Essex Company and received the necessary state and federal permits to begin construction on a new $30-million power plant at the south end of the Great Stone Dam. That plant was put into operation in 1981. The output of its two 8,400-kilowatt generators is sufficient to power nearly 17,000 homes.

Through the application of new technology to a historical resource, the Essex Company has made a new contribution and a lasting commitment to the city that it spawned.

Engineers, draftsmen, and clerks are all hard at work inside the company's Essex Street office, March 1898.

Eagle-Tribune Publishing Company

Irving E. Rogers, Jr., likes to remind his editor that the people who read his newspaper meet him as he walks down the street and aren't a bit shy about telling him what they think.

His father comes into the office each day with coat pockets stuffed full of little pieces of paper. On them are written notes of some of those things people tell him—story tips, situations around town that need correcting, and yes, even complaints.

The two Rogers, senior and junior, are co-publishers of the *Eagle-Tribune* and they are members of a vanishing breed. More than one-quarter of all newspapers in the United States today are owned by 20 large conglomerates, and that rate of absentee ownership rises almost monthly. The Rogers are determined to keep ownership of the *Eagle-Tribune* local, a determination that rises out of a belief that readers are better served by neighbors than by a corporate policy manual.

It is also a tradition, one started more than 100 years ago—on July 20, 1868,—with the formation of the *Lawrence Daily Eagle*, the forerunner of today's *Eagle-Tribune*, a daily and Sunday newspaper which serves a burgeoning Merrimack Valley on both sides of the Massachusetts-New Hampshire border.

The *Evening Tribune* was organized in 1890. As this was happening, the Rogers family was emerging as a force in the Lawrence area. Alexander H. Rogers was born in Scotland, the son of a flax dresser, and emigrated to the United States at the age of three with his father Barnett Rogers, his mother, and eight friends. The band of Scotchmen soon settled in Andover.

Young Alexander's father earned his living in the Smith and Dove linen mills while his son was growing up. But in 1890 he left the firm to open a real estate agency, which actually housed a number of enterprises, including an insurance brokerage and a travel agency that sold steamship tickets. Rogers also built a reputation as an auctioneer, served as the Andover correspondent for the *Lawrence American*, and still found time for civic service. By the time of his death, he had become one of Andover's leading citizens, and on the day of his funeral all business activity in Andover was suspended out of respect.

When Alexander finished his public school education he went to work in the weaving department of Lawrence's Arlington Mills. His inclinations, however, were toward journalism and so when the opportunity arose to serve an apprenticeship on the *Lawrence American* he took it. Soon he moved to the *Lawrence Daily Eagle* as a reporter.

In 1898 young Rogers, using funds made available to him by his father, joined with Henry F. Hildreth to purchase both the *Lawrence Daily Eagle* and the *Evening Tribune*. For the next decade the partnership was responsible for publishing the two papers. When Hildreth died, Rogers bought out his interest and on May 15, 1909, incorporated the Hildreth and Rogers Company.

The history of the *Eagle* and *Tribune* newspapers runs a close parallel to the history of the city of Lawrence: Both have enjoyed continuous growth and have prospered individually, although their fortunes have been closely intertwined.

In the history of Lawrence publishing many newspapers have risen, enjoyed brief successes, and faded from the scene. The *Eagle* and *Tribune* have steadfastly marched forward, ever adding to the number of readers, constantly improving the quality and coverage of news, and proceeding to higher standards and objectives.

Moving forward toward victory in the Lawrence publishing field, nearing the day when the *Eagle* and *Tribune* would stand alone in the local daily publishing field, on November 28, 1928, these papers suffered their most damaging blow. One of the city's worst fires destroyed the easterly half of the building on Essex Street, with a resultant loss of more than $.5 million. The damage rendered publication of the daily editions in the home plant impossible for one week. But no interruption in publication occurred. The *Eagle-Tribune* emerged from the ashes strong and vital. Rebuilt by 1930, the papers were in up-to-date quarters on Essex Street where they would remain for nearly 40 years.

Rogers owned two other business interests, as well. He had inherited a small job-printing department with the papers, the development of which he encouraged. And in 1937—having decided that radio was here to stay—he founded WLAW, a station that he felt

Alexander H. Rogers (third from left) and his colleagues posed for this photograph about 1900 in front of their newspaper and job-printing office at 12 Lawrence Street.

had the potential to serve much of northern New England.

Like his father, Alexander Rogers played a prominent role in civic affairs. He served as a member of the city's Common Council and a host of organizations. Busy as he was, "his office door was never locked to anyone." When he died in 1942, his newspapers were the largest in Essex County.

By the time Alexander died, his only son, Irving E., had been working on his father's papers for almost 20 years. A product of Phillips Academy and Dartmouth College, he entered the newspaper business as a reporter in 1923. After stints in the advertising department and as a photographer, he joined the business section of the paper. He also was responsible for the operation of WLAW.

A resident of North Andover, Irving Rogers had already made his mark in civic affairs by orchestrating the reform of several town bylaws. Like his father and grandfather, his civic service would make its permanent mark on the community: In addition to expanding the Santa Claus Fund started by his father in 1924, he made remarkable contributions to the growth of the Lawrence Boys' Club, the Lawrence General Hospital, and the Bon Secours Hospital. Irving Rogers, more than any other single person, was instrumental in establishing the Joint Hospital Corporation.

Soon after World War II, Rogers began a series of steps leading to expansion. In 1947 he moved the job-printing division into larger space in South Lawrence. In 1948 he purchased the Consolidated Press of Andover, publisher of a weekly and a commercial printing business. In 1949 he reorganized by selling the daily newspaper's commercial printing business to Consolidated, which became a wholly owned subsidiary of the newspaper publishing company. At the same time he incorporated the Andover Publishing Company as owner of the *Andover Townsman*. And in 1953 he sold WLAW.

By the mid-50s traffic congestion and the need for more storage space for newsprint were forcing Rogers to think about a new site for the newspapers. Two of Rogers' three

On August 20, 1982—40 years to the day after he became publisher—Irving E. Rogers, Sr., (right) turned the reins of the Eagle-Tribune *over to his son, Irving E. Rogers, Jr.*

sons, Irving Jr. and Allan, had assumed active roles in the corporation and they urged their father to take a long look at the future of the business.

In 1959 the two newspapers were merged: The new *Lawrence Eagle-Tribune* consisted of a "county" edition in the morning and a "final" edition in the afternoon. Further planning, however, was delayed because of the untimely death of Allan, who had assumed editorial responsibilities.

After necessary adjustments following this sad event, Rogers instructed his oldest son, who was handling all business affairs, to search for a site for a new building. No site could be found in Lawrence. After a great deal of discussion the paper's owner selected a site on Route 114 in North Andover, where there was both adequate space and easy access to the regional highway network. In 1968 the new plant was opened and a new era in the life of the newspaper began.

Relocation, in addition to providing more space and relieving vehicular congestion, also proved to be the occasion for the introduction of state-of-the-art printing technology. Literally overnight, the *Lawrence Eagle-Tribune* became the largest offset-produced daily newspaper in New England. It also gave the paper the best

color-printing facilities in the region, a feature that proved especially valuable a few years later when the corporation purchased the *Sunday Sun*. The Sunday *Eagle-Tribune* that soon followed used color photos liberally and today the Sunday newspaper is more popular than the daily.

Over a century ago, following the appearance of the first edition of the *Daily Eagle*, an enthusiastic reader wrote: ". . . The day has at last dawned when, after our daily toil, we can return to our homes and firesides and peruse a daily Lawrence paper manufactured out of the brains of Lawrence people, and not imported from Hub."

Four generations later, Merrimack Valley residents have the same opportunity.

Alexander H. Rogers (seated) is seen here in the mid-1920s showing his son, Irving, the tricks of the trade.

Export Warehouse Company

William G. deMontigny, son of Emile and Annie deMontigny, was born in Medford, Massachusetts, on August 1, 1922. His father was a builder. Unfortunately, when William was 17 years old, his father died and he was forced to drop out of school. He went to work in the Quincy Market area of Boston and later transferred to the Boston Navy Yard. When World War II began, he was sent to Pearl Harbor, where he worked on damaged ships belonging to the U.S. Navy. William returned home on leave from Pearl Harbor and was married April 14, 1945, to Mary Louder of Medford, his childhood sweetheart.

While he was at Pearl Harbor, his brother Arthur started a trucking business with two other men. They called the business the Jo-Art Express Company. "The Fleet," owned by Jo-Art, consisted of four trucks including a 1931-vintage, 10-ton GMC. Within a few years the two brothers decided to start their own trucking company. It was called Mystic Express Company, and they were the sole owners and partners. For 16 years Mystic Express was busy hauling freight within a 50-mile radius of Boston.

In 1950 William and Arthur constructed a garage for their trucks, realizing only after the fact that its location beside the railroad made it a convenient location for a warehouse. They became a public bonded warehouse known as Mystic Express & Warehouse Company, Inc.

William and Mary deMontigny started their own business in 1960. They incorporated the Export Warehouse Company in Medford, and were able to obtain a permit to serve as a statewide trucking firm. As the demand for the company's services grew, William and Mary began looking for another location. In 1967 they expanded their organization to Andover, Massachusetts, where they constructed a modern, efficient warehouse as well. In 1971 they added a second building at the new location.

During the following decade, William and Mary focused their attention on trucking and warehousing. But when the opportunity to acquire a wholesale lumber company arose in 1981, they decided to add a third operation to their properties. Today they are the proud owners of the York Wholesale Lumber Company, which they intend to develop rapidly in the near future.

Partners in life and partners at dinner: Mr. and Mrs. William G. deMontigny are shown here enjoying a change of pace from their busy schedule.

Ferrous Technology, Inc./ Foundry Technology, Inc.

When George W. Hamblet purchased the land, buildings, and equipment at 30 Island Street, Lawrence, in 1898 he acquired a site that had been used to make machine parts for a quarter of a century.

Hamblet bought the property from John E. Dustin, proprietor of the Dustin Machine Company. Dustin had set up shop there originally with a partner after they were successful in buying Carter's Mill, a machine and repair shop. Dustin and his partner claimed they were steam, gas, and pipe fitters, but they also fabricated gears and shafting for the city's textile mills.

After Dustin became sole proprietor, he concentrated on gears and shafting for a while, but expanded into the manufacture of napping machines and chain ballers (for cotton warp and filling). By the time he was ready to sell the firm to Hamblet he was building the Finlay Paper Cutter, which he modestly labeled "the best in the world."

George Hamblet was in his thirties when he bought out Dustin. A Dracut native, he had worked his way through MIT, graduating with a degree in engineering in 1888. He taught at MIT for a few years following graduation and then decided he wanted to own his own company. In its first appearance in the Lawrence City Directory (1898) the Hamblet Machine Company

offered to make and to repair machinery, and to fabricate pulleys, gearing, and shafting. But its paper cutters were advertised in boldface type, as if to emphasize them.

In fact, the paper industry in New England would, over the next 50 years, prove to be the firm's most important customer. The "Hamblet Sheeter," although never patented, was a radical improvement over other existing cutters. Its job was to convert rolls of paper to sheets, by cutting to length, slitting to width, and stacking. It gave Hamblet a virtual monopoly in the business and the firm prospered.

Hamblet and his wife became parents of six children. The three sons all wound up in the business: Theodore as machine shop superintendent, William as purchasing agent, and G. Warren as president. Like his father before him, G. Warren graduated from MIT where he earned his degree as a mechanical engineer.

The 1930s afforded the Hamblets little opportunity to add to their capital. The shop ran sporadically with most employees serving "on call." When an order arrived, young G. Warren would ask his men to come to work. Between orders they were unemployed. But during World War II the defense industry provided work for thousands of small shops, including Hamblet Machine Company, which made valves for a major defense contractor.

After the war the pent-up demand for paper machinery brought more orders than the shop could handle, but as the paper industry expanded other machine makers entered the market.

By the '60s the future of the organization seemed uncertain. Consequently, when Southworth Machine Company of Portland, Maine, expressed interest, the three brothers decided to sell. In 1970 the Hamblet Machine Company was dissolved.

Meanwhile, G. Warren Hamblet's son, James E., a civil engineer, had entered the business briefly. He had decided, however, to strike out on his own and had leased a small part of his family's property on the site in order to establish Foundry Technology. His small business serviced the durable goods industry by making bronze and aluminum sand castings.

After less than two years in Lawrence, Southworth decided to consolidate in Portland once again and put the local property up for sale. James Hamblet took advantage of the opportunity to buy back the real estate his grandfather, father, and uncles had owned. At the same time in 1971 he incorporated Ferrous Technology, which produced gray iron sand castings.

Hamblet likes to point out that the nature of the sand-casting foundry business has changed very little over the centuries. The critical difference between then and now is in the degree of dimensional and chemical consistency made possible by advances in technology and chemistry.

Frequency Sources, Inc.

Frequency Sources, Inc., typifies the new high-technology firms that have contributed to the reindustrialization of the Merrimack Valley. Founded in 1964 by a Chelmsford physicist, the company today is a wholly owned subsidiary of the Loral Corporation of New York City.

Founder David L. Baldwin left his previous employ in order to explore the possibilities of solid-state technology. He was the right person in the right place at the right time, for as he had believed, an "explosion" in the new technology occurred within the decade. He worked out of the basement of his home for several months before establishing the new venture in a village storefront.

The firm's first product was a solid-state microwave oscillator. By December 1965 Baldwin felt prospects were good enough to justify his doubling the company's space within the village store building. At the same time he also hired a Lowell University undergraduate named Eugene J. Veracka who today is both the corporation's senior employee in terms of service and president of its eastern operations.

Veracka is a native of Maynard, Massachusetts, and the son of a former woolen mill employee. As a boy, he had worked with his father who, after leaving the textile industry, had established his occupation in the radio and television repair business. Then joining FSI, he worked for Baldwin during the day and attended school during the evening.

In 1968 the firm moved again into a rented 12,000-square-foot building. The product line was also expanded at this point to include the semiconductors used in the company's products. A new unit, BLP Devices, was organized to do this; it was headed by Bernard L. Plansky. Plansky later succeeded Baldwin as president of the parent organization. Plansky's original unit was renamed GHZ Devices, Inc., in 1969. GHZ now develops and produces a series of semiconductors for use by the entire microwave industry.

Rapid growth continued, and in 1972 the company acquired Fairchild Camera and Instrument's solid-state oscillator operation and renamed it Frequency-West, Inc. This California-based manufacturing unit catered primarily to the telecommunications market. At about the same time, Frequency Contours, Inc., a new subsidiary, was created and housed at Frequency-West. In 1978 Frequency Sources acquired Wavecom Industries in California, and its Acronetics Division was "folded" into Contours.

By then, GHZ had moved to a site at Maple Road, Chelmsford, and FSI had expanded into two additional buildings in North Chelmsford. In 1977 all of the Chelmsford operations were centralized at the Maple Road location.

The success of the founders and engineers who had developed the original products attracted the attention of Loral, whose principal activity is electronic warfare. Loral acquired FSI on August 15, 1980. The high-technology products now manufactured by FSI were described by Loral's chairman as "among our most promising fields of endeavor." Today FSI supplies many of the prime contractors to the Defense Department, including Raytheon, Westinghouse, Sanders Associates, Hughes Aircraft, and General Dynamics.

The president of FSI is optimistic about the future market for his company's products, and with defense spending continuing at an increasing rate, the demand for FSI's products is positive. But a shortage of engineers and technicians may also occur and is cause for concern. Meanwhile, the firm is providing strong evidence that the Merrimack Valley labor force has been effectively retrained from textiles and shoes to state-of-the-art electronics.

Frequency Sources' early solid-state microwave oscillator was produced in a village storefront. (Photo courtesy of Herb Gallagher.)

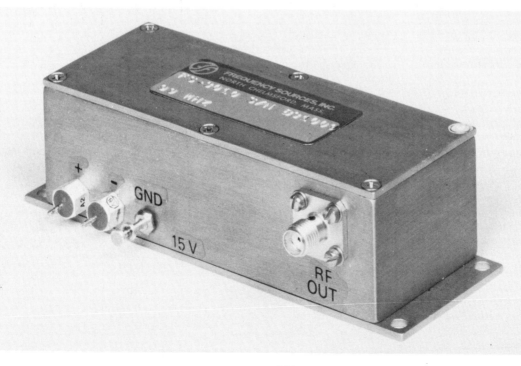

Jackson Lumber Company

The founder of this 36-year-old business, Joseph A. Torrisi, is the son of immigrants. His parents were among the thousands of Italians who came to Lawrence during the first decade of the 20th century to labor in the American Woolen Company's huge Wood Mill.

Young Torrisi was born in 1908. He attended local schools and at age 18 began practicing the carpenter's trade. Not satisfied to work for someone else, however, he soon decided to establish his own business with a friend named George Fichera. Consequently, in the city directory for 1931, Torrisi and Fichera advertised themselves as general building contractors, with "estimates cheerfully given." For the next 15 years the partners built a variety of structures, including synagogues and barracks.

Torrisi had not yet found what he wanted and in 1946 the partnership was amicably dissolved. In its place Torrisi and his brothers Fred and Tom incorporated the Jackson Lumber Company. The firm was located on Jackson Street in Lawrence's central business district. The owners of the new venture went to some lengths to acquire an inventory that would allow them to service area building contractors. Before long, they occupied additional space on nearby Methuen Street, where a millwork shop was outfitted.

In 1950 Torrisi purchased land adjacent to the Boston & Maine Railroad's tracks in South Lawrence, where he erected a warehouse. Unfortunately, not long after, the city's remaining textile mills closed, leaving thousands of residents without work. For the next few years Torrisi and other local leaders were preoccupied with the task of finding new owners and new uses for the historic mill buildings.

As the city struggled to rebuild its economic base a complex urban renewal plan was adopted which ultimately forced the Jackson Lumber Company to relocate. By the time that happened Torrisi had already acquired the former David Brown Bobbin Shop adjacent to his South Lawrence property. The millwork division was relocated there. Nearby he constructed another warehouse as well as a small shopping center on the block he owned.

In 1963 Torrisi's son Alfred, a Notre Dame graduate with a degree in economics, joined his family's company. In 1981, when his father retired, Alfred became the chief executive officer and in 1982 was named president and treasurer. His father continues to serve as chairman of the board, and brother Tom manages the firm's kitchen division. The two uncles, although retired, still help out regularly.

As the area's economy improved, so did the firm's prospects. The only lumber company in Lawrence, it is the largest such operation in the Merrimack Valley. Gross sales climbed from $1.5 million in 1965 to $7.8 million in 1980. Growth in sales made it necessary to expand the physical plant as well. Coincidentally, the major tenant in the nearby shopping center had left and so with help from municipal and banking officials the organization was able to expand its site.

Historically, Jackson Lumber Company primarily has been a regional retail business, but in the very recent past the millwork division has grown significantly. By manufacturing pre-hung doors, movable partitions, and plastic laminate counter tops, this part of Jackson Lumber Company has suddenly generated up to half of the firm's total sales volume. For this and other reasons, Al Torrisi is optimistic about the future of the firm his father started.

This sturdy Ford truck and a hard-working crew delivered dozens of loads of lumber to customers from the company's original location.

Anna Jaques Hospital

Until 1884 residents of Newburyport and its surrounding communities who were injured or ill had only two choices: They could go to the office of the local physician (usually in his home) for treatment, or they could ask the doctor to come to them. In May of that year, however, they were offered a third choice: If the occasion warranted it they could be admitted to the Anna Jaques Hospital. The new hospital was actually a Federal-style house at the corner of Monroe and Broad streets, adapted to care for the ill.

The hospital was created through the combined efforts of a local physician, women committed to good works, and an "angel." In this case the physician was Dr. Francis A. Howe of Newburyport, the women were friends of Miss Alice W. Toppan of that community, and the angel was Miss Anna Jaques of Newbury.

The proposal to establish a hospital in this old seaport had surfaced around 1880; the following year a charter for the purpose was issued. During 1882 Miss Toppan and her band of young friends sponsored several "entertainments," the proceeds from which went to the new hospital fund. But it was Miss Jaques who served as the unlikely catalyst for the project.

Anna Jaques was born in 1800 on her family's farm. Her ancestors had helped to settle Newbury in the middle of the 17th century. Miss Jaques remained on the farm for her entire life, caring first for her parents and then for three siblings, all of whom she outlived.

Variously described as an invalid and a recluse, she counted Newburyport's Dr. Howe among her few friends. It was he who suggested to her near the end of her long life that she help launch the hospital. Her gift of $25,000 provided the corporation with the necessary cash. She made one of her infrequent excursions to view the hospital soon after it opened; satisfied, she returned to the farm, where she died in 1885.

For nearly two decades the hospital served its community well; but by the turn of the century it had become apparent that a larger, more modern facility was needed. In 1901 William C. Todd of Newburyport offered to donate the property he owned on Highland Avenue as a site for a new building; he also pledged $50,000 in cash for the enterprise. Elated, the trustees proceeded to finish plans for a new hospital. Their plans were expanded when Meyer S. Bernheimer, yet another friend of Dr. Howe, gave the corporation a generous sum of money in order to allow an "operating department" to be included in the new hospital.

During the next half-century the hospital did not grow dramatically. A story to a wing, a tuberculosis sanitarium, and an X-ray and laboratory building were constructed.

Beginning in 1954, however, a series of events occurred, the cumulative effect of which has been to transform a small general community hospital into a completely modernized health care facility. The first of several changes in the physical plant was made in 1954, when an addition was constructed which provided the hospital with a modern kitchen, maternity and pediatric services, and an emergency room. In 1957 the hospital agreed to merge with a second community hospital (Worcester Memorial) a 64-year-old institution which then closed its doors.

By 1965 the hospital would boast of

The original building housing the Anna Jaques Hospital, as seen about 1884.

80 beds. A $5-million construction project was completed in 1975, which provided 24 new beds including an intensive care unit, as well as other ancillary facilities. The 1975 building was designed to carry four additional floors. In 1982 an additional floor and several other renovations were completed, adding 32 medical/surgical beds and a 20-bed mental health unit to the hospital's capacity, for a total of 156 beds.

Responsible for this steady growth has been an active board of trustees, a strong management team, and a medical staff, the composition of which has changed over the past 10 years from general practitioners to predominantly specialists. The hospital today serves an area of 50,000 persons.

Busy nurses are tending to the patients in the men's ward in this scene, circa 1905.

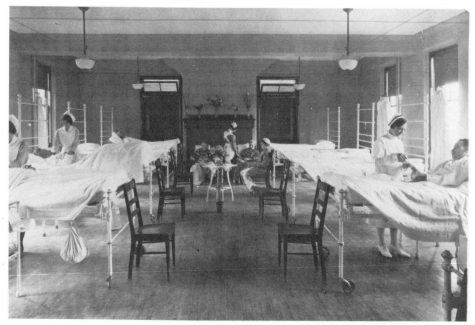

Laughton's Garden Center

One of the Merrimack Valley's largest greenhouse-garden centers is located on the site of a former hayfield in North Chelmsford. The business known as Laughton's Garden Center today was started in 1934 by newlyweds Courtland A. Laughton and Frances A. Hoelzel.

The Laughtons met 50 years ago in Danvers, where he was working in the greenhouses at the Essex Agricultural School. His bride-to-be was earning money for her education by serving as a switchboard operator at the tuberculosis sanitarium.

By the time they married, the new Mrs. Laughton had earned her R.N. degree at Lawrence General Hospital. Mr. Laughton, a graduate of the Essex Agricultural School, had worked in greenhouses and flower shops in Boston and Salem. He had also earned his living for a time at a radio manufacturer's establishment in Lawrence.

After marriage the Laughtons settled in North Chelmsford, where Mr. Laughton went to work in a local textile mill. Mrs. Laughton continued her nursing practice on a part-time basis as they began to raise a family. But they also moved quickly in the direction where their future would be: They rented part of a nearby hayfield, planted some pansies and perennials, and began business.

Although the Depression was not an ideal climate in which to start a small business, each year the Laughtons managed to sell a few more flowers than they had during the previous year. They also invested more money than they received from their business. Nevertheless, in 1936 Mr. Laughton (after discovering he was paying more for help in his greenhouse than he was earning at the mill) became a full-time florist.

When World War II began he went to work for the Raytheon Company as a test engineer in its Waltham plant. He remembers many months of wartime work consisting of 7-day weeks and 12-hour days. In his non-existent "spare" time he continued to care for his greenhouses. Mrs.

Laughton managed their retailing and kept the books while caring for their young daughter and infant son. By now they had purchased the seven-acre hayfield and had built their own house on one side of it. Daughter Judith helped in the florist shop while in grammar school, through college, and even after marriage. She now helps out at holiday times.

When the war ended both Laughtons devoted more and more energy to expanding their greenhouses and flower shop. In 1961 they established a garden center to meet the needs of the suburban communities that were expanding in the area. Their son, Charles, a Cornell University graduate with a degree in horticulture, assumed the active management of garden center operations a few years later and proceeded to expand that part of the business even further.

Neither floods nor fire have discouraged the Laughtons. They watched their land go under water temporarily in 1936 and 1938, but their worst damage from water occurred in 1970, when an earthen embankment at nearby Crystal Lake gave way. A three-foot wave of water swept over most of the property, destroying inventory and damaging equipment. Two-and-a-half years later, when Mr. Laughton had just finished cleaning up the flood damage, a fire caused by faulty electrical equipment swept through the building housing the garden center. Undaunted, the Laughtons called their insurance agency, cleaned up the debris, moved the remaining stock into

A recent view of Laughton's Garden Center suggests the extent of the growth of the business during the past decade.

An early view of the Laughton greenhouse near Princeton Boulevard in North Chelmsford.

greenhouse space, and continued business without interruption. Five months later they opened their new garden center building.

The Laughtons' major project during the past several years has been to develop their nursery operation. Today they own 70 acres in Westford, where they grow the shrubs and trees they sell. Production of nursery stock is now one of the largest segments of the company, which employs over 55 people.

An expanded greenhouse and small florist shop give evidence of Laughton's growth during the first 15 years of the company's history.

Lawrence Pumps Inc.

The centrifugal pump, which is the trademark of this expanding firm, has been manufactured in Lawrence since at least 1886. Owned today by Victor J. Mill, Jr., and Victor J. Mill III, the business was purchased in 1935 by Victor J. Mill, Sr. (1887-1972).

Mill, who had been part owner of a pump manufacturing firm in central New York, held a degree in mechanical engineering from Yale. The business he now owned—Lawrence Machine & Pump Company—had been incorporated by James and Charles Lanigan in 1927. Originally located at the end of Island Street, the firm moved to Market Street in 1922. By then the pumping machinery produced during the past four decades was used extensively in the nation's paper and pulp mills, tanneries, bleacheries, and dye houses. According to an early catalog, they were also used to pump out docks and cofferdams, to raise sewerage, to drain and irrigate land, and to pump sand and "gritty" water.

The most important customer for the new owner and his four employees was the dredging company that was slowly moving thousands of tons of sand and fill from the bottom of Boston Harbor to the point nearby where Logan Airport was being constructed. The pumps made by Mill's company and the "know-how" he provided helped ensure the success of the dredging operation.

But the business quickly suspended pump making when World War II began. Working now with 20 employees, the firm became a subcontractor for the U.S. Navy's submarine program. Within a few months Mill secured a prime contract to construct the main induction valve and its operating mechanism for all the new submarines being constructed on the East Coast.

When the war ended the organizaton quickly converted to pump manufacturing again. For the next few years its fortunes paralleled those of the growing chemical and process industry, which became its primary market. At the same time, the irrigation pumps it manufactured continued to be in demand by both domestic and overseas users. By the early '50s the business employed about 30 persons.

In 1941 Victor J. Mill, Jr., a Yale graduate with a degree in industrial administration, joined his father's firm. Soon he was encouraging his father to strengthen research and development, to improve manufacturing techniques, and to place increased emphasis on quality control.

During the '50s and '60s, the company's original line of pumps was steadily expanded until it included process pumps, slurry pumps, propeller pumps, non-clogging pumps, dredge pumps, self-priming pumps, steam-jacketed pumps, and paper stock pumps. Clients included the petrochemical, mining, metallurgy, utilities, nuclear power, nuclear energy, chemical process, and refinery industries.

During the past two decades, the number of employees has tripled to 150. Plant expansion began as early as 1941; more space was added in 1952, 1960, 1968, and 1976. By 1981 the firm had acquired all the property in an entire city block bounded by Market, Parker, and Foster streets on three sides and by the Boston & Maine Railroad track on the fourth. During 1982 another major expansion effort will be implemented.

The owners feel that Lawrence Pumps' products are purchased because of the organization's reputation for excellent design and high quality. Each pump is custom-made by a team of professional engineers, designers, skilled machinists, and technicians. The firm depends on area engineering and vocational schools for a continuous supply of new talent.

In 1965 a member of the third generation of the Mill family joined the firm. Victor J. Mill III brought with him a bachelor's degree in industrial administration from Villanova University. In 1973 he and his father introduced computer-programmed, numerically controlled machinery into the plant, further improving the quality of their product and the productivity of the labor force. The concept worked so well that during 1982 the entire company will be computerized.

The adoption of new technology may, in fact, be a large part of the reason why an old firm making the same product can survive and flourish. It sheds light, too, on the reason why Lawrence Pumps' newest marketing area—the synfuels industries—acknowledges the firm as a leading pump manufacturer.

Victor J. Mill, Sr., founder of Lawrence Pumps Inc.

Lowell Five Cent Savings Bank

When the Lowell Five Cent Savings Bank was incorporated on April 12, 1854, it became the eighth bank in that busy industrial city. In Massachusetts at that time, only Boston had more banks.

The initiative to establish Lowell's third savings bank came from the Reverend Horatio Wood, whose ministry included the Free Chapel and Free School on Middlesex Street. Three other local ministers agreed to serve as vice-presidents of the new institution. Artemus Tyler, banker and politician, was elected treasurer. The new institution found a home on the premises of the Prescott Bank, where it remained for 20 years.

The Reverend Wood's object was to "get on interest the savings of small deposits among the younger as well as the working class." And that is exactly who showed up on opening day, when 309 depositors left $7,026 in the bank's care. The lenders included 248 persons under 15 years of age. Deposits of five cents were left by 29 young savers. (The new bank was the only one in the city that would accept deposits of less than one dollar.)

By 1874, when the bank moved into its new "marble building" at the corner of Merrimack and John streets, it had more than $2.5 million on deposit from Lowell's laboring class. By mid-1877 deposits exceeded $3 million. (The Five Cent Savings, with more than 10,000 accounts, had more depositors than any other Lowell bank.)

The Reverend Wood resigned and Sewell Mack, son of a Scotch-Irish immigrant, was elected to succeed him. A businessman and politician, he had introduced gas to the city and served as president of the Lowell Gas Light Company.

Mack served as president for nine terms. He was replaced by William S. Southworth, superintendent of the Massachusetts Cotton Mills, who presided over a steady increase in deposits until he moved south with the MCM Corporation in 1898. His successor was John A. Faulkner of the Faulkner Mill family. When Faulkner died the officers voted to have the president, rather than the treasurer, serve as chief executive officer. Austin K. Chadwick, who had served as treasurer for a dozen years, was promptly promoted to president, a post he would hold from 1912 to 1930.

In 1923 the bank constructed a new building at the corner of John and Lee streets (the site it occupies today). A year later Edward F. Lamson, whose entire career was spent at the bank (he had been its first clerk) was serving as treasurer and within a few years thereafter became the chief executive officer. When he retired in 1951 the trustees declared "to him, as much as to any individual, this bank owes the success and prestige which it enjoys today."

The following years, under the leadership of Edward N. Lamson, were a period of expansion: In 1955 the first branch office was opened (in Chelmsford), the bank began offering premiums to depositors, and in 1960 it acquired the assets of the Merrimack River Savings Bank. (In 1939 it had acquired the Mechanics Savings Bank.) In 1962 the bank merged with the City Institution of Savings. During Lamson's term as president, the bank exceeded $100 million in assets. Lamson retired as chief executive officer in 1971. Gerald R. Wallace was elected president and chief executive officer and has remained in this capacity to the present time. Today, at age 128, the bank founded for Lowell's working class has assets of over $188 million.

Home of the Lowell Five Cent Savings Bank.

Originally constructed in 1923, the bank's building is still located at the corner of John and Lee streets.

Macartney's

Macartney's was founded by Robert J. Macartney over 100 years ago. Macartney, who was born and raised in Nova Scotia, came to the United States shortly after the Civil War to work in the textile mills of Lowell. After working all day in the mills he worked part-time at night in the Lowell One Price Clothing Store to earn extra money. It was through this job that he came to love the clothing business. He liked it well enough to open his own store in Lawrence after he had saved enough money to buy his own business, which was located on Essex Street near the M.J. Sullivan Furniture Store.

In those early days of Lawrence it was the custom for retailers to bargain with their customers. It was the era of caveat emptor, "let the buyer beware." The customer paid a price commensurate with his ability to bargain with the merchant. The "one-price" concept changed all that—and Macartney's was one of the first stores in the city to establish a single price for a particular item. And that was the price to all. Everybody was treated alike. The concept brought stability and fairness to the trade.

In those early years Macartney's One Price Clothing Company prospered. And since business was good, Macartney decided to expand. He found that the store where he had first worked at night, the Lowell One Price Clothing Store, was available and he bought it. The two stores grew successfully through the early 1900s and Robert Macartney's two sons, Amherst and Gardner, eventually took over the management of the two stores. A third store was opened in Haverhill a few years following World War I.

Today Macartney's is owned and managed by the same family. The third generation, Robert J. Macartney II and Gardner Macartney, now own and operate three stores in Lawrence, Andover, and Chelmsford. Many changes have taken place through the years, but the principles and policies of the late Robert J. Macartney have endured. Those principles, which have ensured success and prosperity, have embodied three cornerstones: quality,

service, and value. Good-quality merchandise was and is an overriding linchpin. It is accompanied by value through moderate pricing and service carried to the point where satisfaction is a certainty because customers can depend on a store whose first priority is making sure that they get what they pay for.

Robert J. Macartney (left) and his employees pose outside Lawrence's first One Price Clothing Store, about 1880. Note the steamer trunks on either side.

A vertical sign calls attention to Macartney's Essex Street location at the turn of the century.

C.M. McDonald & Company, Inc.

Nailhead Creations, Inc.

C.M. McDonald is the trade name for the various manufacturing, jobbing, and sales operations conducted by Anthony Giannone, Jr., and his wife Lucille in the former Pacific Mills Worsted Mill on Canal Street. This small but prosperous firm opened its Lawrence operations in 1954.

The company, now well-known in the shoe, handbag, and garment industries, is the creation of Anthony Giannone, Sr., son of Italian immigrants who settled in New York City. Although he displayed artistic skills as a youth, his first full-time job was as an employee in the garment industry.

Before long his talent for sketching called him to the attention of his employers and he was assigned to the pattern department. Soon he found himself head of the design department. Eventually he left the company to establish a short-lived partnership with two acquaintances. From then on he was his own boss, with Mrs. Giannone as his only partner. Nailhead Creations (1938) produced nailheads and rhinestone treatments for women's garments, shoes, and handbags. In 1948 he established the Roller Process Corporation, which manufactured glitter fabrics for the American shoe industry.

Anthony Giannone's businesses prospered, but soon after one of his major New York clients moved to Lawrence he decided to open a branch of C.M. McDonald & Company there. In 1954 the silent factories left behind by the departing textile industry offered good, inexpensive space for new businesses.

Although he had worked for his father during summer school vacations, Anthony Giannone, Jr., had elected to strike out on his own after finishing school. But when his parents asked him to take over their Lawrence operation—which was floundering— he returned to the family business.

In 1960 the owners consolidated textile operations in Lawrence. C.M. McDonald & Company became the primary Massachusetts corporate identity, although the earlier names were retained for trade purposes. At about the same time the younger Giannone married the college graduate who would become his business partner as well. A little less than 15 years later they were ready to take over the entire operation. On June 10, 1974, they purchased the business from the elder Giannones, who then retired to their farm.

When the younger Giannones took over, they discovered that the domestic market for their product was drying up. They decided to explore the international market by exhibiting at a Paris trade show; the Europeans loved their product and sales increased. By 1979 approximately 80 percent of the firm's clients were located overseas.

Not content with where they are now, Anthony and Lucille Giannone have plans to expand. They expect to penetrate markets in Africa and South America with their special brand of glitter and related products. At the same time they are exploring opportunities to import "unusual" products, which will complement their present line of goods for the shoe, handbag, and garment industries.

Anthony Giannone, Jr., and his wife Lucille are the husband-and-wife team who have owned C.M. McDonald & Company, Inc., since 1974.

In this 1940 photograph from the family album, Mary Ann McDonald Leahy (second from left) is surrounded by her daughters (left to right) Marie, Margaret, and Catherine Marie. The latter is the wife of Anthony Giannone, Sr.

Merrimack Valley Textile Museum

The Merrimack Valley Museum was founded by members of the Stevens family. John Stevens, an immigrant from England, arrived in Essex County in the middle of the 17th century and helped to settle what is now North Andover. A descendant, Nathaniel Stevens, set up a woolen mill in the community in 1813; from then until 1971 the Stevens family manufactured woolen cloth in their hometown. Today J.P. Stevens & Company is an international firm headquartered in New York City.

The prime mover in the early history of the museum was Caroline Stevens Rogers, assisted by a handful of Massachusetts businessmen, area scholars, and regional museum directors. Although she had spent most of her adult life in Boston, she and her husband "retired" to North Andover in 1953. Devoted to the memory of her father, who had died at a relatively young age, she was determined to see that his collection of American antiques was appreciated by other collectors and students of Americana. She placed much of his collection in the local historical society.

But Mrs. Rogers discovered that her father's interest in textiles and textile tools was so extensive that it merited separate treatment. Consequently, she decided to establish a textile museum and to build it in her hometown.

At the suggestion of Walter Muir Whitehill, the authority on the history of historical museums, Mrs. Rogers decided to hire a graduate of the Hagley Program at the University of Delaware to come to North Andover to manage the project. J. Bruce Sinclair arrived during the summer of 1959 with his newly acquired master's degree in hand.

Between then and 1964 he oversaw the preparation of a charter for the new museum, the construction of a building, the hiring of a curator and a librarian, the accumulation of a collection, and the installation of an exhibit.

When he left (on opening day, September 19, 1964), Sinclair could

rest comfortably with the assurance that he had started a new, specialized museum with great expectations and high standards. The institution he organized is today in large measure a reflection of his vision.

Visitors to the new museum discovered an exhibit that documented and explained how woolen cloth making changed over two centuries. They could see for themselves the tools used in a pre-industrial society and the machines designed for factory-made goods.

After the museum opened, the collection continued to grow by leaps and bounds. By 1967 the library materials had outgrown the space allocated to them and a new wing had to be added to the original building. Four years later the tool and machinery collection was installed in a 30,000-square-foot steel frame structure erected to care for what had now become the largest textile tool and machinery collection in the United States.

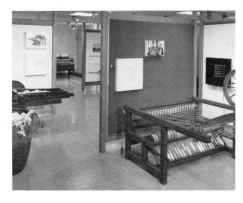

One of the Merrimack Valley Textile Museum's principal galleries is devoted to an exhibit about the way in which cloth making was mechanized during the 19th century. Visitors can watch trained guides operate the antique machinery. (Photo by Warren Jagger.)

With exhibits, library, and artifact collections in place, the museum began to concentrate on field research, education, and publications.

Field research uncovered the evidence which proved that much of the original 19th-century industrial landscape in the Merrimack Valley was intact: The museum staff could only stand by helplessly when the famous Dutton Street boarding houses were torn down in Lowell; but crowds gathered for walking tours of

The Merrimack Valley Textile Museum's original building faces the town common in North Andover's old center. Also visible in this photo are the North Parish Church steeple and the cottage and museum owned by the North Andover Historical Society.

downtown Lawrence, and when the curator nominated the Great Dam (1845) and North Canal (1848) to the National Register of Historic Places, even the local business and political community converted to the cause of historic preservation.

Educational projects have included traveling exhibits, a lecture series in local history, guided bus tours of historic industrial sites, temporary exhibits about Shawsheen Village (Andover) and Machine Shop Village (North Andover), and audiovisual presentations for school-age audiences.

The publications program has served several different audiences: John Borden Armstrong's *Factory Under the Elms* (1969) helped build support for the preservation of Harrisville, New Hampshire; Peter Molloy's *Inventory of Industrial Sites in the Lower Merrimack Valley* (1976) aided planners, architects, and developers; Martha Coon's history of *Linen-Making in Early New England* (1980) revised assumptions about that chapter of American history.

In the recent past, in order to help preserve antique textiles in other collections, the museum established a Textile Conservation Center. Its clients include museums, historical societies, and collectors from all over the United States.

The Merrimack Valley Textile Museum has become recognized as a center for reseach in American textile history. In this way it honors the men and women who made the Merrimack Valley famous.

New Balance Athletic Shoe

William J. Riley of Belmont, Massachusetts, incorporated the New Balance Arch Company in 1906 and began to make flexible arch supports. His product was sold through ads in magazines as well as by a few salesmen. One of them, Arthur Hall of Fall River, had enough confidence in the product to purchase an interest in the small business in 1929. Nearly a quarter of a century later he sold the company to his daughter, Eleanor, and her husband, Paul W. Kidd. Within a few years the Kidds decided to capitalize on their knowledge of orthopedics by designing and fabricating custom-made running shoes.

By 1961 the basement of their Arlington home had become too small, so they opened the New Balance Orthopedic Laboratory in a storefront on Massachusetts Avenue in Cambridge. There each shoe continued to be cut, cemented, and lasted by hand.

The new shoe became increasingly popular with track team members and by 1967 the Kidds were forced to rent more space. In 1968 they moved to a larger location in Watertown. Unfortunately, a freak flood in 1969 did serious damage to their inventory, which was not covered by insurance. But they bounced back. Their mail-order business continued to spread the reputation of their product.

Still, New Balance, after six decades of operation, was a small business. Six people, working in 10,000 square feet of space, could make about 30 pairs of shoes each day. Sales in 1972 amounted to about $100,000.

But 1972 was to be a turning point in the history of New Balance. After nearly 20 years in the business the Kidds decided to sell the company. The willing buyer, James Davis, was a 28-year-old Brookline native who had earned a bachelor's degree at Middlebury College. Davis had been selling computers but was eager to have his own business. Upon examining New Balance he realized the product had what marketing experts refer to as "high acceptance." But he also recognized that the company suffered from low visibility and a poor distribution system.

For a while Davis concentrated on what he has labeled "cosmetic" changes. But in 1976 New Balance was producing its "320," which runners rated the number-one shoe on the market. By then the company was located in Boston's Allston neighborhood, where its corporate offices are located today. By 1978, despite increased production capacity, orders far outstripped the firms ability to keep up with demand.

In the course of studying alternative production sites, Davis discovered that one of the shoe companies in the greater Lawrence area was closing. Assuming that part of that skilled labor force would be available, he decided to expand into the Merrimack Valley. Consequently, New Balance rented space from Rowland Industries, owner of the former Pacific Mills on Canal Street in Lawrence.

The decision proved to be an auspicious one. Sales have doubled every year since 1978 and today New Balance rents about 200,000 square feet of space in the old mill building. Today the Lawrence operation includes running shoe production, research and development, and manufacturing of activewear.

In the course of developing the product line for New Balance, Davis has opened small factories in Ireland, Canada, and England. Within the past two years the firm has also established two facilities in Maine.

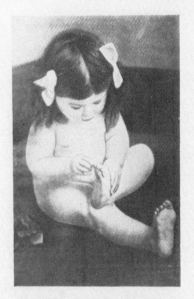

This page from an early advertising brochure stresses a constant theme in the history of New Balance: Its footwear is based on a knowledge of physiology.

Norcross & Leighton, Inc.

The early history of this ancient, family-owned firm is difficult to reconstruct. What is known is that the agency was in business as early as 1846, when the young city of Lowell was only 20 years old. Until 1883 the agency was managed by various officers of another firm, the Traders and Mechanics Insurance Company. At that point, one O.H. Perry sold the business to Edward M. Tucke, secretary of the other firm. Tucke in turn sold the business in 1887 to Nicholas W. Norcross, who promptly named it after himself.

Norcross retired in 1892, leaving the agency to his son. In 1907 Nicholas G. Norcross took James H. Leighton in as a partner. Leighton was active in municipal politics as well as local banking circles. Upon his advent the name of the agency was changed to Norcross & Leighton.

Leighton's son, Howard, joined the firm in 1941 and four years later his father bought out the Norcross interest. When James Leighton died in 1948 his wife, Edith, became president. Her son, Howard, assumed the titles of president and treasurer in 1954.

The company constructed its own building at 170 Appleton Street in 1957; 11 years later the building was more than doubled in size. Meanwhile, the firm had acquired the "good will and interests" of the Daniel J. O'Brien (1964), the Eustace B. Fiske (1967), and the Hodson (1968) agencies.

Howard H. Leighton graduated from Babson Institute in 1939 and worked as an underwriter and special agent before joining his father's firm. During World War II he served as a naval officer. After returning to the insurance business he became active in civic affairs, as well. His most notable contribution to Lowell's civic life was to found the Lowell Exchange Club.

Robert Hill Leighton, the present owner, joined the agency in 1965. A Tewksbury native, he attended the Belvidere School in Lowell and, like his father, graduated from Babson College. His initial job in the firm was as clerk to his father; he later became office manager. When the agency purchased the E.B. Fiske Agency, Leighton managed it for a year as a separate office. He has since served successively as assistant treasurer, treasurer, and president.

Today the agency employs 23 persons and does four million dollars worth of business in gross premiums annually. It offers all lines of insurance, serving both commercial and personal clients. The company's oldest personal client dates to 1913; its oldest commercial client is the Courier Corporation.

What of the future? Leighton notes that today there are only half as many insurance agencies as there were a decade ago. A successful agency needs to gross at least two million dollars in annual premiums, he feels, and predicts that 6 out of 10 agencies won't survive this decade. Leighton's goal? He says he is aiming for $10 million in gross premium income within five years.

Northern Essex Community College

In 1958 the legislature established the Board of Regional Community Colleges and authorized and directed this board to determine the need for education at the community and junior college level, as well as to develop and execute an overall plan to meet this need by establishing and maintaining regional community colleges at appropriate locations throughout the commonwealth. The curricula at the community colleges were to be comprehensive in scope, meeting the needs of those who plan to transfer to senior colleges or universities; those who seek training in preparation for careers in business, industry, the allied health fields, or service occupations; and those who simply wish to study at the college level as part-time students for credit and personal enrichment.

Subsequently, in 1961, the Northern Essex Community College opened its doors to 186 students, most of whom came from Haverhill and the communities immediately adjacent to this former shoe-manufacturing center. Lacking land or buildings of their own, the college faculty met students in a former elementary school that had been declared surplus by Haverhill's city fathers.

President of the new school was Harold Bentley, an English native. Bentley, a Congregational minister, had left the active ministry in 1944 to join the faculty at Worcester Junior College. He later became president, a post he filled until accepting his appointment at Northern Essex Community College.

As president, Bentley was responsible to the Massachusetts Board of Regional Community Colleges. But a local advisory board, composed of civic and business leaders, helped shape the distinct character of each community college.

The new institution quickly outgrew the small school in Haverhill's Bradford neighborhood. Additional space was found in the city's former high school, in church basements, and in a Grange Hall. Meanwhile, plans for

a permanent campus were adopted, and in 1971 nearly 2,000 students were enjoying the benefits of a 106-acre campus near Kenoza Lake, only a stone's throw away from Interstate 495.

When Bentley retired in 1975 he was succeeded by John R. Dimitry, a native of Detroit whose professional career has been spent in community college teaching and administration. Dimitry, who had earned a doctor of education degree from Wayne State University, was president of Macomb County Community College, the largest such school in Michigan.

Under Dimitry the enrollment and curriculum at NECC developed and expanded in the occupational and technical program area; nearly 70 percent of today's student body is enrolled in professional and career programs. Programs of community service were expanded, and cooperative educational programs with area businesses and industries were instituted and began to flourish.

In 1981 the governance of the college was reorganized. New legislation provided for a board of regents to oversee all public institutions of higher learning in the commonwealth. Each institution, however, is managed by a nine-member local board of trustees. In the case of Northern Essex, the governor has appointed seven trustees, including an alumnus. Alumni elect

The Northern Essex Library first opened its doors in 1971, when the college moved from the former Haverhill High School site to the new campus on the shores of Lake Kenoza. The library was later designated the Harold Bentley Learning Resource Center in honor of the institution's founding president.

one representative to the board, as do members of the student body.

Today the college serves 8,000 students from nearly four dozen communities stretching from Lowell to Newburyport in the Merrimack Valley. Northern Essex offers a comprehensive selection of programs and services and is now the largest community college in Massachusetts.

The College Center is the focal point for a wide variety of college and community activities. The most recently constructed of the campus' seven buildings, the facility opened in 1973.

Pellon Corporation

As a beginning for what is now a large, diverse multinational activity, Pellon Corporation manufactured its first interlining products in Lowell, Massachusetts, in 1951. The company was founded by a Polish immigrant who already had established a prosperous distribution business in New York City and was looking for new opportunities to expand. While on a visit to West Germany in 1950, he came across a unique textile product in a drapery shop, traced it back to Freudenberg & Company in Weinheim, West Germany, and in due course purchased its distribution rights for the United States.

Recognizing the need for local manufacture, the new Pellon Corporation (the name derives from the Spanish word "pelo," meaning wool fibers) capitalized on the availability of skilled labor and existing plant space in Lowell. Initial operations were established with imported, used equipment in leased space at 221 Jackson Street, Lowell, in what was originally a textile machine building that was also used by General Electric during the war. Today the firm occupies more than 600,000 square feet of factory, warehouse, and office space in Lowell and Chelmsford, Massachusetts, and Hopkinsville, Kentucky.

Initial products made in Lowell were somewhat experimental and primitive compared to the sophisticated range of nonwoven fabrics offered today. Combinations of basic ingredients included various synthetic and natural fibers—among them human hair from China. Such material became available at that time because the new Chinese government was enforcing removal of men's braids to signify the transition to a new regime.

The first Pellon-manufactured products were sold primarily for home sewing, the dress market, and custom tailoring trades. But sales efforts were soon directed to the mass market represented by the American apparel industry. Within a few years a nationwide network of exclusive distributors was established to serve the specialized needs of the apparel industry, and that organization remains in place to this day. Emphasis was subsequently given to the development of opportunities for industrial and technical applications of Pellon nonwoven products.

In 1959 Pellon added a new plant on the Jackson Street property to expand manufacturing and warehousing facilities. A building at 491 Dutton Street was purchased for converting operations in 1962. To keep up with the expanding business, another plant was erected in Lowell the following year, and further additions were made to the Jackson Street complex in 1969, 1971, and in 1972.

Another expansion of the Pellon complex was initiated in 1972, with the erection of a manufacturing facility in Cornwall, Ontario, Canada. A new plant was erected in Chelmsford in 1974 to serve as warehouse and office space for a variety of administrative functions, and a new manufacturing facility was completed in Hopkinsville in 1975.

When the original owner withdrew from the business in 1956, Freudenberg & Company assumed full ownership of Pellon, and it rapidly became one of its leading enterprises in

Pellon Corporation's new headquarters in Chelmsford.

the United States.

Today the Pellon corporate headquarters is located in Chelmsford, with a principal marketing office and application laboratory in New York City. In the apparel industry, Pellon's name has become synonymous with nonwoven interlinings, largely because of its ability to adapt products to meet the particular requirements of its customers. New industrial applications are constantly being discovered, as evidenced by direct sales to corporate customers for filtration, battery separators, polishing, and data storage discs.

Pellon Corporation has come a long way since its modest beginnings in downtown Lowell, and its prospects for further growth continue to be favorable.

The company's Lowell facilities.

Pepsi-Cola Methuen Bottlers Incorporated

The soft drink that is now a household word was introduced to Merrimack Valley residents during the Great Depression. The Pepsi-Cola Company used the same secret formula then as it does today to make the concentrate that serves as the base for the famous soft drink. The concentrate was distributed to a handful of bottlers who were then responsible for the finished product. These independent bottlers would actually sell the product by the case to hundreds of retail outlets.

Pepsi-Cola was first bottled in the Merrimack Valley in 1941, when the original plant on Broadway in Methuen was completed. Hundreds of thousands of gallons of Pepsi have been bottled there during the past 41 years.

The key figure in the early history of Methuen's Pepsi-Cola bottling company was Mrs. Florence "Dixie" Robertson. She, along with her son, Clyde Fore, managed the local bottling company until 1957 when it was sold to Michael J. Lattif of Syracuse, New York, who operated the plant until the franchise was purchased by David R. Coffman in 1959.

Coffman was a native of Chicago who had grown up in Cleveland before going to work for the Coca-Cola company in Lansing, Michigan, in 1938. After World War II, when he saw service in the Navy, Coffman worked for General Motors. His career was then interrupted by the Korean War when he was called back into the Navy. But while on duty he met a former business acquaintance who asked him to come to work for Pepsi-Cola. Consequently, he worked in the sales area for Pepsi between 1953 and 1959 when he took advantage of the opportunity to purchase the local franchise.

Along with a business that needed better leadership, Coffman found he had inherited at least two key employees. Robert Allen, who had started working for the local bottling company in 1941, would stay on to be his production manager, a position he holds today. And Thomas A. DiMauro, who had been a member of the sales force since 1949, remained to become the general manager.

Coffman determined that in order to succeed, his bottling company would have to maintain the quality of its product, add to the sales department, and hire its own driver/salespersons rather than subcontract through independent distributors. It would also be necessary to increase productivity in order to keep the price of the product within range of the average consumer's pocketbook. Today a line that originally had a capacity for filling 120 bottles a minute can fill 640 bottles in the same length of time. New semiautomated equipment has also eliminated much of the manual labor previously involved. Quality control— essential to continued consumer satisfaction—is emphasized at every point.

Coffman has witnessed a number of other changes during the 23 years he has owned the company. The artesian wells on the property once capable of supplying all the water needed, now produce about half of the daily requirement. The other half comes from the municipal system and is treated and purified in the plant. Per capita consumption of Pepsi's product has increased tenfold during those years.

Today the Methuen plant is kept busy filling glass and plastic containers with Pepsi-Cola, Diet-Pepsi, Pepsi-Light, Mountain Dew, Hires Root Beer, Orange Crush, and Schweppes.

As the man who has developed the franchise to its current size approaches retirement, a second generation has been brought into the management framework. Donald H. Sorrie, Coffman's son-in-law, came to work about five years ago as plant manager. Recently he has been promoted to assistant general manager. It will be his job to ensure that Merrimack Valley residents continue to drink their share of Pepsi.

An early view of the Pepsi-Cola bottling plant includes the original on-site advertising symbol and an example of a delivery truck. Visible in the background is part of Lawrence's Arlington Mills complex.

J. George Picard and Son

Soon after the beginning of the 20th century a French-Canadian farmer and his wife left their Quebec village to seek a better life in New England. They settled briefly in Willimantic, Connecticut, where Joseph George Picard was born in 1902. A few years later they emigrated to Canada, but when their son reached adulthood he returned to the United States to look for work.

Young Picard settled in Lowell, where he soon joined a small construction crew and mastered the craft of carpentry. By 1934 (in the depths of the Great Depression) he was ready to strike out on his own. During the next two decades his small business would earn a reputation for quality remodeling, sympathetic additions, and custom-made new residential construction.

George J. Picard, the oldest of six boys in the family, joined his father's business in 1948. His brother Ronald entered the company a few years later. At the initiative of the two sons, the scope of the firm's work was expanded to include commercial and industrial construction.

The venture was incorporated in 1964 and in 1970, after operating out of the family home on Ursula Street for 30 years, was moved to rented space on Pevey Street. Within a few years Paul and Richard Picard, the two youngest sons, also had joined the firm as it completed a record volume of business with the largest crew in its history.

But size and volume turned out to be less desirable trademarks than quality. Soon after the elder Picard died on April 23, 1975, George J., Paul, and Richard left the firm. Ronald then assumed the reins as president, treasurer, and sole owner. No new residential work was taken on as the business concentrated on commercial and industrial construction. Volume declined but profitability improved. In 1981 the company enjoyed the most prosperous year in its 47-year history.

Today's crew of 12 to 15 men is long on experience: Several craftsmen have been employed by Picard for two to three decades. This seems especially fitting as J. George Picard and Son is now the oldest general contractor in Lowell.

J. George Picard, Sr., founder of the company that bears his name, is seen here at his desk shortly before his retirement.

Typical of the work done by the Picard firm is the Towne House Motor Inn in Lowell. Restored in 1955, the original structure now has additions at either side.

Preston Fuels

The owner of this small business likes to point out that—although his company is only a century old—his family has been selling fuel in New England for more than 200 years. The Campbells, his maternal ancestors, hauled wood from New Hampshire into Boston during the 18th century.

The paternal side of the family entered the fuel business much later. Frank Preston, the founder, in 1879 decided to go into the wood, coal, and ice business with his brother-in-law. For the first few years wood was the most popular fuel they sold, although the soft coal purchased by many local factories was also an important part of the business. Near the end of the century, the partners began handling a new type of domestic fuel. Named after the German scientist who perfected the process, ''Otto coke'' was adopted slowly and with great reluctance by domestic consumers.

Since Frank Preston had been willing to introduce coke into Manchester, his suppliers, New England Coal and Coke Company, asked him to help them enter the Lowell, Massachusetts, market. John H. Preston, his son, was given the assignment and in 1903 moved to the lower Merrimack Valley to establish a

new retail outlet for wood, coal, and coke.

Until World War I, wood and coal continued to be the most salable products of Preston Fuels. Because of its bulk and abrasive features as a product sold by the bag, coke was considered inconvenient. But a postwar strike by miners caused the coal supply to dwindle dramatically. The Preston yard was filled to overflowing with coke, and homeowners who had resisted change were now forced to buy the product. For the next 20 years coke was popular

In this pre-World War I photograph, two freight cars of coal stand in the yard ready to be unloaded into the bins at the side.

In 1908 Jim and Jerry were the reliable team that delivered bags of coal, wood, and coke by wagon to residents of the Lowell area.

and the firm prospered.

In 1933 John H. Preston returned to Manchester, New Hampshire, to take charge of his father's business. His son, John C., then assumed the management of the Lowell office. He was quite familiar with the business, having been introduced to it at a relatively young age.

After World War II, the pent-up demand for consumer goods stimulated manufacturers to produce more. Production required energy. Among the solutions to the problem of inexpensive and apparently inexhaustible sources of supply was oil, which soon replaced coal and coke as the popular agent. Preston Fuels, slow to enter the fuel oil business, suffered the consequences.

During the '50s and '60s the company diversified its product line on several occasions, without dramatic results. When the energy crunch arrived in the '70s, however, the organization was ready; the coal and wood burners it had sold for years became popular again. So did its fuels; in one decade, the demand for coal increased tenfold.

As it entered the '80s the firm was busy selling coal, its oldest product. But solar and wind power were also among its sources of potential energy. Owner John C. Preston says, ''When the company was founded, we were in the wood and coal business; today we are in the energy business.''

St. John's Hospital

The seven Sisters of Charity who organized St. John's Hospital in 1867 held strong opinions about the conduct of their patients: The first set of regulations to be printed forbade smoking, spitting, and littering. Relatives of patients were, at the same time, warned that in the event of death no "wakes" were to be conducted on premises "under any pretense whatever."

The old yellow house in which the first patients were lodged sat hard by the red brick mills bordering the Merrimack River. A tenement for many years, it was home for some 30 worker's families. After renovation it could accommodate 30 sick persons. The honor of being the first patients fell to eight chronically ill women.

Two years later, with funds borrowed from the Lowell Five Cent Savings Bank (q.v.), the directors of the hospital constructed a four-story brick building which incorporated "all the best conveniences and appliances to be found in a first-class hospital."

As the population of Lowell doubled between 1870 and 1900, the hospital expanded its physical plant several times. By 1903 the original wooden structure had to be torn down to make room for a large steam laundry. By that time the hospital's principal volunteer corps, the Ladies of Charity (now the Ladies of St. John's), had been organized.

But from the turn of the century until well after World War II, the hospital, like the city, grew intermittently. In 1961 the Sisters of St. Martha assumed responsibility for managing the hospital and soon the Joseph E. Sullivan Building (named after the hospital's first chairman of the board of governors) was added to an otherwise aging physical plant. During the 1960s, under the leadership of the hospital's president, Sister Maria Loyola, and with the guidance of her staff and the hospital's governing board, a master plan was developed which led to the hospital's greatest period of expansion and modernization.

In an attempt to anticipate the health needs of the greater Lowell area for the next 30 years, hospital officials broke ground late in 1973 for a $13-million facility which was dedicated three years later. Named for the late John F. Reilly, Sr., a prominent Lowell businessman, the new structure gave the hospital a 256-bed capacity, as well as the most modern physical plant of any hospital in New England.

During the same period the governing body of the institution was reorganized. In place of an advisory system, an active and energetic board of governors was elected, consisting of 42 business, religious, and civic leaders. By 1980 the hospital was serving more than 100,000 patients a year and the chairman of the governing board could report that the institution was in "good health." A modern physical plant, widespread use of the latest health care technologies, a well-trained staff, and strong community support all served to confirm the claims of hospital leaders.

St. John's Hospital (left), erected in 1869, as seen from across the Merrimack River in this 1887 photograph. The Church of the Immaculate Conception (right, background) was constructed in 1872.

St. Joseph's Hospital

Today's 232-bed hospital was originally established in 1839 as the Lowell Corporation Hospital, the nation's first industrial hospital. By actively assessing and responding to the medical needs of its community, the Lowell Corporation started a tradition of providing health care based upon social involvement which has been nurtured by the present St. Joseph's Hospital Corporation.

Dr. Gilman Kimball, a Lowell gynecologist, was an early advocate of the establishment of a hospital to care for the city's mill workers, most of whom were women. Appointed the Corporation Hospital's first superintendent, Kimball reported to a board of directors comprised of representatives of each of Lowell's manufacturing companies.

The Corporation Hospital turned away no patients for lack of money. If the mill workers were unable to pay for their care, the mills for which they worked reimbursed the Corporation.

While Lowell's mills flourished, the Corporation Hospital kept pace with the advancement of medical technology and expanded its services to meet the medical needs of the city. By the 1920s, however, most of the cotton mills had been moved to the South. The Corporation could no longer afford to maintain its hospital, so it put the building up for sale.

Unable to find a buyer, in 1930 the Corporation donated its hospital to the Archdiocese of Boston with the stipulation that the hospital would continue to serve the Lowell community. Placed under the auspices of the Franco-American Oblates, the hospital was renamed in honor of St. Joseph. Father Louis G. Bachand, O.M.I., the leading proponent of the Oblates' acquisition of the hospital, was chosen as the first president of St. Joseph's Hospital. Management of the new institution was entrusted to the Grey Nuns of the Cross of Ottawa. Sister St. Alphonse Rodriguez, the first administrator, and Joseph Legare, a Lowell banker and philanthropist, worked together and earned community support and professional accreditation for the hospital.

The Kirk Boott House, site of the Lowell Corporation Hospital. Boott was the treasurer of the Merrimack Mills.

Since 1930 a combination of religious and lay people has labored to make St. Joseph's Hospital a leader and an innovator in the delivery of health care, especially in the treatment of dialysis patients.

St. Joseph's Hospital was designated in 1969 as the Regional Dialysis Center for the 23 communities of the Merrimack Valley. Along with conventional hemodialysis, the hospital offers alternative methods of treatment to give the dialysis patient more personal freedom. A pioneer in the implementation of Continuous

Ambulatory Peritoneal Dialysis (CAPD), also known as "walk-around dialysis," the hospital also provides training for at-home dialysis.

An eight-station satellite dialysis facility was opened in Merrimac, Massachusetts, in January 1982. It was the first free-standing dialysis unit in New England owned and operated by a hospital.

Today St. Joseph's Hospital continues to adapt to the health care needs of greater Lowell by constantly striving to make the benefits of modern medical care more accessible to all the area's residents.

St. Joseph's Hospital's Paul A. Gagnon Pavilion, dedicated in January 1975.

Sutton Travel Service, Inc.

William Sutton, like hundreds of other English immigrants, came to the Lawrence area to work in the Arlington Mills. Not content with the meager wages of an operative, he launched a series of income-producing ventures with his wife. In 1908 Sutton convinced the officers of Cunard and White Star lines to appoint him as their local travel representative. Many of the customers in his grocery store needed help in returning to the Old Country or in bringing relatives to the United States. He knew a great deal about the condition of the neighbors and their relatives abroad, because they relied on him, as the neighborhood postmaster, for assistance in many things.

After World War I many prewar immigrants wanted to visit their native land again, but were reluctant to travel on their own. Thus in 1922 Sutton began offering his annual conducted excursions by the great liners that operated weekly from Boston to Great Britain. Later he organized a "grand tour" for those who wanted to visit Europe as tourists.

During World War II the agency was, for all practical purposes, closed. When it reopened in 1945 at the corner of Common and Lawrence streets, a travel revolution had begun. The bulk of prewar passenger fleets had been sunk or converted to troopships. But now, the airplane had come of age and air travel became available to all. Sutton became the local agent for American Overseas Airlines (later to become Pan Am) in 1946. Most travelers over 50 years of age had never flown before and were very reluctant to try it. Sutton organized his first air excursion to London in 1946 and filled it with 50 first-time fliers. Later that same year the Suttons flew to the Caribbean to celebrate their 50th wedding anniversary, accompanied by their granddaughter, Betty Couilliard, who was to carry on the travel business. By emphasizing how safe and convenient air travel could be, clients were encouraged to use air to various destinations for vacations as well as to visit relatives.

Ms. Couilliard joined her mother, Mrs. Minnie Tryon, in the family business in 1955 when there was little money for pleasure travel in the Lawrence community because the local textile industry was dying. However, soon new commerce and industries replaced the old. Air travel for these new commercial travelers was the best way to reach their markets. At this time, the agency was able to secure the first postwar Polish visa for a member of the local Polish community and Sutton's reputation for reuniting Polish families made the firm one of the most productive agents to this destination. Because of this Ms. Couilliard was invited by Sabena to travel trans-Atlantic on the very first passenger Boeing jet aircraft delivered to any commercial carrier.

Jet travel and the new immigrants in Lawrence meant a repeat of the early century travel flow to and from the Old Country. Lower air fares to exotic vacation spots and expanded business made it necessary to move to larger quarters on the opposite corner of Common and Lawrence streets in 1964, and at the same time to open a

Mr. and Mrs. William Sutton were the founders of the agency that bears their name today.

second office in Andover at the corner of Lowell and Main streets. By now, Ms. Couilliard was a certified travel counselor and replaced her mother as agency manager. Sutton Travel was the first agency to be computerized in the Merrimack Valley. Ms. Couilliard now plans to add to her list of over 100 countries visited and to follow in her grandfather's footsteps when she again escorts a tour—this time to China and the Orient.

Organized and guided by the Sutton Travel Service, this group of Lawrencians tour-bused its way around Britain in the late 1920s.

Tripoli Bakery

When Rose and Rosario Zappala and their young son, Charles, arrived in Lawrence in 1908 they settled in a neighborhood that was crowded with other Italian immigrants like themselves. Tenements and small shops dominated a six-block area immediately north of the east end of Essex Street, the city's main thoroughfare. Just a short walk away, on either side of the Merrimack River, were the giant mills that had attracted thousands of laborers. The newest and largest of these was the Wood, named after the president of the American Woolen Company. Many of the Zapalas' neighbors worked there.

Mill work, however, was not what Rosario Zappala chose as his means of livelihood. Instead, he opened a poultry store on the north side of Common Street, just a few steps away from the second-floor tenement where he lived with his wife and growing family. He would manage his poultry business (pigeons and rabbits were also available) at this location for 40 years, while his family expanded until there were three sons and four daughters.

Across the street from Mr. Zappala's store was a small bakery where, about 1923, his sons, Angelo and Charles, went to work. Their job was to help make deliveries of each day's fresh bread. When one of the bakers decided to buy the shop from the current owner, Mr. Zappala gave his friend a $2,500 mortgage on the property. But the new owner-manager decided within a year that he did not want to continue in the trade and so, in 1925, Mr. Zappala found himself in the bakery business. Beginning with sales that averaged 250 loaves of bread a day, the small business enjoyed some success during the next few years. Charles' untimely death in 1932 altered the family's plans, and Angelo took over the business.

The bakery struggled through the remainder of the Depression; with the advent of World War II and the temporary revival of the textile industry, business picked up. By the end of the war young Stephen Zappala

Rosario Zappala (1885-1960), founder of the Tripoli Bakery.

was old enough to join his brother and the bakery's dozen employees. By then Tripoli was delivering the products to many small stores as well as to a few restaurants. While Italian bread had been the main prewar product, the postwar years saw the addition of "American" bread, a variety of pastries, and rolls for the newly popular submarine sandwiches. Soon after the war Angelo introduced pizza to the summer colonies at Salisbury Beach on the Atlantic shore just 20 miles away.

Rosario Zappala retired from the bakery shortly before his death in 1960. But his wife, Rose, who had always worked there, continued to come to the bakery on a regular basis for the following decade. Today she is retired.

From the beginning, the Zappala family has wholesaled as well as retailed the products of its ovens. Its wholesale customers include two local supermarkets—Messina's and Barcelo's. Area schools and restaurants are also on its list of customers. But the firm's 62 employees see most of their products exit the Common Street store carried by old and new customers who come there for breads, rolls, and pastries. Today, as was the case 50 years ago, members of the family help prepare the 3,000 loaves of bread, 1,000 dozen Italian rolls, and the variety of other rolls and pastries that come out of the ovens each day.

This two-story wooden frame building on Common Street, Lawrence, in the heart of the immigrant Italian community, was the original home of the Tripoli Bakery.

Mrs. Rosario Zappala, with a package of rolls, stands behind the counter at her family's bakery (circa 1972).

USCI Cardiology & Radiology Division of C.R. Bard

This prosperous firm is a product of World War II. Until then, American physicians had relied on French and German manufacturers for the urological catheters used in the nation's hospitals. When the international crisis interrupted that supply line in 1941, a group of Glens Falls, New York, entrepreneurs organized the United States Catheter and Instrument Corporation. In addition to the constant civilian demand, thousands of war casualties also required catheters; employees of the young company worked around-the-clock seven days a week during much of this period. The quality of their product was so high that Army and Navy officials awarded the firm an "E" for excellence.

After the war the organization expanded its product line. In 1946 Dr. Andre Cournand and USCI scientists designed a heart catheter that significantly improved success rates in the critical area. Consequently, Dr. Cournand was awarded a Nobel Prize for Medicine. Today the corporation manufactures a range of cardiovascular catheters and probes which incorporate balloons, electrodes, and sound-sensing elements. Most are composed of polyethylene, polyurethane, and woven Dacron materials.

In the 1950s, following successful collaboration of a faculty member at the University of Alabama, a Chemstrand scientist, and the USCI staff, nylon and Teflon arterial grafts were introduced. In collaboration with Dr. Michael DeBakey of Baylor University, in 1960 Dacron arterial grafts became available. Since then this line has expanded to include lightweight grafts and internal and external velour grafts. The firm also manufactures and supplies fabrics used in hernia repair, intracardiac patching, and hip-joint repair.

USCI was acquired in 1966 by C.R. Bard, a New Jersey corporation. A few years later the officers decided to

conduct a national search for a new site. Three factors were important, according to president David Prigmore: a close relationship to a major medical center, especially one that specialized in heart surgery and cardiology, to help in the evaluation of products, offer the opportunity for clinical studies, and assist in the development of new ideas; a reliable source of technical staff including engineers, plastic chemists, and textile technologists; and a good work force. After weighing all these factors the project managers elected to relocate in Billerica, where Bard already owned real estate. When the move was made in 1973, many former Glens Falls employees took advantage of the opportunity to move to a more cosmopolitan area.

The 1,000-person work force in

This skilled technician is knitting bio-grafts that will be used as artificial arteries in bypass surgery.

Billerica today manufactures products that serve an international hospital market. They are perhaps proudest of one of their newest products, the Gruntzig Catheter—of Swiss origin but licensed to USCI in 1978. The unique device offers patients and surgeons an alternative to open-heart surgery; in 1981 at least 7,000 such operations were avoided by its use. Instead, surgeons were able to insert the catheter, inflate a tiny balloon, and clear the affected artery.

The history of USCI in the Merrimack Valley has been one of impressive growth. According to the present management there is no reason to think this pattern will change.

University of Lowell

The University of Lowell was formally established in 1975 as a result of the merger of Lowell State College and Lowell Technological Institute. Those two prominent schools of higher education were founded in the late 19th century, each evolving over the years until the final transition, which created the new University of Lowell. The university is situated in the historic textile-manufacturing city on the Merrimack River, which is the first city in the United States to be designated a National Historical Park.

In 1894 Lowell State College began training teachers, and the next year Lowell Technological Institute was established as a textile school, offering diplomas in cotton and wool manufacturing, textile chemistry, and other skills related to the city's primary industry. James T. Smith, native-born secretary to the board of trade, was the prime mover of the technological project in Lowell. He felt, as did the owners and managers of the Lowell mills, that a better-trained work force would be able to produce "fine and fancier fabrics." A majority of the trustees, naturally enough, were mill presidents, treasurers, agents, and superintendents from the Lowell-Lawrence region.

When the merger took place in 1975, both institutions had become multipurpose schools with programs in the arts and sciences and excellent reputations in their respective specialties. Today the university's seven colleges cover over 100 acres on both the north and south sides of the Merrimack River. Its more than 450 full-time faculty members teach more than 15,000 students in undergraduate, graduate, and continuing education programs.

Students who qualify to enter the University of Lowell can obtain a superior education in any one of 70 undergraduate degree programs. Students are involved in scholarly research, creative and artistic achievement, and original inquiry. The university's interactions with area service agencies, health-care facilities, and industries provide students with state-of-the-art knowledge of the latest

developments and needs in their chosen field. The University of Lowell is one of three state universities in Massachusetts and is accredited by the New England Association of Schools and Colleges.

Set in an area that was once Pawtucket Indian territory and later chosen as the site of a unique industrial experiment, the University of Lowell, steeped in history, continues to grow and evolve with its neighboring region.

Students who apply to the University of Lowell have Scholastic

Southwick Hall, on the campus of the University of Lowell, is the building that housed the Lowell Textile Institute. It is the oldest structure extant on the original campus. (Photo courtesy of James Higgins.)

Coburn Hall is the oldest remaining building on the University of Lowell campus, where the Massachusetts State Normal School at Lowell was originally established.

Aptitude Test scores that are considerably higher than the national average for applicants to four-year institutions. A majority of students enroll in career-oriented undergraduate programs—engineering, music, pure and applied science, education, management science, health professions, and in liberal arts specialties such as technical writing and law and justice. The University of Lowell is one of the largest sources, in New England and in the United States, of professionals educated in engineering and technological fields.

Wang Laboratories

The founder and chief executive officer of this spectacularly successful computer corporation, An Wang, was born and raised in China. In 1940 he earned his bachelor of science degree at Chiao Tung University in the busy port city of Shanghai. At the conclusion of World War II he left his native land to enroll as a graduate student at Harvard University. In 1948 he was awarded a Ph.D. in applied physics. Because China was then in the throes of political change Dr. Wang elected to remain at the university, where he became a research fellow at Harvard's Computation Laboratory. The focus of the laboratory at the time was on the development of early computers. Dr. Wang has since recalled that he was "in the right field at the right time . . . ," as it was (his invention of) the core memory that "nurtured the rapid growth of modern computers."

In 1951, as the university de-emphasized research into computer technology, Wang left Harvard and established the predecessor of Wang Laboratories in downtown Boston. The firm's first year was singularly uneventful; after 12 months had passed the founder felt justified in hiring one part-time college student. By this time Wang had married and become a father and thus did not lack motives to make his enterprise a success.

During its first decade Wang Laboratories was just that—a place where experiments could be conducted and a "shop" where one-of-a-kind electronic digital instruments could be fabricated for industry and for the federal government. One of the early successes—now in general use—was the hardware necessary to allow machine tools to be computer programmed.

Yet, a decade after the firm had been established, Wang Laboratories was still working on product development for other companies to manufacture and distribute. This was the case, for example, with one of the first computers for justifying type for typesetting, called the Linasec; another corporation marketed the instrument Wang had developed.

Wang then made the decision that would spur his organization's unprecedented growth: "We saw it would be more beneficial, and more profitable, to control the distribution of our products, and to interact directly with the end-user." In order to

Dr. An Wang, founder of Wang Laboratories.

manufacture multiple units, new plant space was necessary. Fortunately for the Merrimack Valley economy, Wang decided to build a plant in Tewksbury, next to Route 495, a recent addition to the federal highway network. Consequently, in 1964 the business earned one million dollars for the first time in its history.

In 1965 Wang introduced its desktop computer, called LOCI. Later that year the firm produced its first electronic desk calculator. As a result of these and other technological breakthroughs, the company's revenues doubled annually for the remainder of the decade. By 1972 annual income amounted to $32 million.

Perhaps the most significant achievement of the 1970s was the introduction of word-processing systems and multi-terminal data-processing systems. Within a short time Wang emerged as the leading worldwide supplier of word-processing systems and the second largest supplier of small data-processing systems. A further advance was made in 1979, when integrated information systems for combined data and word processing were produced.

As Wang's research and

Introduced in 1970, the Wang 600 series of scientific and engineering calculators was the forerunner of the company's small-business computing systems.

The corporate headquarters for Wang Laboratories dominates the skyline near the Lowell Connector and Interstate Route 495.

development efforts succeeded time after time, revenues began to grow geometrically. During the fiscal year ending December 31, 1982 (the company's 31st year), revenues amounted to $1.195 billion. By then the firm employed 19,000 people and occupied more than three million square feet of manufacturing and development space in old and new buildings in the Merrimack Valley. Along the way it had become, appropriately enough, an international organization; overseas manufacturing facilities and overseas markets are today a key part of the Wang empire.

Dr. Wang's achievements have been widely recognized. He now holds eight honorary degrees. He serves as a bank director, is an overseer at Harvard, a trustee of two other universities, and a member of the commonwealth's board of regents. He is also founder and president of the Wang Institute of Graduate Studies, which he founded in 1979.

Today's Wang INTEGRATED Systems allow many people to share information, and to have access to word processing, data processing, telecommunications, and many other capabilities—all through one system that makes "the office of the future" a reality today.

Watts Regulator Company

Joseph E. Watts, a brass finisher with good business instincts, established his company on Essex Street in 1874. He relocated twice before erecting his own plant in 1893 on Lowell Street near Broadway. The new structure was described at the time as "... the best-built and most completely equipped machine shop in the limits of the city of Lawrence."

When Watts died two years later, the plant and good will of the business was purchased by two "enterprising young men" named Pickels and Dodson. R.I. Pickels, a native of Lawrence, was a mechanical and electrical engineer who had studied at MIT. C.W. Dodson was an Andover native who had studied at Cornell. Together they "made their mark" with the firm they ran for about 20 years.

In 1918 the company was sold to Burchard Everett Horne and two partners. Horne soon bought out his partners; the firm has since been controlled by the Horne family. (Horne's son, George B., succeeded his father and his son, Timothy P., manages the corporation today.)

The organization Horne had purchased, although healthy, was small, employing only a handful of people. He and his chief engineer—a man named Wendell Dillon—designed a number of relief and regulatory products for the plumbing and heating industry in order to increase sales. Still, until World War II, the company employed fewer than a dozen men.

When Horne's son, George, joined the firm in the '30s, he brought a salesman's flair and an optimist's vision with him. A new building was constructed in 1937 (the site of corporate headquarters today), and research and development efforts were accelerated.

The formation of certain national valve standards and safety codes led to the widespread application of many of Watts' proprietary products, especially its famous temperature and pressure relief valves for protection against the potential explosion of water heaters.

Other new specialized valve products, such as water and steam pressure regulators, led to national distribution and the period of expansion had begun.

By the late 1950s the company employed 360 persons and a third-generation Horne, Timothy, joined the family firm. Watts then began a process of decentralized manufacturing for future growth by constructing a major facility in Franklin, New Hampshire. Today there are six plants in the United States, one in Canada, and one in Holland.

Over 1,200 employees are part of an ever-expanding organization with higher-technology product lines extending Watts' presence from its traditional plumbing and heating markets into additional major markets, including municipal waterworks and the chemical-processing industries. Over a century of progress can be traced from the firm's modest origins.

The corporate headquarters of Watts Regulator Company, Lawrence.

Westford Anodizing Corporation

Westford Anodizing Corporation is the creation of David A. Allen, who started the business in 1971 and incorporated the firm on November 1, 1972.

Born in Newburyport in 1940, Allen joined the U.S. Navy after finishing high school and served as an enlisted man for four years. When he left the Navy he went to work as a truck driver for a Newburyport anodizing company. While working his way up to plant foreman he enrolled as a mechanical engineering student at Northeastern University's evening division.

Like many of the Merrimack Valley's first entrepreneurs, Allen decided that owning a business would be preferable to working for someone else. After finding the equipment he needed (another anodizing firm recently had failed) he rented space in one of Westford's 19th-century machine shops.

Allen's venture succeeded and by 1976 he felt confident enough to buy out his partner and become sole owner of a business which employed 20 persons in its basement location. He then purchased and restored what is reputed to be Westford's oldest mill building, a two-story granite structure erected about 1860 for the Abbot Worsted Company.

Today Westford Anodizing employs a work force of 40 persons. The company has about 170 regular customers. Gross sales income rose from $18,500 in 1972 to $500,000 in 1977 to more than one million dollars in 1981.

Metal finishing—the process of coating an object with a layer of another metal or paint—is an old technique. (Today, of course, the object as well as the coating may be plastic.) Advances in chemistry and in engineering make the results more predictable today, but the basic processes remain the same: The object to be treated is inspected, cleaned, plated, rinsed, dried, inspected again, packed, and shipped.

Westford Anodizing Corporation finds most of its clients among the high-technology firms in northeastern Massachusetts and southern New Hampshire that are leading the reindustrialization of the Merrimack Valley. Perhaps 85 percent of his company's business comes from firms such as Wang, Centronics, Honeywell, and Data General, Allen estimates.

Anodizing requires relatively large amounts of electricity and water and thus the energy crunch and environmental movement of recent years have had a major impact on Allen's plans. To meet Environmental Protection Agency standards he installed a complete wastewater pollution control system in 1979. In 1982 he hopes to reactivate an old water turbine that he is relying on to produce the electricity he needs during at least eight months of the year.

And thus the water in Stony Brook, in Westford's Graniteville section, will continue to create jobs for the great-grandchildren of yesterday's immigrants.

An artist's rendering of the stone mill built for the Abbot Worsted Company in the 19th century and renovated recently for Westford Anodizing Corporation.

Patrons

The following individuals, companies, and organizations have made a valuable commitment to the quality of this publication. Windsor Publications and the Merrimack Valley Textile Museum gratefully acknowledge their participation in *The Valley and Its Peoples: An Illustrated History of the Lower Merrimack.*

Alco Electronic Products*
Alexander's Markets*
Ames Textile Corporation*
Avco*
Bennett & Hodge Travel, Inc.*
Berkshire Manufactured Products*
Bethany Homes, Inc.
Blue Cross and Blue Shield of
    Massachusetts*
Bride, Grimes & Co., Inc.*
Cantor Insurance Agency*
Central Industrial Laboratories, Inc.*
Alfred F. Contarino

Courier Corporation*
H.J. Doerr Painting, Inc.*
Eagle-Tribune Publishing Company*
Essex Company*
Export Warehouse Company*
Family Products, Inc.
Ferrous Technology, Inc./Foundry
    Technology, Inc.*
Frequency Sources, Inc.*
Haverhill Co-operative Bank
Jackson Lumber Company*
Anna Jaques Hospital*
Laughton's Garden Center*
Lawrence Pumps Inc.*
Lowell Five Cent Savings Bank*
Macartney's*
C.M. McDonald & Company, Inc.*
    Nailhead Creations, Inc.
New Balance Athletic Shoe*
Norcross & Leighton, Inc.*
Northern Essex Community College*
Pellon Corporation*

Pepsi-Cola Methuen Bottlers
    Incorporated*
J. George Picard and Son*
Preston Fuels*
St. John's Hospital*
St. Joseph's Hospital*
Sutton Travel Service, Inc.*
Tau-Tron, Inc.
Tripoli Bakery*
USCI Cardiology & Radiology*
    Division of C.R. Bard
University of Lowell*
Wang Laboratories*
Watts Regulator Company*
Westford Anodizing Corporation*

* Partners in Progress of *The Valley and Its Peoples: An Illustrated History of the Lower Merrimack.* The histories of these companies and organizations appear in Chapter 9, beginning on page 137.

Acknowledgments

The author wishes to extend special thanks to the following: Donna Mailloux (Pollard Memorial Library, Lowell); Pam Chicklis (Lowell Historic Preservation Commision); Jeffrey R. Brown (North Amherst, Massachusetts); Ralph Fasanella (Ardsley, New York); Christopher Snow (Newburyport, Massachusetts); Daniel Lombardo, (The Jones Library, Amherst, Massachusetts); Sally Pierce (Boston Athenaeum, Boston); Marsha Rooney (Andover Historical Society); Florence Bartoshevsky (Baker Library, Cambridge, Massachusetts); Louis T. Karabatsos (Lowell, Massachusetts); Martha Mayo (University of Lowell); Nicki Thiras (Addison Gallery of American Art, Andover, Massachusetts); Mary Flinn and Martha Larson (North Andover Historical Society); Anne Farnam, Bettina A. Norton, Dean T. Lahikainen, and Marylou Birchmore (The Essex Institute, Salem, Massachusetts); Julia P. Fogg (Chelmsford Historical Society); Ellie Reichlin (Society for the Preservation of New England Antiquities, Boston, Massachusetts); Howard Curtis and Greg Laing (Haverhill Public Library); Dan Jones (Peabody Museum of Archeology and Ethnology, Cambridge, Massachusetts); Mary Allis (Fairfield, Connecticut); Kathy Flynn, John Grimes, and John Nove (The Peabody Museum of Salem); John Roberts (North Andover, Massachusetts); Frederick Johnson and Eugene Winter (Robert S. Peabody Foundation for Archeology, Andover, Massachusetts); Wilhelmina Lunt and D'Arcy G. van Bokkelen (The Historical Society of Old Newbury, Newburyport, Massachusetts); Harriet Ropes Cabot (Cotuit, Massachusetts); Thomas E. Leary (Slater Mill Historic Site, Pawtucket, Rhode Island); Eartha Dengler and Jonas Stundza (Immigrant City Archives, Lawrence, Massachusetts); Russell Reeve (Stevens Memorial Library, North Andover, Massachusetts); Betsy Woodman (Newburyport, Massachusetts); Ronald Bourgeault (Hampton, New Hampshire); Sue Nault (Merrimack College, North Andover, Massachusetts); Paula Newcomb (Amesbury, Massachusetts); Ernest Price (Rowley, Massachusetts); Regina Tracy (Custom House Maritime Museum, Newburyport, Massachusetts); Arthur L. Eno, Jr. (Lowell, Massachusetts); Patricia O'Malley (Bradford College, Haverhill, Massachusetts); Elizabeth Sholes (Pawtucket, Rhode Island); Marion Hall, Patricia Markey, Jessann Freda, Nancy Leonardi, and Robert Hauser (Merrimack Valley Textile Museum, North Andover, Massachusetts); Mrs. Stuart L. Potter and Charles Steans (Billerica Historical Society); Richard Koke (New York Historical Society, New York, New York).

Suggested Reading

Bailey, Sarah Loring. *Historical Sketches of Andover (comprising the present towns of North Andover and Andover), Massachusetts*. Boston, 1880 (reprint 1974).

Barber, Russell. *The Wheeler's Site: A Specialized Shellfish Processing Station on the Merrimack River*. Cambridge, 1982.

Chase, George Wingate. *The History of Haverhill, Massachusetts, From Its First Settlement in 1640 to the Year 1860*. Haverhill, 1861.

Coburn, Frederick. *History of Lowell and Its People*. 3 vols. New York, 1920.

Cole, Donald. *Immigrant City: Lawrence, Massachusetts, 1845-1921*. Chapel Hill, North Carolina, 1963 (reprint 1980).

Currier, John J. *History of Newbury, Massachusetts (1635-1902)*. Boston, 1902.

_____ . *History of Newburyport, Massachusetts*. Boston, 1905 (1977 reprint).

Dublin, Thomas (ed.). *Farm to Factory: Women's Letters, 1830-1860*. New York, 1981.

Dublin, Thomas. *Women at Work: The Transformation of Work and Community in Lowell, Massachusetts, 1826-1860*. New York, 1979.

Eno, Arthur L., Jr. (ed.). *Cotton Was King: A History of Lowell, Massachusetts*. Somersworth, New Hampshire, 1976.

Fuess, Claude M. *Andover, Symbol of New England: The Evolution of a Town*. The Andovers, 1959.

Greenslet, Ferris. *The Lowells and Their Seven Worlds*. Boston, 1946.

Gregory, Frances W. *Nathan Appleton, Merchant and Entrepreneur, 1779-1861*. Charlottesville, Virginia, 1975.

Hazen, Henry A. *History of Billerica, Massachusetts with a Geneological Register*. Boston, 1883.

Holden, Raymond P. *The Merrimack*. New York, 1958.

Hurd, D. Hamilton (ed.). *History of Essex County, Massachusetts, with Biographical Sketches of Many of its Pioneers and Prominent Men*. 3 vols. Philadelphia, 1888.

_____ . *History of Middlesex County, Massachusetts with Biographical Sketches of Many of its Pioneers and Prominent Men*. 3 vols. Philadelphia, 1890.

Josephson, Hannah. *The Golden Threads: New England's Mill Girls and Magnates*. New York, 1949.

Labaree, Benjamin W. *Patriots and Partisans: The Merchants of Newburyport, 1764-1815*. Cambridge, Massachusetts, 1962 (paperback 1975).

Massachusetts Historical Committee. *An Archaeological Survey and Documentary History of the Shattuck Farm, Andover, Massachusetts*. Boston, 1981.

Meader, J.W. *The Merrimack River; Its Sources and Its Tributaries*. Boston, 1869.

Merrill, Joseph. *History of Amesbury, including the First Seventeen Years of Salisbury, to the Separation in 1654; and Merrimac, From its Incorporation in 1876*. Haverhill, 1880.

Moorehead, Warren King. *The Merrimack Archaeological Survey: A Preliminary Paper*. Salem, Massachusetts, 1931.

Nason, Elias. *A History of the Town of Dunstable, Massachusetts from its Earliest Settlement to the Year of Our Lord, 1873*. Boston, 1877.

Perry, Gardner. *History of Bradford, Massachusetts*. Haverhill, 1820.

Roberts, John L. *The Glacial Geologic History of North Andover and the Surrounding Area*. North Andover, Massachusetts, 1977.

Robinson, Harriet H. *Loom & Spindle or Life Among the Early Mill Girls*. Boston, 1898 (reprint 1976).

Roddy, Edward G. *Mills, Mansions and Mergers: The Life of William M. Wood*. North Andover, Massachusetts, 1982.

Sears, John Herny. *The Physical Geography, Geology, Mineralogy and Paleontology of Essex County, Massachusetts*. Salem, Massachusetts, 1905.

Stevens, Horace Nathaniel. *Nathaniel Stevens, 1786-1865. An Account of His Life and the Business he Founded*. North Andover, Massachusetts, 1946.

Walters, Ronald G. *American Reformers, 1815-1860*. New York, 1978.

Waters, Wilson. *The History of Chelmsford, Massachusetts*. Lowell, 1917.

Index

Partners in Progress

THIS BOOK WAS SET IN
PONTIAC AND CASLON TYPES,
PRINTED ON
ACID FREE
70 LB. WARRENFLO
AND BOUND BY
WALSWORTH PUBLISHING COMPANY